FROM RECESSION⋅ RENEWAL

The impact of the financial crisis on public services and local government

Edited by Joanna Richardson

First published in Great Britain in 2011 by

The Policy Press
University of Bristol
Fourth Floor
Beacon House
Queen's Road
Bristol BS8 1QU
UK

Tel +44 (0)117 331 4054
Fax +44 (0)117 331 4093
e-mail tpp-info@bristol.ac.uk
www.policypress.co.uk

North American office:
The Policy Press
c/o International Specialized Books Services (ISBS)
920 NE 58th Avenue, Suite 300
Portland, OR 97213-3786, USA
Tel +1 503 287 3093
Fax +1 503 280 8832
e-mail info@isbs.com

British Library Cataloguing in Publication Data
A catalogue record for this book is available from the British Library.

Library of Congress Cataloging-in-Publication Data
A catalog record for this book has been requested.

ISBN 978 1 84742 699 4 paperback
ISBN 978 1 84742 700 7 hardcover

The right of Joanna Richardson to be identified as editor of this work has been
asserted by her in accordance with the 1988 Copyright, Designs and Patents Act.

The statements and opinions contained within this publication are solely those
of the editor and contributors and not of The University of Bristol or The Policy
Press. The University of Bristol and The Policy Press disclaim responsibility for
any injury to persons or property resulting from any material published in this
publication.

The Policy Press works to counter discrimination on grounds
of gender, race, disability, age and sexuality.

Cover design by Qube Design Associates, Bristol
Front cover: image kindly supplied by www.alamy.com
Printed and bound in Great Britain by TJ International, Padstow
The Policy Press uses environmentally friendly print suppliers

FSC
Mixed Sources
Product group from well-managed
forests and other controlled sources
Cert no. SGS-COC-2482
www.fsc.org
© 1996 Forest Stewardship Council

Contents

List of figures, tables and boxes   iv

Notes on contributors   v

Acknowledgements   x

Foreword by Ken Livingstone   xi

Part One: Context

one   Introduction: the scope and challenges of the financial   3
crisis
Joanna Richardson and Colin Copus

two   The historical context of the global financial crisis: 25
from Bretton Woods to the debacle of neoliberalism
George Lambie

three   Financial crises, governance and cohesion: can   51
governments learn up?
Stuart Holland

Part Two: Policies and issues

four   Public policy responses to fiscal debt or deficit: is there   73
a difference?
Fred Mear

five   Protecting the community from the effects of the   89
financial crisis
Joanna Richardson

six   Exploring the local political context of the recession   111
Steve Leach and Mark Roberts

seven   Efficiencies in public service delivery   135
John Seddon and Brendan O'Donovan

eight   Choice, empowerment, personalisation: taking forward   157
public services in a recession
Tim Brown and Nicola Yates

nine   Governing the mix: how local government still matters   179
Helen Sullivan

Part Three: Conclusion

ten   Conclusion: from recession to renewal?   199
Joanna Richardson

Index   221

List of figures, tables and boxes

Figure

1.1   Changes in PSND since the mid-1970s   5

Tables

1.1   Recent history of the financial crisis   6
1.2   Responses to recessions   11
1.3   Recession 'waves'   16
7.1   The DWP-promulgated design for housing benefits   143
9.1   Options for 'enabling' local government   192

Box

6.1   Conditions for successful neighbourhood working   122

Notes on contributors

Tim Brown is Director of the Centre for Comparative Housing Research at De Montfort University, Leicester. He is a Corporate Member of the Chartered Institute of Housing and is a Local Improvement Advisor for the Improvement and Development Agency. Tim is course leader for the MSc in Business for Housing and teaches on a wide range of undergraduate and postgraduate programmes, including MBAs. He has written widely on choice-based lettings in academic journals and has contributed to two government good practice guides on this topic. Tim has spoken at national and international conferences on the challenges of adopting a customer approach in social housing. Currently he is working on projects on urban regeneration and network theory as well as on a total capital pilot that is investigating the potential of area budgets.

Colin Copus is Professor of Local Politics in the Department of Public Policy, De Montfort University, Leicester. His main research interests are local party politics, local political leadership and decision making, the changing role of the councillor and small-party and independent politics. Colin has recently concluded two major research projects: the first was a Leverhulme-funded project exploring the role and impact of small political parties, independent politics and political associations in local government; the second was a Nuffield-funded comparative project examining the roles, responsibilities and activities of councillors across Europe. He has conducted research for DCLG and co-authored publications including 'Making the Most of the New Constitutions' (2003), 'The Development of Overview and Scrutiny' (2002) and 'New Council Constitutions' (2000). Colin is the author of two major recent books: *Leading the Localities: Executive Mayors in English Local Governance* (Manchester University Press, 2006) and *Party Politics and Local Government* (Manchester University Press, 2004).

Stuart Holland has been involved in national and international policy making since he was an economic and political assistant to Harold Wilson in the 1960s. He drafted Labour's industrial and regional policies in the 1970s, was elected Member of Parliament for Vauxhall in 1979 and was shadow Minister for Development Cooperation from 1983 to 1987 and shadow Financial Secretary to the Treasury until 1989. He coordinated a group which influenced the commitment of the 1986 Single European Act to economic and social cohesion, left parliament in 1989 to help Jacques Delors design policies and financial instruments for this, and advised on their extension in the Lisbon Agenda. He currently teaches in the Faculty of Economics of the University of Coimbra, Portugal. Stuart's publications include: *The Market Economy: From Micro to Mesoeconomics* (1987) and *The Global Economy: From Meso to Macroeconomics* (1987), both published by Weidenfeld and Nicolson, London and St Martin's Press, New York, as well as *The European Imperative: Economic and Social Cohesion in the 1990s* (1993) (with a Foreword by Jacques Delors), published by Spokesman Books, Nottingham.

George Lambie is a Principal Lecturer in the Department of Public Policy at De Montfort University, Leicester, where he teaches International Political Economy and Latin American Politics at undergraduate and postgraduate levels. He has published three books: one on Cuba's relations with Western Europe; the second on the influence of European politics of the interwar years on Latin American intellectuals; the third book is entitled *The Cuban Revolution in the 21st Century* (2010). He is co-editor of *The International Journal of Cuban Studies*. From 1995 to 2000 he was Co-director, with Cuba's Minister of Finance, of the first major European Commission cooperation project with Cuba. His work on the contemporary financial crisis includes an article entitled 'Nemesis of "market fundamentalism"? The ideology, deregulation and crisis of finance' (*Contemporary Politics*, vol 15, no 2, June 2009, pp 157–77). He is currently researching the Labour Party's Alternative Economic Strategy of the 1970s and its objective of challenging the forces that led to globalisation.

Steve Leach joined the Department of Public Policy (Faculty of Business and Law), De Montfort University, Leicester, as Professor of Local Government in January 1996, after 18 years at the Institute of Local Government Studies (University of Birmingham). His research interests include political leadership, local politics, strategic planning and management, and local government structures. He has published numerous books and articles including: *Local Political Leadership* (with David Wilson; The Policy Press, 2000), *The Changing Role of Local Politics in Britain* (The Policy Press, 2006) and *Botched Business: The Damaging Process of Local Government Reorganisation 2006–08* (with Michael Chisholm; Douglas McLean, 2008). Steve has worked as an advisor for the Local Government Leadership Centre, carrying out diagnosis of leadership capacity needs and opportunities in Dorset County Council, Salford City Council and Rochdale Metropolitan Borough Council.

—

He has worked with Lincolnshire County Council and the seven Lincolnshire districts in developing a preferred option in response to the Miliband agenda, which was presented to David Miliband in June 2006. With Michael Chisholm, he produced a critical appraisal of the two unitary proposals in Cheshire for Crewe and Nantwich Borough Council (May 2007).

Ken Livingstone began his political career serving on Lambeth and Camden councils before becoming leader of the Greater London Council in 1981 until Margaret Thatcher abolished it in 1986. He then served as Labour MP for Brent East from 1987 to 2001. Ken was elected Mayor of London in May 2000 and was re-elected for a second term in June 2004. With strong ideas about how the capital should be run, Ken has never been afraid of controversy. He had the courage and vision to introduce the congestion charge and a transformation of the city's ageing transport infrastructure to free up London's traffic. He also successfully restored beat police and bus services. He took the decision to bid for the Olympic Games and was the driving force behind the capital's successful 2012 bid; his leadership vision was for strong and diverse growth for London and successes in which all Londoners could share. With the government he led the preparations to deal with terrorist attacks such as those on London in 2005. Fundamental improvements in environmental management are also central to Ken's vision, and in 2007 he produced a climate change action plan which showed how London could reduce its carbon emissions by 60% in 20 years and by 80% to 90% by 2050. He has written two books, *If Voting Changed Anything They'd Abolish It* (1987) and *Livingstone's Labour* (1989). Ken has a radio show on LBC (London's Biggest Conversation) every Saturday and he has recently been working on his autobiography.

Fred Mear is a Principal Lecturer in Accounting and Finance, specialising in Public Finance. Fred trained as an accountant and worked in local authorities before joining De Montfort University, Leicester. He has a particular interest in transitional situations and has experience in transitional and developing economies. He has worked on tax and financial reform in Cuba, becoming Technical Co-ordinator for the EU-funded project advising on the development and implementation of a taxation system for the self-employed, and training taxation officers, and, in addition, advising on accounting reforms. Fred was also involved in a number of projects with former Soviet countries in their transition to market economies. He has been a trustee of Skillshare International (an international aid organisation) since 1993 and has seen the impact of globalisation in the developing world. He has worked with or in a number of developing (especially in sub-Saharan Africa) and transitional economies and situations.

Brendan O'Donovan is Head of Research at Vanguard Consulting, working alongside John Seddon. He has recently completed an MSc in Operations Management at Cardiff Business School. Having previously worked for a city council, Brendan is now a Visiting Research Associate at Cardiff University and has recently co-authored a report for the Wales Audit Office on the subject of systems thinking in the Welsh public sector.

Joanna Richardson is a Principal Lecturer in the Centre for Comparative Housing Research at De Montfort University, Leicester. She is programme leader for the Chartered Institute of Housing MSc and the Professional Diploma courses, and she teaches on undergraduate and postgraduate housing programmes. Jo has written *The Gypsy Debate: Can Discourse Control?* (2006) and *Providing Gypsy and Travellers Sites: Contentious Spaces* (Joseph Rowntree Foundation, 2007). She has undertaken planning research for Lord Avebury and the Derbyshire Gypsy Liaison Group as well as a number of Gypsy and Traveller Accommodation Assessments and projects to develop strategy in this field. Her research also focuses on policing, and on representation of Gypsies and Travellers in the media, and she has had a number of chapters published in this area. Jo is also editor and contributing author of a book, *Housing and the Customer* (2010), for the Chartered Institute of Housing.

Mark Roberts is Visiting Research Fellow at the Local Governance Research Unit at De Montfort University, Leicester. Mark trained as a social worker and before joining De Montfort was Head of Child Care and Deputy Director of Social Services at Sandwell Metropolitan Borough Council in the West Midlands. His main research interests are concerned with urban politics, race and faith, and he is currently co-authoring a book on institutional theory. His most recent empirical work has focused on neighbourhood management in Derby, Leicester, Birmingham, Nottingham and Edinburgh.

John Seddon is an occupational psychologist, management thinker and leading authority on change in organisations. He is a vociferous critic of centralised 'command and control' management of the public sector. John insists that managers will discover they would be far better off if they knew how to manage for flow rather than aiming to create economies of scale. He is credited with translating the principles behind the Toyota Production System (TPS) for service organisations. John is a Visiting Professor at Cardiff and Derby Universities, and is managing director of Vanguard Consulting. He is author of *Systems Thinking in the Public Sector: The Failure of the Reform Regime and a Manifesto for a Better Way* (Triarchy Press, 2008).

Helen Sullivan is Professor of Government and Society at he University of Birmingham. Her research and writing explores the changing nature of local governance, with particular emphasis on the impact of collaborative working on politicians, professionals and the public; developments in neighbourhood governance; and the evaluation of complex policy initiatives. She has received research funding to examine these issues from the ESRC, the Joseph Rowntree Foundation and government departments (in all areas of the UK). She has published widely on local governance in academic and practitioner journals. She is author of *Power, Participation and Political Renewal* (with Marian Barnes and Janet Newman; The Policy Press, 2007), *Building Capacity for Health Equity* (with Marian Barnes et al; Routledge, 2005) and *Working across Boundaries: Collaboration in Public Services* (with Chris Skelcher; Palgrave, 2002).

Nicola Yates is Chief Executive of Kingston-upon-Hull City Council and was previously Chief Executive of North Shropshire District Council and Services Director at Harborough District Council. Nicola is also an Honorary Research Associate at the Centre for Comparative Housing Research at De Montfort University, Leicester. Under her leadership, she has guided Hull City Council to become the most improved council in the country. At North Shropshire, she led on the delivery of a programme of service improvements. The Audit Commission in its Comprehensive Performance Assessment (CPA) in 2008 rated the local authority as 'good' compared with 'poor' in 2004, and highlighted the significant improvements in services outcomes for customers and local communities. At Harborough District Council, Nicola led on the development and delivery of the first district-wide choice-based lettings scheme in Britain. She has written articles and chapters for books and good practice guides on a wide range of subjects including partnerships, choice-based lettings and supporting people. Nicola received an OBE in 2010 for her services to local government.

Acknowledgements

The editor would like to thank a number of people who have informed the debate in this book, offered advice and read drafts of some of the chapters. Particular thanks are due to George Lambie, whose original idea it was to have a public policy debate at De Montfort University on issues related to globalisation and the financial crisis. Thank you to all of the contributors to this book for your insight and good humour in meeting deadlines. Colleagues in the Centre for Comparative Housing Research have been a good source of advice, most particularly Tim Brown and Peter King, and I have also benefited from the helpful suggestions of Emily Watt, Leila Ebrahimi and Jo Morton at The Policy Press. Thank you to David and Edward Richardson, and to my parents, for their patience and support.

The contributing authors would also like to thank Professor Joaquim Feio of the Faculty of Economics at the University of Coimbra for the ongoing discussion of themes in Stuart Holland's work in Chapter Three; also Vivien Lowndes and Steve Griggs for their advice and suggestions on Helen Sullivan's Chapter Nine.

Foreword

With the world economy at several crucial turning points and the new 'Con-Dem' coalition preparing a package of tax increases and spending cuts there can't be a better time to re-evaluate our economic strategy.

Postwar economic history fits into two neat segments: the broadly social democratic agenda from 1945 to 1976, followed by the monetarist fundamentalism which exploded both here and abroad in 2008. In the main Western economies the first 30 postwar years were the most successful period for gross domestic product (GDP) growth with a strongly redistributive tax policy (a top rate of 98% in 1950s Britain and 90% under Republican President Eisenhower). The proceeds of GDP growth sustained high levels of public and private investment and closed the inequality gap. In Britain in 1979 the richest 10% of the population were worth four times the poorest 10%, not merely due to benign governance but coinciding with the apex of trade union influence over the economy.

Thirty years after Margaret Thatcher and Ronald Reagan launched their economic revolution, trade union power is diminished and the richest 10% are now worth eight times the poorest. According to the monetarist script, we should have gone from strength to strength vis-à-vis the rest of the world, but investment has collapsed and on the human side the casualties have been immense, with the growth of an underclass in poorly paid and insecure employment and, in some areas, no prospect of employment for themselves or their children. Yet the parents of the 'broken Britain' generation were the lower middle class and skilled working class who had well-paid and secure employment throughout the 30 years after the Second World War.

This shift of power and wealth upwards has not revived the economies of Britain and America. Contrary to the Thatcherite mantra that 'public investment squeezes out private investment', there was no corresponding increase in private sector investment as Thatcher reduced public investment from a postwar average of 5.5% to 1% of GDP. To its shame, Tony Blair's government challenged little of the Thatcherite consensus and merely raised public investment to 1.5% of GDP.

With the smashing of trade unions and the collapse of the communist 'threat', restraints on capitalism were removed, with corporations taking an ever-increasing share of profit for dividend payments and obscene salaries at the top while cutting investment. Skilled manufacturing was written off and growth came from a massive expansion of the financial sector based on escalating risk taking. Privatisation saw the elimination of job opportunities for skilled workers, leaving whole regions with little choice other than public sector employment or a life on benefits. For many the only way of surviving was borrowing or holding down two jobs, with all the associated consequences for family life.

As Thatcher and Reagan began leading the West into this economic dead end, Deng Xiaoping set China on the path to becoming the world's most successful economy, doubling its GDP more rapidly than any other nation in history and then going on to do it again and again. As monetarists in the West kept revising predictions of a collapse of the Chinese model, 600 million Chinese were lifted out of poverty. In real purchasing-power parity terms, China is already the world's second largest economy and may overtake the US as early as 2018.

Deng's success was based on an understanding of what really matters in economic theory. He saw that Britain secured 100 years of global domination by being the first nation to achieve a level of investment of about 7% of GDP. After its civil war the US laid the foundations to dominate the 20th century by driving investment up to 19%. West Germany led postwar Europe to broad parity with the US by achieving 25% investment in 1973. Japan leapt to second place in the economic league table by achieving 38% in its best year. Before the current crisis China was investing 43% of GDP, and in response raised that to 46%. In contrast, Britain and the US responded to the crisis by reducing investment.

The election of Manmohan Singh as Prime Minister of India in 2004 brought another economist to power, who took India's rate of investment from 20% to 35% today, guaranteeing his re-election. It is unlikely that India will overtake China because the absence of dividend payments leaves China with an additional 7% of GDP for investment rather than inefficient consumption by the wealthy. But even with that disadvantage, as early as 2030 we could see a G3 of China, India and the US controlling a majority of global GDP. The increasing nationalism and lack of confidence that besets politics in Europe will prevent Europe from speaking with the one voice that is necessary to be part of the top table.

The obvious lessons for the West are that we must increase our level of investment and heed the powerful argument in Wilkinson and Pickett's *The Spirit Level* (Allen Lane, 2009) about the huge social and human benefits of a more redistributive tax system.

This book outlines the context of the financial crisis and examines a range of policies and issues that encompass the debate about the role of public services, national and local. These are the choices that face us and they require a substantial change of direction from the policies of the last 30 years.

We will see whether the new Con–Dem government protects investment or puts in train the changes necessary to give all our citizens a chance to achieve their potential. Unless we make such changes we had better revise the school curriculum to make Mandarin compulsory for all pupils.

Ken Livingstone
May 2010

Part One
Context

ONE

Introduction: the scope and challenges of the financial crisis

Joanna Richardson and Colin Copus

Dear chief secretary, I'm afraid there is no money. Kind regards – and good luck! (Byrne, 2010)

This book aims to analyse the impact of the financial crisis on public services and local government. Public debt in Britain is high[1] and to tackle this, the Conservative–Liberal Democrat Coalition government elected in May 2010 confirmed immediate reductions in public expenditure in 2010/11. The general election, however, was fought on the basis of not 'if' but 'when', and by whom, such reductions would be made and how the consequences of these reductions would be managed. It is the impact for providers and users of public services, and more widely for government and governance, which will be explored in the book. This chapter will set out a brief historical context and outline some of the emerging debates, responses and concepts in the rest of the book.

The Governor of the Bank of England captured the essence of the frustration of many at the handling of the financial crisis:

never in the field of financial endeavour has so much money been owed by so few to so many. And, one might add, so far with little real reform. (King, 2009)

A number of government interventions, not only in Britain, but in the US and around the globe (see further Chapters Two and Three), sought to shore up the viability of the banks because of the view that they were 'too big to fail'. The hold of the financial services sector over government actions from 2007 infuriated those who felt that similar support should be shown for the car industry and other key manufacturing industries such as steel, not forgetting small businesses too. The government supported the financial services sector, but the injection of public cash into the banks did not lead to increased liquidity, indeed loans to businesses were drastically curtailed, again hitting small business and individual home owners. The considerable support provided to the banks (effectively the nationalisation of private debt), at the expense of the taxpayer, resulted in only negligible change in behaviour by the banks. Indeed, the question of individual bonuses paid to some bankers, and the scare tactics of the loss of 'the best' of the banking industry if Britain enforced a regulatory cap on bonuses, indicated that little had changed. Banks were reporting huge profits in 2010, thanks to the range of stimulus measures provided by public money; meanwhile, the state of the public finances was getting worse. There remained a feeling that nothing had changed for the banking sector; whereas the pain for the public sector, and society, was becoming all too vivid and the potential for a 'double-dip' recession resulting from harsh cuts was increasingly seen as a possibility.

Recent history of the crisis: setting the scene

While it is important to set the scene, the intricacies of the shadow banking system, and the subsequent near collapse of the financial services sector, will not be the focus of this book. There is a range of texts (Bootle, 2009; Cable, 2009; Gamble 2009; Tett, 2009; Lewis, 2010; Stiglitz, 2010) which examine the recent history and politics of the crisis.

Nevertheless, a brief and recent history of the crisis is necessary to give context to the debate in the remainder of the book. The current financial crisis in Britain began with a severe credit crunch in 2007, but had its roots in wider themes and issues, and is linked with historic economic and political decisions. The financial crisis began with a predominant discourse of private debts – mostly in the banking sector. It moved to other areas of the private market, and by late 2009 and early 2010 when private markets and banks were rallying, the debt problem in the public sector had become the key focus – sovereign debt was the issue for politicians and ratings agencies. The chart in Figure 1.1 shows the changes in Public Sector Net Debt (PSND) as a percentage of Gross Domestic Product (GDP) since the mid-1970s.

In 2007–08 PSND as a percentage of GDP was 36.5%, by November 2008 it was 49.6%, in November 2009 it was 60.2% and in March 2010 it was 61.9% (2010 Budget). Some industry commentators suggested that PSND could head towards 80% unless strict measures were taken to curb debt and the Coalition government's emergency budget and public sector cuts were a response to this concern. In Table 1.1, we set out the journey towards the most recent financial crisis – using the same time frame from the mid-1970s. The journey that Britain has undertaken reflects a series of structural, economic and political

Figure 1.1: Changes in PSND since the mid-1970s

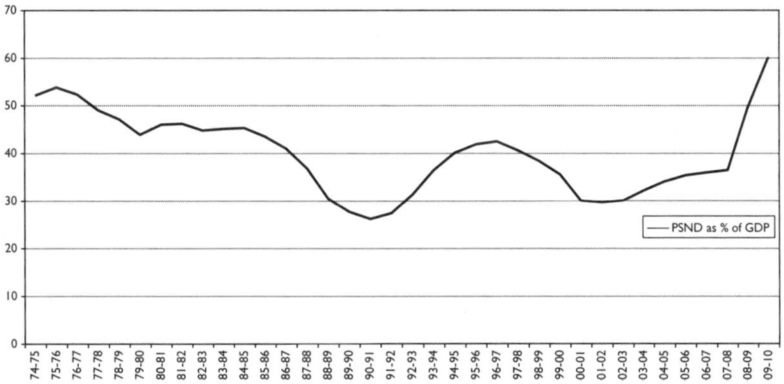

Note: Figures up to and including 2007–08 are from the 2009 Budget, but 2008–09 and 2009–10 figures from November each year are from the Office for National Statistics.

problems; including the effect of embracing the service and financial sectors as a ready alternative to a manufacturing base.

This brief recent historical analysis of the current financial crisis has highlighted some of the key themes and issues for government, public sector and private sector in understanding the impact of the financial crisis and developing suitable measures to mitigate it.

'Crisis' in context

> What makes it a crisis is that even in periods of relative calm the underlying causes and conflicts which give rise to dramatic episodes and decisive confrontations have not gone away. (Gamble, 2009, 40)

The language of recession as 'crisis' indicates either a level of panic among those seeking to come to terms with its implications, or the use of a deliberately emotive description to galvanise action and force recognition of the seriousness of public debt. Dramatic labels have been employed – such as the 'Armageddon' scenario painted by Bundred (2009). Blastland (2008), however, reminds us that caution is required in interpreting figures, labelling issues and apportioning blame or praise when talking about government debt. Indeed, Reinhart and Rogoff (2008) refer to 'the "this time it's different" syndrome [which] is the false belief that domestic debt is a novel feature of the modern financial landscape'.

Table 1.1: Recent history of the financial crisis

Britain in recession 1974–75	
1970s	Recession in the middle of the decade (1974–75) public sector net borrowing (PSNB) was 7.3%[a] of GDP in 1975 (the Pre-Budget Report at the end of 2009 had public sector borrowing requirement (PBR) at 6.4% of national income – a similar level to that in 1975). A key feature of the 1975 recession was the rising level of inflation that preceded it. Britain still had a reasonably strong industrial and manufacturing base which could aid the recovery of the economy (although these sectors were eroded in favour of the financial services sector from the end of the decade onwards). Unemployment breached the one million figure (this was seen as unacceptably high at the time, and was part of the context for the 'Labour isn't working' slogan in the Conservative election campaign in 1979). 1976: the International Monetary Fund (IMF) provided a £2.3 billion rescue for the British economy. 1977: the Community Reinvestment Act (CRA) was introduced as a federal law in the US to encourage banks to loan to those on lower incomes.[b] 1979: a new Conservative government under Thatcher was elected.

Britain in recession 1980–81	
1980s	The decade started with a recession. Thatcher's Conservative government eased off controls in the exchange market, which empowered globalisation and the rise of international financial markets. The rise of the Eurodollar market[c] in the 1970s had also increased multinational corporations' access to private international capital, furthering the globalisation of markets. Greece joined the European Community in 1981 (Spain and Portugal joined later, in 1986). The EU regional aid programme was expanded to bring poorer Mediterranean countries into line with the more affluent West. Increasing development of the derivatives market and the 'shadow banking' system. Commodities such as wheat and gold, as well as debt, were the subject of a gamble on their future value. There was a great deal of financial innovation unfolding at this time (see further Lambie (2009) and Chapter Two in this book). In the early 1980s the special circuit of building society mortgage lenders, supported and regulated by government in the UK, came to an end when banking reform allowed building societies to demutualise and offer products that banks offered. Introduction of the Right to Buy (RTB) in Britain, in 1980, encouraged those on low incomes and already in social housing to buy their homes. Thirty years later and over 2 million homes sold at a discount to their occupiers resulted in a net loss of publicly owned housing. Housing bubbles in the 1980s and 1990s gave inflated values of these newly bought assets; RTB owners obtained loans leveraged against these inflated house prices, which resulted in negative equity, repossessions and homelessness. The London Interbank Offered Rate (LIBOR) was introduced in 1984 to offer consistency in the interest rates charged on interbank loans. Basel Accord in 1988 required banks to set aside capital to deal with debt default problems that might occur, but it fundamentally allowed banks to circumnavigate the provisions in the US Glass-Steagall Act (1933).[d] Further reduction in the strengths of UK manufacturing industries; alongside increased freedom from regulation for financial traders. The financial services sector has grown unimpeded, to the extent that it is now seen as 'too big to fail'. Coal mining, ship building, car production and steel manufacture have not been so protected.

Table 1.1: continued

Britain in recession 1990–92	
1990s	Britain joined the European Exchange Rate Mechanism (ERM) in 1990. 'Black Wednesday' – September 1992. Britain left the ERM in 1992 after speculators launched an attack on sterling. This was a defining moment in the rise of global capital, which, it seemed, was empowered to take on a central bank and win. Not being part of the ERM has allowed the government to pursue a track of quantitative easing during the current recession. From the end of the 1990s recession and during the remainder of the decade, there was continued and uninterrupted growth, ending in December 2007 with the recession.[e]
Late 1990s to mid 2000s	The financial services sector continued to grow in Britain and the US. Thatcher/Major hands-off approach to the finance sector continued under Brown's 'light-touch' regulation. Continued innovation in hedge funds and derivatives products. The euro was launched in the late 1990s (Spain and Portugal were founder eurozone members and Greece was admitted in 2001). 1999 saw the repeal of the Glass-Steagall Act in the US. 'Sub-prime' lending in America saw a rapid growth between 1999 and 2008. Britain's gold reserve was sold on the market for an average price of $276 per ounce between 1999 and 2002 (Benedictus, 2010). Money was invested in the euro and other foreign currencies.[f] Increasingly aggressive sub-prime lending, in the US particularly, but also in the UK, with proactive strategies on new lending from banks. Risk was seen to be minimal as loans were backed with the increasingly valuable asset of houses. Creation and development of risk distribution products such as Credit Default Swaps (CDS)[g] and Collateralised Debt Obligations (CDO).[h] CDOs epitomised the globalisation of risk and debt as bundles were unpacked, repackaged, relabelled with new risk ratings and sold on around the world. The debts (originally supported by real estate values inflated by easy credit, but by 2007 rapidly falling in value) were not easily located in these CDO bundles. The US hedge fund Long Term Capital Management collapsed in late 1999. Collapse of Enron, in the US, in 2002. The subsequent hearings in Congress uncovered the complexities of the operating arrangements using subsidiary companies and derivatives products. This was closely followed by collapse of Arthur Andersen, in Britain. In the US William White[i] warned the Kansas City's Symposium at Wyoming that 'We need to find solutions that strike the right balance between intervention and market processes' (Borio and White, 2003, 32) and suggested two modifications: firstly, that policy decisions should be based on longer horizons and, secondly, that greater weight should be assigned to the balance of risks. In 2004 the Treasury in Britain knew it did not have the processes in place to deal with a failing bank. A subsequent House of Commons Public Accounts Committee report (June 2009) concluded that 'the pace with which [the Treasury] acted to remedy these shortcomings was leisurely'. This combination of poor scenario planning and light-touch regulation of the shadow banking system had an impact on events in 2007. 2004 saw the Basel 2 Accord, which supposedly introduced a tighter alignment of risk control and bank capital.

Table 1.1: continued

Britain in recession 2007-10	
2007 to mid 2008	In his Budget statement in March 2007, Gordon Brown told the House of Commons: 'And we will never return to the old boom and bust.' Later in 2007, the value of housing fell in the US and Britain.
	Problems in the US sub-prime mortgage market became more apparent.
	There was divergence between LIBOR and the Bank of England interest rate; this represented the mistrust between banks because of the inability to identify the location of toxic debt. Banks stopped lending to each other, resulting in a lack of liquidity in the market, which became known as 'the credit crunch'.
	The credit crunch – mostly hidden from public view, but felt by financial institutions constrained by lack of liquidity in loans between banks – became prominent in the 'run' on the Northern Rock bank in September 2007; this followed reports in the media that the bank had received 'emergency' funding from the Bank of England because of liquidity difficulties and cash shortage.
	Northern Rock was nationalised to protect customers in February 2008, after failure to find a private buyer.
	Spike in world oil prices, rising to $140 a barrel. There was a spike in gas prices and a rise in food and other commodity prices too at this time.[j]
Autumn 2008	Collapse of Icelandic bank. A number of British local authorities had made large investments and lost money.
	Scandal of Madoff's Ponzi scheme in the US and the global effect on individual and organisational investors.
	In March 2008, Bear Stearns was on the brink of failure, but Federal Bank of America stepped in to support it. JP Morgan took over the company.[k]
	Fannie Mae and Freddie Mac,[m] whose role in the US was to provide mortgage liquidity to the market through loans, were brought under US government 'conservatorship' (US government guaranteed the debt). Between the two institutions they had a huge responsibility for the mortgage market in the US – over $5 trillion (Cable, 2009).
	Collapse of Lehman Brothers in the US – an example of a bank that the US Federal Reserve Bank did not think was 'too big to fail', although this was the largest bankruptcy known, with a debt of over $600 billion.[n] The ripple effect of this bankruptcy led to an 'end of capitalism' discourse for a time.
	It also hastened the merger and buy-out of a number of distinguished US banks.
	In Britain, Woolworths went into administration resulting in job losses and vacant shop fronts across the country.
2009	The previous 'end of capitalism' discourse seems to have been firmly replaced with 'Armageddon' of public debt levels.[o] A certainty of the need for public spending cuts took hold in public and political discourse.
	The government allowed the Bank of England to start a Quantitative Easing (QE) programme (essentially expanding the Bank's monetary base to buy back government and other bonds from banks). £200 billion had been spent by mid 2010.
	Housing markets in both Britain and the US saw some stabilisation, and in areas of Britain, month-on-month growth in the market value of houses.
	HM Government published its asset portfolio as part of the operational efficiency programme (HM Government, 2009c), which included suggestions of public asset sales.
	Northern Rock was divided into a 'good bank' and a 'bad bank' so that 'toxic assets' were separated out from the commercial bank.
	The Pre-Budget Report in December 2009 announced an increase in taxation through a rise in National Insurance contributions, and a cut in public service expenditure from 2011. The UK public sector deficit for the year was estimated at £178 billion.
	By Christmas 2009, 30,000 small firms had been bankrupted since the start of the crisis (Kingsmill, 2009).

Table 1.1: continued

2010	The debate moved from individual mortgage debt to national sovereign debt as Iceland refused to repay debt to Britain and the Netherlands. This built on the warning from both the International Monetary Fund (IMF) and Standard and Poor's ratings agency in 2009 that Britain's AAA credit rating may be under threat unless the government reduced public debt.
	The dependency of currencies such as the euro was in doubt with the potential domino effect across the eurozone of the state of Greece's economy, as well as others including Portugal, Ireland and Spain.
	At the end of March 2010, UK unemployment had increased to 2.51 million.
	The price of gold per ounce stood at over $1,100 per ounce in April 2010 (Benedictus, 2010)ᵖ and the people of Britain were encouraged to 'cash my gold'!
	2010 Budget downwardly revised the public sector deficit for 2010 to £167 billion.
	By the end of April 2010, ratings agency Standard and Poor's had downgraded Greece's debt status to 'junk' and both Spain and Portugal also had been downgraded. There were fears of a spread of sovereign debt crises across Europe; but the 750 billion euro bail-out package to Greece calmed the markets a little and the euro rallied briefly.
	A Conservative–Liberal Democrat alliance formed the new UK government in May 2010; their coalition agreement made clear that the £6 billion efficiency savings to start in 2010, as included in the Conservative manifesto, would remain in place.
	The Queen's Speech at the end of May outlined a number of Bills in the Conservative–Liberal Democrat government's programme, including a Bill from the Department for Work and Pensions on benefits changes.
	Details of the £6 billion cuts to be made in 2010 were also announced at the end of May by the new Chancellor (Osborne), eg over £500 million cut from quangos, £900 million from the Business and Innovation and Skills Department and £200 million from universities.
	In the US, Obama signs the Dodd-Frank Wall Street and Consumer Protection Act in June 2010, designed to reform financial regulation.
	The Emergency Budget published by the Coalition government in June 2010 announced deep and rapid cuts in public sector budgets, as well as tax increases, such as the rise in VAT to 20% from January 2011.
	Quangos continued to be abolished through 2010, and regional planning bodies were abolished and replaced with Local Enterprise Partnerships (LEPs). Government Offices in the Regions were also axed, together with the Financial Services Authority, the Food Standards Agency and the Film Council, and the Tenant Services Authority was put under review – to name but a few.
	A number of budgets were cut with immediate effect too – including the Building Schools for the Future programme, child trust fund payments, and capital funding for Gypsy and Travellers sites, among many others. Concerns were raised over the disproportionate effect on the poor and vulnerable (see further Chapter Five in this book).
	The Budget at the end of June 2010 and the Comprehensive Spending Review in Autumn 2010 continued the new tightening of government expenditure on public services. Central government departments, along with local councils, were working on financial scenario planning of cuts in budgets of between 25% and 40%.
	In September 2010 Connaught, the property services group specialising in social housing, went into administration.
	The 'Big Society' takes centre stage in the ideology of the Coalition government, local councils pilot initiatives as localism 'Vanguards' and individuals are asked to contribute ideas on where efficiencies can be found as part of the 'spending challenge'.

Notes to Table 1.1

[a] The measure of PSNB has changed since 1975 and would measure 6.9% now (Clark and Dilnot, 2002).

[b] Some commentators blame this Act for the sub-prime crisis in the US, although many institutions lending in the most recent crisis were not bound by the CRA. The Conservative–Liberal Democrat government coming into power in May 2010 in the UK was reportedly considering a similar piece of legislation.

[c] US dollars deposited in European banks (now further afield around the globe too) and paid out on short-loan period. The relevance of the deposit in Europe was the facility to escape US Federal Reserve regulations (see further, Chapters Two and Three of this book, and Friedman, nd).

[d] Following the US stock market crash in 1929 and then the collapse of large sections of the banking sector in 1933, two financial bills were brought together in one Act. The Glass-Steagall Act formally separated investment and commercial banking functions.

[e] Originally it was thought that the recession started in March 2008, but revised figures on GDP showed that the start date was more probably in December 2007.

[f] By 2010 the euro and some other currencies were devaluing fast as the extent of sovereign debt became more apparent in countries such as Greece.

[g] A package which backed up the validity and viability of the investment – a little like the additional insurance one might buy to offset the risk of failure of a new TV or fridge.

[h] Bundling together a range of debt products and selling them on with a rating to denote their risk of failure. See further Tett (2009) for a good account of the financial services sector and its products.

[i] Head of the Bank for International Settlements.

[j] A McKinsey report in March 2009 refers to growth in energy demand fuelling future price spikes – it made recommendations on energy efficiency to help combat the growing demand.

[k] See further Cable (2009) for an interesting account of this period.

[l] The Federal National Mortgage Association.

[m] The Federal Home-Loan Mortgage Corporation.

[n] Sandler and Fortado (2009) also reported that fees involved in administering the bankruptcy could reach $1.4 billion.

[o] Steve Bundred, former Chief Executive of the Audit Commission.

[p] Worth around $800 an ounce more than it was sold for.

Gordon et al (2009) examined the responses from UK local authorities in the three recessions during the period 1980–2008. Some of the key contexts, principles and issues are shown in Table 1.2.

The title of this book (*From Recession to Renewal*) suggests that the authors are relatively optimistic about the outcomes of the financial crisis in relation to public services and governance – that is not to say that we suggest repairing the status quo, but that there is an opportunity

Table 1.2: Responses to recessions

	Early 1980s recession	**Early 1990s recession**	**Late 2000s recession**
CONTEXT	National economic strategy exposed whole economy to intense competitive pressures. Impact concentrated in North and on middle-aged/elderly production industries – substantial parts lost or long-term decline. Recurring high unemployment.	Recession seen as the puncture of mid-1980s boom. Anti-inflationary macro-economic policies in place following mid-1980s boom. Impact of recession felt in service areas this time, but the industrialised sectors in the North still not recovered from previous recession. Effect on housing market, fall in house prices, reduction in new development, negative equity and repossession.	Loss of confidence in financial markets seen to trigger recession (see Table 1.1), similar to 1990s recession in perception of puncturing a boom caused by house-price growth and credit-based personal consumption. Suggested that focus was in and around London region with substantial job losses. Similarity to previous recessions in the demand side of housing market, but more rapid decline than in previous decades. Some commentators suggest more similarities with 1930s than the two most recent recessions.
GOVERNMENT RESPONSE	Political environment at time saw intervention to counter market forces as inappropriate. Alternative Economic Strategy developed from 1973 to 1983 by Labour, as well as some local authority (LA) activism in attempt to react to neoliberal government policy. LAs constrained by lack of finance and reduced borrowing powers. Localist approaches to service delivery. Right to Buy introduced but receipts went to the centre rather than LAs.	Muted response from LAs because of tight expenditure controls, e.g. arrival of poll tax as well as disappearance of more activist LAs. More lobbying for central discretionary funds, development of regeneration and urban policy making to deal with longer-term structural issues in areas. LAs responded to homelessness issues, but housing associations, with wider borrowing powers, provided some assistance to limit repossession, and some social purchase of private sector homes.	Perhaps less need for regionally focused response or spatially targeted boosts to LA activity. A need identified for more intense LA response to homelessness issues – central funds such as the Homes and Communities Agency's mortgage rescue scheme, and local policies to mitigate homelessness seemed to be instigated quite quickly; but crunch in building industry hampered new development. Distinction from previous two recessions in lack of funding for mortgages and small business loans. Impacts in number of areas, including private and social building as well as LAs' own capacity to invest.

Source: Adapted from Gordon et al (2009, 2–3).

to change the current paradigm of market-led governance to a more balanced approach of benefit to all in the changing global society. There is a potential for renewed focus on governance, as well as on the practical services provided by the public sector and its partners, and a chance to reconsider the role of the public sector more generally. Government and governance have an integral role in shaping public society as it emerges from the financial crisis and can do so in a positive and invigorating fashion that builds on the position of the public sector and its contribution to economic and social recovery. We hope for a new debate, not the same old sterile, private versus public sector argument, where the left or right argue for their favoured sector to be the most powerful. What is tantalisingly alluded to is a new relationship between the public and private sectors which recognises and builds on mutuality and recognition of the benefits of each to the other. The new political alliance which built a Conservative–Liberal Democrat government in May 2010 offered a potentially new paradigm for such a debate; however, it quickly became apparent that, in relation to the economy, reductions in the cost and role of the public sector was still the only political discourse in town. As reductions in public expenditure continued to be announced throughout 2010, there seemed to be less rationale for optimism coming out of the new government's discourse of rolling back the state. Only a critical perspective of the development of government thinking about what exactly is the 'Big Society' and what is meant by 'localism' within a unitary state, and the impacts of these and of reductions in state spending power, will tell whether recession is followed by renewal or retrenchment of government and governance.

Initial and emerging responses to the financial crisis

Fundamentally, there are three key responses that a government can take to a financial crisis:

(1) 'print' money through a programme of quantitative easing;
(2) cut public spending;
(3) raise income tax,

or it can take a mixed approach, using all three measures.

These responses have to be very finely balanced so that a fledgling recovery is not put at risk by quick withdrawal of economic stimulus. The International Monetary Fund (IMF) warned of the need for finely balanced measures (IMF, 2010) and offered potential solutions to taxing banks and bankers (IMF, 2010a). In its *World Economic Outlook* report

(IMF, 2010b) it referred to the fragile recovery and warned that fiscal stimulus packages should be fully implemented throughout 2010, with fiscal consolidation as more of a focus from 2011.

The previous Labour government's Pre-Budget Report in December 2009 and the Fiscal Responsibility Act 2010 set out an initial plan for the economy which embraced a mixture of a managed reduction in public spending over 8 years, and some rises in tax income. While there were different approaches across the political spectrum in the run-up to the election on the depth and speed of government measures to implement reductions in spending (Conservatives, 2009; Clegg, 2010), there was a consensus that reductions were necessary to lower the national public debt; and the new Conservative–Liberal Democrat government speedily confirmed a package of £6 billion efficiency savings in public sector spending to be made in 2010–11.

Commentators on government responses to the crisis in 2009 and 2010 were mixed. From a US perspective, Stelzer felt that the government needed to wake up to the severity of the public debt and he suggested that the financial markets did not believe there was a credible plan to deal with the issue (Newsnight, 2010). A view which chimed with those in the private sector, such as Lea (2009) and other industry figures, suggested that only a downgrading of Britain's credit rating would prompt the cuts in the public debt that would be necessary. The Institute for Fiscal Studies (2010a) suggested that the main political parties in the run-up to the election were 'vague' in their plans for dealing with public debt and that they were 'overambitious' in the amount that could be saved in public sector spending.

The issue of regulating the shadow banking system and its products was a sporadic part of the debate in 2010. Beyond the one-off bankers' tax and the Fiscal Responsibility Act 2010, the discourse had moved from one of 'the end of bankers and capitalism' to one of 'public debt' and this was reflected in the government's initial responses in the crisis. White (2009) argued that this discourse of 'can't lean [against upswing of a credit cycle] but can clean [up after the bust]' was unsatisfactory. He suggested that 'monetary policy should be more focused on "pre-emptive tightening" to moderate credit bubbles than on "pre-emptive easing" to deal with the after effects' (p 1). The government in early 2010 seemed to be cautious in overly 'tightening', in the face of threats from the financial services sector to leave the country. Only a medium- to long-term view will show whether the government's response will include some 'leaning' as well as the current 'cleaning' operation, although the IMF report to the G20 in April 2010 certainly suggested 'leaning' approaches in its proposals for a financial stability contribution tax to mitigate against bail-out costs in a future crisis, and a financial activities tax on profits and pay of bankers (IMF, 2010a).

By April 2010 there was a Europe-wide fear of the spread of sovereign debt, its effect both on the euro and British economic recovery, particularly following the downgrading of Greece's debt status to 'junk' by Standard and Poor's, and the subsequent wrangling on bail-out measures by eurozone members. There was a fear for other European countries, in particular those with similar debt levels to Greece, but also concern over the effect of the fall in value of Greek bonds held by other European governments and banks, and the potential fall in value of other European downgraded bonds, such as those of Portugal and Spain. The links between European and global banks and governments were inextricable, and the effects appeared to be virtually contagious, – but were soothed, for a time, by the balm of a €750 billion bail-out package to Greece. Britain's debt, and the commentary by private industry, international experts, the IMF and ratings agencies, meant that the new government felt compelled to make the reduction of the public sector debt a priority in its planning.

In May 2010 the new Conservative–Liberal Democrat government confirmed intentions to reduce public spending immediately by £6 billion in 2010–11, a plan which front-loaded the tightening of public expenditure and which some warned could lead to a double-dip recession. Once the full impact of the 2010 Budget started to be felt, concerns were raised not only by public sector agencies, but by private companies whose main clients were in the public sector; this led to an emerging fear, in the late summer of 2010, of another recession.

Local responses

On a more local level, some interesting solutions emerged. The Audit Commission (AC)[2] in 2009 reported that local authorities had taken steps to support businesses, labour markets and vulnerable households. They referred, however, to 'waves' of impact on the economy, on society and as a result of uneven recovery across geographical areas and different groups of society. It was suggested that city borough councils would be worst hit, with districts in more rural areas suffering a lesser impact (AC, 2009, 21). Experian (2009) found in its analysis that councils in the North East and in Wales would be hardest hit (p 7). Moreover, what remains of the British industrial sector faced renewed pressure, with the announcement by Ericsson in November 2009 of the closure of its research and development plant in Coventry; with Corus's announcement in December 2009 of the end of steel production in

Teesside, because of reduced global demand; with Kraft confirming in early February 2010 the closure of the Cadbury factory in Keynsham, and, also in February, the announcement by AstraZeneca of the closure of its Loughborough plant. The respective regional impacts of these plans further undermine notions of imminent recovery.

The public sector, often a major employer in some areas, was also announcing job cuts and mergers in some services, which would have an impact on the local employment landscape. CEDOS/ADEPT (2010) reported (p 7) that an estimated 6,700 jobs had been lost in councils in the six months to May 2009, and that predicted job losses in local authorities would continue at the same rate over the next year. Just one example among many reports was the merger by Coventry and Warwickshire councils of certain services, as well as undertaking joint working between agencies, in order to provide £12 million in savings (*Coventry Telegraph*, 2010). While the issue of unemployment was felt most starkly in the private sector at the beginning of the recession, by 2010 the public sector was starting to feel the impact and was predicting more of the same in the years to come. The Chartered Institute of Personnel and Development (CIPD, 2010) suggested a two-speed recovery for jobs and the economy (particularly in the South, where the impacts of previous recessions were not still as obvious and deeply manifest as in some areas of the North), with private sector firms seeing a return to positive growth for the first time in over 18 months, with benefits particularly in private sector services and manufacturing.

The 'wave' analogy used by the AC (2009) allowed analysis of complex and multiple facets of a recession and their impact on local government and wider society. Three waves of impact were suggested, along with the responses necessary from local government, as set out in Table 1.3.

The AC (2009) reported that, while all councils responded to the impact of the crisis, 'most responses have been basic and low risk' (p 35) but some councils have prepared for the social 'wave' by investing in, for example, crime and social disorder partnerships to mitigate social impact (p 37). The report examined the detailed financial impact on councils' own resources; for example, in one metropolitan borough, their stated financial and social issues included:

- reduction in treasury management income
- reduction in council tax and business rates collection
- increase in rent arrears
- increase in housing benefit applications

Table 1.3: Recession 'waves'

Wave	Response
1: Economic A relatively short period of economic decline – this can include firms reducing staff numbers, rise in unemployment and fall in real incomes.	*1: Protect* The role of central government is to protect key industries and provide stabilisation in the economy, as well as to continue to provide the welfare safety net. Local councils should protect local businesses and help local people.
2: Social A longer period where economic growth may improve, but unemployment continues, which can be linked to housing and health issues.	*2: Support* Councils have an increasingly important role, as local people increasingly need their services. Local government will deliver central programmes, but also develop specific responses for local priorities.
3: Unequal recovery Economy and investment grow, but some areas will take longer to benefit from recovery in the economy.	*3: Recover* Investment is provided in areas slower to recover, by both central and local government agencies, through training, labour market and social programmes.

Source: Adapted from AC (2009, 13).

- reduction in revenue from planning application, building control and land search fees
- increase in number of abandoned vehicles
- increase in jobseeker allowance applications
- reduction in capital receipts. (Adapted from AC, 2009, 42)

In *Surviving the Crunch*, the AC (2010) reported differing proposals on the speed of cuts and concluded: 'Cuts can be made quickly; delivering more for less is harder and takes longer' (p 43). It outlined a framework in stages of difficulty and expediency, with the quickest and easiest step being (1) 'Same for more – Cuts', which includes increasing fees, charges and taxes (see Mear's Chapter Four in this book for a full debate on these options, as well as Brown and Yates in Chapter Eight on the 'easyBorough' model); followed by (2) 'Less for less – Cuts', which includes redundancies, demand management through restricting access and service cuts; (3) 'Same for less – Efficiency', comprising recruitment freeze, outsourcing, 'efficiencies' in back-office systems and savings through partnerships as well as efficient procurement and asset management; and finally, the most difficult and timely option, (4) 'More for less – Redesign', which refers to partnership delivery, reducing need to reduce demand, prevention and service redesign (p 43). The option of delivering more for less has to be the most attractive option for the future, but as the AC notes, it is the more difficult and time-consuming option. Clearly, at a national level the

Conservative–Liberal Democrat Coalition government decided to cut hard and fast, rather than assessing the situation for longer-term gain, and in so doing immediately impacted on local government budgets, services and strategies.

The financial crisis and politics

Political structures and culture in the UK have shaped our experience of the financial crisis. Equally, the financial crisis can be said to have reshaped politics and shown a perceived weakness of government when faced with global forces. When voters look to government to take immediate action to tackle certain economic pressure points they can be left with little doubt that government either will not or cannot protect them from, say, threatened redundancies. The take-over of Cadbury by Kraft in the early part of 2010 and the uncertainty over possible loss of jobs that arose left a sense of powerlessness for all concerned, not least the government. Short of taking drastic political action that might see potential buyers withdraw and a take-over deal collapse, with the subsequent loss of even more jobs, government can do little to force action in a global market. Politicians expressed anger at the take-over and made reference to protection measures in their election manifestos. The reality, however, of what may be possible in a globalised economic model, held up by both political left and right as a beneficial way of doing business, has yet to be seen.

The role of the state – and not just at times of crisis – became the political battleground in the pre-election period. The simplistic views of the state as a tax-and-spend bureaucracy that consumes resources and wealth generated by the private sector, or as a modern-day Robin Hood that redistributes wealth and controls the actions of a greedy market are both designed for public political consumption. The complex reality is that while the state has a role in society and in the economy, that role is designed to meet not just a set of existing social, economic and political requirements, but also a political ideology. Yet, the simplistic views set out above also reflect the effect that state economic and political action can have and the balance that needs to be drawn when the state acts in times of recession, particularly when public sector debt plays such a dominant role in how economies respond to recession. Globalisation has changed the power relationship between 'transnational' businesses and nation states; and this will be discussed in more depth by Lambie in the following chapter. The public sector has a vital and powerful role to play in the way in which Britain emerges from recession and in drawing out the lessons from the current experience. While the public-versus-private, state-versus-capital arguments will continue from their ideological bunkers, how the public sector can and does support the private sector, and vice versa, is likely to receive less attention. There is not just what the central state does during a recession, but also what local government can do in an economic downturn, and what councils can do to regenerate local economies. The economic development budget for local authorities, however, is a soft target when it comes to reductions in expenditure and is likely to suffer while attention is focused on core services.

Politics has shaped the discourse of the financial crisis in Britain, along with the former Labour government's and the new Conservative-Liberal Democrat Coalition government's responses to the need to cut debt. The crisis has, however, also seemed to shape a new politics, one which the electorate wanted to see less on party lines, and more on consensus and alliance. Despite all the warnings from various commentators and ratings agencies that a hung parliament would send the markets into turmoil, the people of Britain clearly thought differently in May 2010 and they voted for a 'new' politics, resulting in a coalition government. How that new politics finally plays itself out will rest on a number of issues: the nature and impact of expenditure reductions and the public reaction to them; the direction of subsequent budgets; the emerging debates around the development of the 'Big Society' and localism (which appear 'home turf' for the Liberal Democrats); the campaign and result of the referendum on the alternative vote; tensions within the coalition cabinet and government backbenches, particularly personal differences and thwarted political ambitions; relationships with the EU; constitutional change and parliamentary reform; the future of Trident; and, any foreign policy challenges that may emerge.

Structure and key arguments of the book

The book is divided into three main parts: (1) Context; (2) Policies and issues; and (3) Conclusion. Part One provides a context for the financial crisis with in-depth political and economic insight into the events leading up to the recession and analyses of lessons that can be learnt. This first chapter has given an overview of the financial crisis and introduced some of the key themes emerging in the impact on the public sector. Chapter Two examines the economic, political and ideological processes that have led to the rise of globalisation driven by 'market fundamentalism'; and it considers how states have been compromised and offers options that may still remain for them to intervene so as to prevent systemic failure. Chapter Three provides a detailed European context for the crisis and asks searching questions on the future of European governments and markets in a global economy.

In Part Two of the book (Chapters Four to Nine) the key policies and issues emerging from an examination of the impact of the crisis on local government and public services in Britain are examined. Chapter Four provides information on financial instruments and mechanisms that have been available to local government and other public sector agencies in responding to the fiscal deficit, and it argues that current economic models will not work for the future.

The financial crisis has an impact on communities, and particularly on vulnerable groups – how can the most vulnerable groups be protected and, what support can be given? Chapter Five examines the issues for vulnerable people and more generally for community cohesion. A range of different examples is used to demonstrate the need for support, and the response from public agencies to protect community members. As a potential multiplier of social exclusion and inequality, the financial crisis is examined in this chapter for its effect on those already seen to be vulnerable.

An analysis of how the recession will affect financial viability, and particularly the community leadership role of councils, is presented in Chapter Six. It examines options for the role of local authorities, such as the service emphasis or community leadership options. The debate on public services and the public sector is also teased out further here and the authors outline a conceptual framework which facilitates an understanding of how councils might respond in this time of change.

Chapter Seven argues that current centrally dictated 'command and control' methods of public service management are inherently wasteful and have only made services worse at higher cost. Instead, an alternative 'systems thinking' methodology is outlined and its application is illustrated through examples from UK public services. If applied more widely, it is suggested, these methods have the potential to create better services at much lower costs while also reintroducing local responsibility for improving these services.

In Chapter Eight, the viability of the choice, personalisation and empowerment agenda in delivery of public services across local government is examined in the context of the financial crisis. The publication of the previous Labour government's (2009) public service reform paper *Building Britain's Future* and the subsequent Conservative–Liberal Democrat Coalition government's ideas on the 'Big Society' promised empowerment of the public consumer, but how viable is this in the recession? Particular attention is paid to different models for the future delivery of services and their implications for the choice, empowerment and personalisation agenda. The authors argue that innovative approaches are likely to be developed only at a local level.

There seems to be a discourse in government that ignores the need for governance in the delivery of services and the management of neighbourhoods. The marketisation of a range of public services, from health to housing, has resulted in a focus on service delivery rather than governance. Chapter Nine examines the orthodoxy of governance and unpicks some of the assumptions in this debate, and it asks who provides public services and does it matter – do we need government?

In Part Three, the concluding chapter, Ten, summarises the debates in the book and pulls out key themes and ideas as we strive for a recovery from the financial crisis in the public sector that is equitable – and not a recovery that rewards vested interests at the expense of more vulnerable sections of society.

There are key, cross-cutting themes in the book, for example the role of government is the focus of Chapters Six and Nine, but is also an underlying current throughout the different debates in most of the chapters. The notion of empowerment of citizens is also a central tenet of Chapter Eight, but again, ideas on the role of citizens, society and government and the changing power structure of government and governed are touched upon in a number of discussions across chapters. Our aim for this book is to examine the impact of the financial crisis on public services in local government – this is achieved within a framework of broad ideas and themes related to the current changes in government and the future of government and society. We do not attempt to predict exactly how much local budgets will be cut by when, and exactly which services will be affected – a range of reports, including government budgets, think-tank analyses and local government budgets concentrate on this level of detail. Instead, our book takes a step back to provide a broader framework for thinking about the impact of the financial crisis.

Notes

[1] The 2010 Budget gave figures showing a deficit of £110 billion, public sector net borrowing of £149 billion and public sector net debt at 61.9% of GDP at the end of March 2010.

[2] The Coalition government announced in August 2010 that the Audit Commission would be abolished to make way for an 'army of armchair auditors' and to create savings for the public purse.

References

AC (Audit Commission) (2008) *Crunch Time: The Impact of the Economic Downturn on Local Government Finances*, London: AC.

AC (2009) *When it Comes to the Crunch ... How Councils are Responding to the Recession*, London: AC.

AC (2010) *Surviving the Crunch: Local Finances in the Recession and Beyond*, London: AC.

Benedictus, L. (2010) 'Nothing says wealth and power like gold. So what should we make of Labour's disastrous sell-off and the national mania for postal cash?', *The Guardian*, G2, 12 April, pp 6–9.

Blastland, M. (2008) 'The myth of record debt', *BBC News Magazine*, http://news.bbc.co.uk/1/hi/magazine.

Bootle, R. (2009) *The Trouble with Markets: Saving Capitalism from itself*, London: Nicholas Brealey Publishing.

Borio, C. and White, W. (2003) 'Whither monetary and financial stability? The implications of evolving policy regimes', Paper presented to the Federal Reserve Bank of Kansas City's Symposium, Wyoming, 28–30 August.

Brown, G. (2007) Budget Statement, 21 March, London, House of Commons.

Bundred, S. (2009) 'Our public debt is hitting Armageddon levels', *The Times*, February 27, www.timesonline.co.uk.

Byrne, L (2010) Letter from former Treasury Chief Secretary, Liam Byrne, to his successor, David Laws, 6 April 2010, as cited in P. Owen, (2010) 'Ex-Treasury secretary Liam Byrne's note to his successor: there's no money left', *Guardian Online*, 17 May, www.guardian.co.uk.

Cable, V. (2009) *The Storm: The World Economic Crisis and What it Means*, London: Atlantic Books.

CEDOS/ADEPT (Chief Economic Development Officers' Society and Association of Directors of Environment, Economy, Planning and Transport) (2010) *Recession Report 3*, February 2010, CEDOS/ADEPT.

CIPD (Chartered Institute of Personnel and Development) (2010) *Labour Market Outlook*, Quarterly survey report, Spring 2010, London CIPD/KPMG.

Clark, T. and Dilnot, A. (2002) *Measuring the UK Fiscal Stance since the Second World War*, London: Institute for Fiscal Studies.

Clegg, N. (2010) 'Four Steps to a Fairer Britain', Speech, 11 January, www.libdems.org.uk.

Conservatives (2009) *Reconstruction Plan for a Strong Economy*, www.conservatives.com.

Coventry Telegraph (2010) 'Councils draw up plans for massive cuts', 6 April, www.coventrytelegraph.net.

Experian (2009) *The Insight Report – Quarter 4, 2009,* London: Experian.

Friedman, M. (nd) 'The euro-dollar market: some first principles', Selected Paper No 34, Graduate School of Business, Chicago: University of Chicago.

Gamble, A. (2009) *The Spectre at the Feast: Capitalist Crisis and the Politics of Recession,* Basingstoke: Palgrave Macmillan.

Gordon, I., Travers, T. and Whitehead, C. (2009) *Local Authorities and the Downturn: A Review of Issues, Experience and Options,* Spatial Economics Research Centre, Policy Paper 3, London: LSE/ESRC/BERR/CLG.

HM Government (2009a) *Putting the Frontline First: Smarter Government,* London: HM Stationery Office.

HM Government (2009b) *Building Britain's Future,* London: HM Stationery Office.

HM Government (2009c) *Operational Efficiency Programme: Asset Portfolio,* London: HM Treasury Publishing Unit.

HM Treasury (2010) *Budget 2010: Securing the Recovery,* London: The Stationery Office.

House of Commons Public Accounts Committee (2009) *Thirty-First Report – The Nationalisation of Northern Rock,* June, www.publications. parliament.uk.

Hutton, W. (1995) *The State We're In,* London: Jonathan Cape.

IMF (International Monetary Fund) (2010) *Exiting from Crisis Intervention Policies,* www.imf.org.

IMF (2010a) *A Fair and Substantial Contribution by the Financial Sector,* interim report for the G20, April 2010, IMF.

IMF (2010b) *World Economic Outlook, April 2010, Rebalancing Growth,* IMF.

Institute for Fiscal Studies (2010) Post Budget Briefing 2010, opening remarks by Robert Chote, Director IFS, London: IFS.

Institute for Fiscal Studies (2010a) 'Filling the hole: How do the three main UK parties plan to repair the public finance?', 2010 Election Briefing Note No 12, London: IFS/Nuffield Foundation.

King, M. (2009) Speech by Mervyn King, Governor of the Bank of England, to Scottish business organisations, 20 October: Edinburgh, Bank of England.

Kingsmill, D. (2009) 'Rescuing small business', *Management Today,* December, p 24.

Lambie, G. (2009) 'Nemesis of "market fundamentalism"? The ideology, deregulation and crisis of finance', *Contemporary Politics,* vol 15, no 2, pp 157–77.

Lea, R. (2009) 'The IMF is right: quicker action needed on the public finances', *Arbuthnot Banking Group Perspective*, www.arbuthnot.co.uk.

Lewis, M. (2010) *The Big Short: Inside the Doomsday Machine*, London: Allen Lane.

McKinsey and Company (2009) 'Averting the next energy crisis: The demand challenge', www.mckinsey.com.

Newsnight (2010) Panel discussion, BBC2, 5 January, introduced by Paul Mason and including Jeremy Paxman, Will Hutton, Irwin Stelzer and Gillian Tett.

Reinhart, C. and Rogoff, K. (2008) 'This time is different: A panoramic view of eight centuries of financial crises', Harvard University, www.economics.harvard.edu.

Sandler, L. and Fortado, F. (2009) 'Lehman fees could reach $1.4 billion, besting Enron', *Bloomberg News*, 23 October, www.bloomberg.com.

Stiglitz, J. (2010) *Freefall: Free Markets and the Sinking of the Global Economy*, London: Allen Lane.

Tett, G. (2009) *Fool's Gold: How Unrestrained Greed Corrupted a Dream, Shattered Global Markets and Unleashed a Catastrophe*, London: Little Brown.

White, W. (2009) 'Should monetary policy "lean or clean"?', Federal Reserve Bank of Dallas, Globalization and Monetary Policy Institute Working Paper no 34, www.dallasfed.org.

TWO

The historical context of the global financial crisis: from Bretton Woods to the debacle of neoliberalism

George Lambie

The global financial crisis, which began in 2007 and was temporarily contained in 2009 by national-level government interventions, still holds deep and worrying implications for the future. As nations have accrued huge deficits to prop up transnational financial institutions, the problems remain of large amounts of overvalued assets on banks' balance sheets, and unknown liabilities in off-balance-sheet vehicles. However, most significant and immediate for the theme addressed in this book is the British government's decision to maintain and increase spending in response to the crisis. This has led to an unprecedented peace-time budget deficit that now necessitates both cuts in public spending and increases in taxation, against a background of rising unemployment and sharply falling tax revenues. The root of this quandary, at the international and UK levels, lies not just in the mismanagement of the international monetary system by banks and governments, but in globalisation itself; a process in which a significant proportion of the power once held by nation-states has been ceded to transnational business (Strange, 1997).

The aim of this chapter is to provide a background to the current crisis of public finances in the UK by tracing the historical developments which have resulted in a transfer of power by states to global forces. The starting point for this analysis is the Bretton Woods conference of 1944 when the wartime Allies, led by the United States and Britain, met to establish a financially regulated order of nation-states which would contain the excesses of free capital movements. A study will follow of those actors, principally private international financial interests and emerging multinational corporations, that sought to undermine this order and replace it with a deregulated global market. Although leaders in some states attempted to resist this process, others, like

Margaret Thatcher in Britain and Ronald Reagan in the US, became champions of the new 'private' global system. Interventions by these neoliberal politicians, who in turn were influenced by academics and intellectuals who gave theoretical justifications to such notions as the 'efficient market hypothesis', consolidated the belief that the state's role was to facilitate the transnationalisation of market forces, rather than to seek to manage capitalism on behalf of the nation. It will be argued that the current crisis is a consequence of this faith in 'market fundamentalism' (Soros, 2008). To conclude, possible scenarios which may result from the crisis will be briefly suggested.

The above analysis will pay particular attention to the regulation and deregulation of finance since the Second World War. While this is not the only reason for the demise of Keynesian-style mixed economy and social democracy, and its replacement by neoliberalism, it is a major part of the processes that influence the motion of history under capitalism. A wider perspective on this transition is given by such writers as Coates (1980), Clarke (1988) and Brenner (2009).

Bretton Woods: bringing order to the vagaries and dangers of unrestrained capitalism

When the allied nations met at Bretton Woods in New Hampshire, US Treasury Secretary Henry Morganthau stated in his opening address to the conference (echoing President Roosevelt's 1933 inaugural speech) that the underlying objective of the proceedings was to reach an agreement that would 'drive the usurious money lenders from the temple of international finance' (Helleiner, 1994, 4). The most influential economists at the conference, including Britain's John Maynard Keynes and America's Harry Dexter White, believed that the largely unregulated flows of capital during the previous era of laissez-faire had led to the crash of 1929, the Great Depression that followed and, indirectly, the Second World War. In designing a new world order, the errors of the past had to be avoided, and as Keynes (1980, 17) stated, rejecting market liberalism in favour of the state management of capitalism, 'what used to be a heresy is now endorsed as orthodox'.

As early as 1933, Keynes had argued in an essay entitled 'National Self-Sufficiency' (Keynes, 1933) that while 'ideas, hospitality, travel' belonged to the international sphere, goods should be 'homespun whenever it is reasonably and conveniently possible' and governments should 'let finance be primarily national'. This last point was particularly important because he believed that, to achieve a nationally orientated strategy, countries must be able to organise their affairs without the disruptive influence of speculative capital movements. In the planning for Bretton Woods this objective was prioritised by Keynes and White, who argued that 'national' goals should take precedence over the financial interests of a small percentage of a country's population. In particular they felt the new 'welfare state' had to be protected from capital flight, driven either by political reasons or to avoid the 'burdens of social legislation' (Horsefield, 1969, 31). Such ideas had been supported by Roosevelt since the early 1930s, and were first tested during the state-led social planning programme of the New Deal. Even before Roosevelt, some American leaders had been fearful of the power of finance. For instance, when the US Federal Reserve was established by private financial interests (as was the Bank of England in 1694), Congressman Charles Lindbergh claimed, 'This Act [Federal Reserve Act, 23 December 1913] establishes the most gigantic trust on earth. When the President [Woodrow Wilson] signs the Bill, the *invisible government* [author's emphasis] of the Monetary Power will be legalised ...' (Roberts, 1984, 33).

Although the intentions of the main participants at Bretton Woods were to create a stable international system managed by nation-states, an overbearing reality was the newly assumed hegemonic status of the US: 'At the end of the war the USA controlled some 70% of the world's gold and foreign exchange reserves, and more than 40% of its industrial output while Europe and Japan had been devastated by war and the Third World was still locked into colonial servitude and contained less than 1% of the world's industrial capacity' (Brett, 1985, 63). But despite America's new role as world leader, which generated vast opportunities to benefit from previous centuries of European colonial expansion and acquisition, the first task was to ensure the survival of world capitalism after the devastation of the war. There was also a new Communist super-power, the Soviet Union, whose real threat was perhaps not so much its military might but the prospect of an alternative to capitalism, which could become more attractive if the latter did not adopt a human face.

Bretton Woods established the US dollar, backed by gold, as the key world currency against which other currencies would be pegged in a system of semi-fixed exchange rates. The power of the US after the war gave it the 'exorbitant privilege' (Giscard d'Estaing, cited in Gourinchas and Rey, 2005) of being able to print limitless paper certificates in the form of dollars, which could be exchanged for imports from other countries at no cost to the issuer. The former hegemon, Great Britain, had enjoyed a similar privilege in the 19th and early 20th centuries, based on the gold standard and the international role of sterling.

Although America's financial advantage can be seen as a means to advance its imperial power, a dominant and stable 'fiat' currency was essential for world economic recovery, and Bretton Woods represented the first attempt to establish an international financial and trading order among independent nation-states. The World Bank, the International Monetary Fund (IMF), and the General Agreement on Tariffs and Trade were also planned at the negotiations and their role was to regulate finance and trade in the postwar world economy.

The system that emerged was an incomplete Keynesian model of world development that emphasised the management of capitalism by synchronised international and state institutions. Vital to this project was the ability of states to impose capital controls to protect internal development strategies from capital flight, and an international system of semi-fixed exchange rates that would encourage economic stability and curb speculation. Keynes felt the role of capital was to provide the lubricant for production and trade, and speculative activities were in direct contradiction to this objective.

However, even before the Bretton Woods Agreement was passed in July 1945 by the US Senate, the New York and international banking community was anxious to shape its outcome in its favour, especially when Truman, who was more sympathetic to its cause than Roosevelt, became President in April (Helleiner, 1994, 52). Principally, it sought to make sterling convertible at the earliest opportunity so that American capital could penetrate the protected Sterling Area that had been established at the beginning of the war. Disregarding the 'transitional' period that had been agreed at Bretton Woods, Britain was encouraged to take a US loan and return sterling to convertibility in July 1947. But in the event, this premature opening was unsustainable and Britain was obliged to retreat back into the Sterling Area, frustrating the bankers' strategy. This later led to the European Recovery Programme (Marshall Plan 1948–52), when the US pumped $12 billion into the economies of Europe and Japan to facilitate their reconstruction and keep up demand for US industrial goods after the war. The Plan was sold to the American public, and Congress, as a means to turn the 'Red Tide' (perceived support for Communism), particularly in France and Italy, but there was little evidence that such a threat existed. Marshall aid certainly made an important contribution to postwar reconstruction; however, European recovery was already under way by 1948 (Milward, 1984). 'Marshall dollars' therefore were needed not so much to buy goods, but to provide offsetting finance to cover purchases already made in the US and continuing capital flight to America despite regulatory controls. In support of their argument for a rapid move to currency convertibility, the bankers had accurately identified that it would be very difficult to curb all speculative capital movements. Indeed only by imposing cooperative controls could such flows be stopped, but the US remained reluctant to implement this measure because of the benefits it accrued from foreign capital receipts and its new position as the world's banker. Resulting from these problems, and Britain's desire to protect the Sterling Area, it was not until the late 1950s that conditions in the international system were suitable for the full implementation of the Bretton Woods financial order based on the convertibility of currencies (Burnham, 2003).

Although the establishment of Bretton Woods was problematic and delayed, the quarter century from 1945 to 1970 was the most successful period of economic development ever recorded, especially in the industrialised world. Moreover, during the years from 1950 to 1970 gains were made not just by the owners of capital and the means of production, but also for ordinary working people as welfare reforms, trade unions and national economic planning helped to improve job security and standards of living. High levels of Keynesian-style domestic investment and a sustained increase in world trade drove this long boom of the postwar period. The aim of the system was full employment, growth, development and limited wealth redistribution under the control of national elites, professional managers and a bureaucratised welfare state. Worker involvement was mainly through trade unions, which were encouraged to accept the logic of a system that was willing to socialise consumption, but fell short of offering industrial democracy and control of production, which would have necessitated unacceptable levels of worker democracy that could not be contained within capitalism.

The new postwar regime of accumulation was founded on the 'Fordist' mode of production, which was dependent on national-level controls to support demand management and provide the welfare underpinnings of the system. According to some theorists, this nationally orientated model of development required a certain level of 'class compromise' (Aglietta, 1979). But from a Marxist perspective, it was a necessary new phase of capitalism which presented less of a 'compromise' if one takes into account that capital enjoyed a high level of profitability in the 1950s (Coates, 1980, 180), and labour productivity grew significantly (Yaffe, 1973, 48) in the immediate postwar years. The sociologist Braverman (1974) argued that advanced technology, mass production, conformity to the work ethic and modern management techniques deepened workers' alienation and exploitation rather than liberating them. Nevertheless, this economic model did lead to sustained growth and a significant increase in equality, especially in the developed countries, creating an expansion of the middle classes which sociologists termed the 'embourgeoisement' of society.

From the mid-1940s to the 1970s, the state in the major developed countries took charge of the 'commanding heights of the economy' and managed national developmental processes, and key industries in both the state and private sectors were run by a patrician elite who presided over a wider system of social and national responsibility. In the US this mode of organisation was termed the 'technostructure' by Galbraith (1968), in which corporations were no longer controlled by capitalist owners and shareholders, but by professional managers whose principal concern was the maintenance of a 'social enterprise', into which workers were incorporated as 'subordinate' partners, rather than simply factors of production. The industrial nations' preference for a Keynesian mixed economy was reflected in the post-colonial and Third World by state-led approaches to 'development'.

The challenge to the 'established order' by international finance and multinational corporations

Despite the general success of the Bretton Woods system, by the late 1960s deep internal problems were beginning to weaken this postwar model of economic and social organisation. These included: an over-extension and over-valuation of the US dollar (exacerbated by the escalating costs of the Vietnam War), which resulted in insufficient gold reserves to back the dollars in world circulation; failure in the US to keep up with labour productivity and export competitiveness in Western Europe and Japan (by 1960 the Common Market's combined exports exceeded those of the US; Engdahl, 2004,106); and growing demands from organised labour and welfare states in the industrial powers for a greater share of national wealth. These factors, and particularly the last one, helped to precipitate a falling rate of business profit (Harvey, 1990, 141; Reich, 1991, 75–6), causing reluctance on the part of capitalists to invest. In an attempt to restore profitability, holders of private finance and emerging multinational businesses sought to break free from the restrictions of national-level state control (Coates, 1980). While the ensuing struggle presented itself as a battle between different factions of capital (financial against industrial, and national against international), underlying this process was a deeper structural crisis, one which had its roots in a problem of over-accumulation, in which the Keynesian-style capitalist form had reached its limits of expansion within existing national-level institutional and social structures (Clarke, 1988; Brenner,

2009). The real struggle in this latter context is between multinational capital and the majority of the world's population: a contest which is becoming more visible as globalisation enters its first transnational crisis.

To explain the rise of globalisation, it is essential to understand the key role that was played by Britain in facilitating the re-establishment of the influence of international private capital. During its period of Empire, Britain was the world's greatest power, and the City of London the centre of international finance, with an average of 60% of the world's trade conducted in sterling backed by gold. In the early 1950s, 50% of world trade was still conducted in sterling (Burnham, 2003, 2). Britain's enduring involvement with its former Empire and other members of the Sterling Area continued to place the City in a powerful international position. This produced a rather contradictory situation concerning the management of the British economy, because while governments (Labour and Conservative alike) were committed to defending national autonomy to pursue social democracy, they knew that the international financial interests of the City brought benefits, such as invisible earnings and influence abroad. This balancing act would eventually tip in favour of private finance.

A crucial factor in facilitating the liberation of multinational (global) forces was the existence in London of the Eurodollar market. This took the form of an arrangement in private banks in which dollars were held on a special account outside the jurisdiction of the issuing and host countries. One observer has described Eurodollars as 'the most dramatic financial innovation in the postwar period' (Schenk, 1998). Continental European governments and the Japanese authorities only allowed their banks to play a limited role in the Eurodollar market. Because none of their currencies held the same international status as sterling, they were less exposed to speculation and capital movements, but volatile expatriate dollars could increase such risks. The Bank of International Settlements (Annual Reports, cited Callao, 1982, 208) estimated that the size of the Eurodollar market grew as follows: 1964 – $9 billion; 1967 – $17.5 billion; 1970 – $57 billion and 1979 – $475 billion. In comparison, US reserves averaged just under $16 billion during this period (ibid).

Because of legislation in the US to restrict the export of capital, many US banks opened branches abroad. In 1968, 26 US banks had 375 foreign branches with $23 billion in assets, but two years later 79 banks had 536 branches overseas with over $52 billion in assets (Moffitt, 1983, 48). Many of these expatriate banks located in London where they had access to the Eurodollar market and the City's vast international experience. By the mid-1970s America's main banks were reaping more profit from their foreign business than from domestic transactions. While America needed a massive internal injection of capital to modernise its economic and social base, a small and powerful group of New York banks, with vast concentrated financial power, were looking abroad for more lucrative investment opportunities. Some of these were promised by the growing power of Multinational Corporations (MNCs), whose financing and investment needs were increasingly being satisfied in the London markets. A French analyst, Servan-Schreiber (1968, 11), estimated that as early as 1965, of the $4 billion invested by US multinationals in Europe, 55% came from the private Eurodollar market.

By the early 1970s, London's Eurodollar market had become the centre for the activities of private international finance, but actions in other parts of the world also served to increase the power of the emerging forces of globalisation. In 1971 pressures on the dollar, and especially the huge disparity between dollars in circulation and gold reserves, resulted in President Nixon taking the world-altering decision to remove the gold parity pledge. The subsequent devaluation of the dollar alleviated some of the strain on the American economy by making US exports cheaper, but it also destroyed the anchor which had held the Bretton Woods system in place. Moreover, while serving the interests of American exporters in the short term, it ultimately jeopardised the future of American manufacturing and New Deal-style social development, benefiting instead the East Coast bankers with global ambitions. Once currencies were able to float, there were greater opportunities for financial speculation, private investments and the emergence of currency futures. As Engdahl (2004, 129) states, 'When Nixon decided no longer to honor U.S. currency obligations in gold, he opened the floodgates to a worldwide Las Vegas speculation binge of dimensions never before experienced in history'.

In 1973, partly as a consequence of the falling value of the dollar, but also as a reaction to US support for Israel during the Yom Kippur Arab-Israeli war, the Organisation of Petroleum Exporting Countries (OPEC) increased the price of oil. This resulted in a vast inflow of dollars to the OPEC nations. They were initially fearful that a disenchanted US might confiscate these 'petro' dollars if they were invested in America, therefore, large quantities were moved into the Eurodollar market. By the late 1970s, the City was established as the hub of emerging global financial power, and was seen by MNCs as a conduit and resource in their quest for the 'transnationalisation' of their operations. As Denis Healey (1989, 412–13), Britain's Labour Chancellor of the Exchequer between 1974 and 1979, notes:

> In 1974 the Treasury, like most economists, believed that
> exchange rates were mainly determined by a country's
> rate of inflation and balance of payments relative to those
> of other countries. By the time I left office they were
> determined by the faceless men who managed the growing
> atomic cloud of footloose funds, which has accumulated in
> the Euromarkets to evade control by national governments
> ... in my time as Chancellor the revolution was already
> underway ... No previous Chancellor had faced such
> problems.

Besides the increasing hegemony of transnational forces, new actors
were also appearing at the national level whose activities helped to
promote the rise of markets and the power of money. Again Britain
was at the centre of such developments with the emergence of the
'takeover movement' in the 1960s and 1970s, led by entrepreneurs like
Jim Slater and James Goldsmith who discovered a formula for buying
up shares and engaging in hostile take-overs of public companies
(Curtis, 1999). These 'corporate raiders' claimed they were rationalising
and restructuring British industry to make it more competitive, an
argument accepted by Conservative and Labour governments at the
time. In retrospect, they simply broke up industry and asset-stripped
it to free cash for distribution to shareholders, with no benefit to the
industrial base or the long-term earning power of the nation. They
did, however, enrich themselves and those of their new middle-class
following who bought the shares. The tycoon Tiny Roland played a
similar role in the British Commonwealth, and especially in Africa
(Curtis, 1999). Lured by the profits generated through these take-
overs, and the power they injected into the stock market, the 'raiders'
were followed into this kind of investment activity by the banks, the
insurance companies and the pension funds. This last case is ironic,
because it was only after decades of struggle with capital that workers
were able to win the concession from employers to contribute to their
support in retirement. Now the agencies that managed these resources
became themselves engaged in destroying the economic structure that
had formed to protect their members.

The British Labour left mounts a challenge to the emerging forces of globalisation

At the time global capital was establishing its hegemony, some
members and supporters of the Labour Party in Britain realised that the

social–democratic Keynesian model of postwar development was under threat. One of the leading intellectuals taking this position was the economist and MP (1979–89) Stuart Holland (who also contributes to this book), a former adviser to Harold Wilson's government in the 1960s and the principal architect of the economic component of Labour's Programme 1973. Holland brought together his theoretical observations on contemporary capitalism in his book *The Socialist Challenge* (1975). In this text he cast doubt on the traditional revisionist stance in the Labour Party, based on the belief that the advanced social-democratic state was able to control the market:

> The current crisis of Capitalism is not simply a matter of inflation. It reflects fundamental changes in the structure of power which have undermined conventional post-war orthodoxies on society, the State and economic management. Recent acceleration in the trend to monopoly and multinational capital has eroded Keynesian economic policies and undermined the sovereignty of the capitalist nation state. (p 9)

Specifically, he identified take-overs, product diversification and growing multinational links, which in turn increased opportunities for transfer pricing, inter-firm trade, leads and lags in payments, as the processes and mechanisms by which big business increasingly evaded state control. Among these new trends, transfer pricing (an accounting practice in which profits are declared in low-tax zones, even though made in other areas with higher tax requirements), was held to be a particularly damaging form of evasion because it deprived the state of an important source of revenue. The deregulation of finance and the growing ease of capital movements provided a fertile environment for such activities.

Holland claimed that while the Conservatives, and Labour revisionists, placed the blame for Britain's lack of productivity and lacklustre economic performance on the excessive power of workers and trade unions, more consideration should be given to the activities of big business that was 'failing the nation on a massive scale and represents a dead weight on the backs of working people who, through taxation, subsidize distributed private profits' (p 69).

When Wilson's Labour government came to power in October 1974, misrepresentation of the 1973 Programme by the press, a largely revisionist Cabinet and increasing global pressures, frustrated its implementation. This was a missed opportunity in the context of

Britain's postwar social-democratic model, because Holland's economic strategy was based on strengthening cooperation between the state and business, which, as well as appealing to some of the left in the Party, also had a following among the centre and the right (Holland, 2009). Moreover, sectors of business accepted the need for an improved relationship with the state. Of particular interest to Holland and his advisers was the example of the Italian state holding company, the Instituto per la Riconstruzione Industriale, which gave the government significant control over production and its sources of finance without engaging in full nationalisation.

In response to the failure to implement much of Labour's Programme 1973, the left in the Party led by Tony Benn, the Minister for Industry, along with support from his followers, and intellectuals like Michael Barrett Brown, Ken Coates and a group of economists from Cambridge University, then designed a more radical programme, which became known as the Alternative Economic Strategy (AES). One of the most advanced contributions to the AES came from the Cambridge Political Economy Group (Ellman et al, 1974). Of particular significance to their argument was the realisation that 'any attempt to plan the economy and implement progressive social policies must come to terms with the realities of Britain's international position' (p 13). A key objective therefore would be to 'fight the power of international capital' (p 15), and its command centre in the City of London.

In Wilson's cabinet reshuffle of June 1975, Benn was removed from Industry to become Secretary of State for Energy, weakening his ability to promote the AES. Benn (1989, 390) believed his Prime Minister's decision was influenced by the country's financial elites; a view taken by the *Guardian*, whose headline on 11 June read, 'Wilson gives Benn's head to the City'. The move also satisfied the Labour right, the Conservatives and the Confederation of British Industry (CBI).

But while the left sought a radical social-democratic solution to Britain's problems, the Conservative New Right was developing a diametrically opposed neoliberal response. As Desai (2002, 9) claims, by the mid-1970s the 'intellectual' revolution of the New Right was gaining momentum and the 'majority of younger economists were now willing to admit the relevance if not superiority of the monetarist framework in explaining the hyperinflation of 1974 and 1975'. The right in the Labour Party was also beginning to be influenced by the neoliberal current, as indicated by Callaghan's address to the 1976 Labour Party conference in which he questioned aspects of state management of the economy and identified high wages as a cause of rising unemployment.

Although the left was weakened by these developments, growing problems in the British economy kept the AES alive, at least in the minds of its advocates. In 1976 there was a renewed opportunity to bring it out into the open when, after a series of loans were made to the UK to deal with balance of payments shortfalls, further funding was only offered by the IMF based on the acceptance of pre-set conditions. This request was consistent with IMF procedure (Burk, 1994), and the Labour government was already voluntarily taking some of the measures required by the Fund, but it was the first time a major industrial power had been asked to make adjustments to its domestic policy and spending to satisfy the demands of an international institution. It therefore became a defining moment in the battle between national social democracy and globalisation and its supporters. On the side of IMF conditionality, which was designed to put a cap on what was seen as the excesses of British social spending, were the Conservatives, elements in the Treasury and the Bank of England, the City of London, the CBI and the right wing in the Labour Party, which ultimately included the Prime Minister and his Chancellor of the Exchequer, Dennis Healey. In opposition were the left in government led by Tony Benn, sections of the Trades Union Congress which understood the implications of the loan, and initially, the centre left in the Party led by Foreign Secretary Anthony Crosland. The situation came to a head in December 1976 when the IMF adopted an intransigent position, and Benn was able to suggest policies in line with the AES at cabinet meetings (Cabinet Office, 2006). Eventually the IMF gave some ground, allowing Callaghan and Healey to gain the support of the centre, leaving the left isolated.

This struggle was viewed with considerable interest and trepidation around the world, and particularly by right-wing forces in the US that understood the importance of London to their globalising ambitions. Conscious of the gravity of the situation, and especially the proposal within the AES to curb the activities of the City financial markets, former (1969–73) US Secretary of State William Rogers commented:

> We all had the feeling it [the initial attempts to deregulate finance] could come apart in quite a serious way. As I saw it, it was a choice between Britain remaining in the liberal financial system of the West as opposed to a radical change of course because we were concerned about Tony Benn precipitating a policy decision by Britain to turn its back on the IMF. I think if that had happened the whole system would have begun to come apart. God knows what Italy

might have done; then France might have taken a radical change in the same direction. It would not only have had consequences for the economic recovery, it would have had great political consequences. So we tended to see it in cosmic terms. (Cited in Glyn and Harrison, 1980, 97)

With the acceptance of the IMF loan and its conditions, the Labour government increasingly fell under the power of global financial forces and the ideology of the neoliberal right.

Had the AES been adopted in its most radical form at any time in the mid- to late 1970s, it would have not only faced huge domestic and international pressures, not least a massive run on sterling, but also confronted the issue of the role of the state itself. The determination of a left political leadership to implement a national-level economic defence strategy would not have been sufficient alone to challenge the power of capital. What was needed was a radical restructuring of the state apparatus to include increasing workers' control of production, complemented by powerful and effective channels of popular democracy which would allow for greater integration of the state and civil society. This in turn would have required the mass mobilisation of the working class, which at that time was outside the political scope of the trade unions and beyond the capabilities of popular movements. The AES did contain provision for an extension of 'industrial democracy', but the prevailing conditions might have made this difficult to implement. The support of other nations and their working classes, especially in Europe, would also have been essential to the survival of this radical initiative. In retrospect, the struggle of the Labour left in the 1970s to deepen social democracy in Britain may have been too sanguine, but it did bring into sharp focus those forces whose hegemonic power would be established in neoliberal globalisation. The challenge they posed is an important lesson to politicians and ordinary people today, as the global era enters a period of crisis.

Consolidating the power of capital

It is not surprising, given Britain's central role in facilitating the deregulation of international finance, that it should produce, in Margaret Thatcher, the first leader of a major power dedicated to neoliberal principles and willing to champion the forces of emergent globalisation. One of Prime Minister Thatcher's first acts on gaining office was to lift exchange controls, allowing banks to raise capital anywhere in the world and further boosting the international power of London. Deregulation and the emergence of private international banking and credit markets in the 1970s and early 1980s paved the way for the growth of securities markets. Securitisation led to the relative decline of conventional loan business conducted by banks and an explosion in the issuing of marketable bonds. In the 1980s securities firms, stimulated by financial deregulation such as the 'Big Bang' in the London Stock Exchange in 1986, sprang up offering to connect borrowers and investors throughout the world.

Financial deregulation has allowed the growth of 'derivatives', which provide businesses and other financial market participants with options to 'hedge' against interest rate changes, exchange rate fluctuations, commodity price movements, and virtually anything that invites speculation. Besides exchange-traded instruments, derivatives also take the form of 'over-the-counter' instruments by which participants deal directly between themselves, assuming all counter-party risk, as they shift huge monetary volumes outside established exchanges (Thomson, 1998). These activities are almost completely unregulated. By avoiding official controls, players in this market can engage in risk arbitrage at reduced cost, but in doing so they add to systemic financial instability. By 2008 this system, which is dominated by large securities and banking houses, and has been legitimised and sanctioned by states, had produced the deficient financial products, and the conditions to distribute them worldwide, that precipitated the financial crisis (Lambie, 2009).

With Britain leading the way in financial deregulation, the US followed, after the election of Ronald Reagan as President in 1980. America's equivalent of the UK's 'corporate raiders' was the 'junk bond' phenomenon, pioneered by banker Michael Milken. Interestingly, Milken was supported by British raiders such as James Goldsmith. As in the UK, when US industry was 'downsized' and brought under increasing control by the stock market, it was exposed to the predatory interests of global capital. From the mid-1980s onwards, with the UK and the US fully committed to neoliberalism and financial deregulation, the rest of the world was obliged to follow suit in a process of competitive deregulation. Countries like France, which, under the Mitterand presidency, attempted to challenge these forces of globalisation, were easily swept aside by the international capital markets. A moment of truth concerning who ruled in this new world order was in 1992 when the Conservative British government of John Major sought to defend Britain's membership of the European Exchange Rate Mechanism. To protect sterling from destabilising speculation, the Bank of England briefly attempted to raise the interest rate to 15%, but the markets realised this was unsustainable and continued selling pounds, immediately forcing the government to accept defeat and allow a devaluation. One of the key speculators against sterling, George Soros and his Quantum Fund, shorted £10 billion and made a profit of £1.1 billion when the British currency collapsed. There was now no question that it was markets that ruled states, rather than vice versa. In a more generalised sense, capitalism was moving into a new phase of accumulation – globalisation. For the first time, all barriers to capitalism's activities would be challenged, except the inevitability of its own internal contradictions: over-accumulation and the necessity to substitute effective demand with the generation of credit.

Globalisation

For the contemporary theoretical champions of globalisation, including Redwood (1994), Barnevik (2001) and Wolf (2004), it represents a logical and necessary extension of market forces into transnational space. In a human context it is succinctly described by Thompson (1992, 182), who writes of an atomised world of individuals existing as 'free standing agents, each equipped with his or her distinctive set of preferences, and each transacting on an equal footing with whosoever it pleases him or her to transact with'. Globally, 'it is not just the world financial village that is in the making. It is the international car, global fashions, intercontinental telecommunications, worldwide brands, and the global consumer ... people ... choosing that have similar ambitions and styles' based on 'democracy and capitalism' (Redwood, 1994). Such ideals are defensible in theory, but in practice difficult to implement successfully.

The liberalisation of capital in a period of advanced modernity helped to facilitate the globalisation of production, and the formation of enterprises that 'know no national boundaries' (Reich, 1991,124). Since the 1980s these twin processes have transformed the organisation of world production, distribution, the apportionment of profits and patterns of consumer demand into a truly global system described as 'the end of geography' (O'Brian, 1992). But this 'transnationalisation' of capitalism in finance and production, understood by neoliberals as the logical extension of markets into global space, has also resulted in the formation of partial and self-seeking interests that have little concern for national citizens or even the 'global consumer'. Sklair (2001), for example, has identified a 'transnational capitalist class (TCC)' which owes no allegiance to nation-states and tends to seek oligopoly rather than competition. The enormous pressures of globalisation on countries, and the actions of politicians sympathetic to market liberalisation and the TCC, have also led to what Robinson (1999) has termed the 'transnational state'. This is formed not just by supra-national agencies like the IMF and World Trade Organisation, but also national, and even local, governments which are increasingly organised to conform to the 'rule of money', and indirectly serve the interests of global capital.

Contrary to the claims of its advocates, globalisation has not created an idyllic world for the global consumer based on 'democracy and capitalism', but a concentration of elite power in transnational space. As we have seen, in the postwar pre-globalisation era, nations, and especially developed ones, largely contained productive forces within their geographical boundaries, and therefore social classes were obliged to negotiate for 'who gets what' through democracy and a consensus on the functional logic of a mixed economy. Once the nation-state began to lose control of finance and production, these ties and responsibilities were broken, as ruling elites were able to manage the process of accumulation globally, diminishing the role of politics (Boggs, 2000) and weakening the effectiveness of democracy at the national level. Today 'democracy' is promoted as a 'world good' by the major powers, but as Robinson (1996) argues, what we have is a questionable form of 'procedural' democracy which he has termed 'polyarchy', a system in which populations are 'free' to choose between competing elite groups who, by preference or obligation, all support the same free market system controlled by the interests of transnational capital. Robinson further claims that in this context 'democracy promotion' becomes an instrument to enhance the interests of these unaccountable global forces, usually to the detriment of the citizens who are engaged in the 'democratic' process. It is not surprising, therefore, that voter turnout in elections is generally poor, nor that one author (Nye, 2001) speaks of a 'democratic deficit'.

Although neoliberal globalisation appears superficially to be dynamic, modern and able to sweep all before it in a wave of unprecedented growth, studies have shown that this is part of its mythology rather than reality. For example, in a well-researched article entitled, 'The emperor has no growth: Declining economic growth rates in the era of globalisation' (Weisbrot et al, 2001), the authors show, using generally accepted economic performance measures, that compared to the 30 years of Keynesian-style economics from 1945 to 1975, the subsequent two-and-a-half decades of world development were mediocre at best.

On a national level, the Centre for Research on Socio-cultural Change (CRESC) at Manchester University recently (December 2009) produced a report entitled, 'Undisclosed and unsustainable:

Problems of the UK business model'. The main conclusion is that 'since 1979 the expanding private sector is increasingly state sponsored and supported as successive Tory and Labour governments have promoted privatisation, PFI [Public Finance Initiative], subcontracting and outsourcing while in many different ways subventing private business' (p 17). Consequently, the British economy, outside of London and the South East, has relied on the state and the state-dependent 'para state' (not included in official figures for government spending) sectors for the majority of employment for nearly two decades. In the Midlands, for example, 73% of new jobs between 1998 and 2007 relied on funding generated from state sources (p 21). As for the financial sector, its ability to create employment has been 'dead flat since 1991' and accounts for only 1.5 million people out of a workforce of 26.6 million (p 13). Clearly the migration of British industry abroad has not been replaced by a dynamic and sustainable service sector, but rather by a 'nanny' state which, through a combination of deregulation and 'subvention', has served the interests of global capital while temporarily averting a political reaction to a decaying economy. Writing on Ireland, Fintan O'Toole (2009) produced a devastating critique of globalisation's effects on that country, in which neoliberal dogma, combined with national peculiarities, has led to an era of graft, corruption and incompetence that has sunk the 'Celtic Tiger'. The same forces have produced disastrous results in most of the former socialist countries, with the Latvian debacle being perhaps only the tip of the iceberg. We are also now seeing an impending implosion in the EU, as the PIIGS (Portugal, Italy, Ireland, Greece and Spain) face a period of austerity in an attempt to bring their unmanageable debts under control. Analyses of the effects of neoliberal globalisation on these countries and many others would undoubtedly be similar to O'Toole's exposure of Ireland, except for the distinct ways in which different national players became engaged in the same game. Not surprisingly, there is abundant evidence to suggest that, rather than resolving problems of poverty and inequality, globalisation is exacerbating them. United Nations Development Programme's (UNDP) Human Development Reports since the mid-1980s have indicated that there has been a growing disparity in wealth, both on a global scale and within countries. In 2000 the UNDP claimed that between 1970 and 1998, the richest 20% of the world's population increased their share of income from 70% to 85%, while the share of the poorest 20% declined from 2.3% to 1.4% during the same period. In 2005 the World Bank carried out the first International Comparison Programme, which established Purchasing Power Parities (PPP) in 146 economies. This method calculates a population's real spending power and is more accurate in assessing actual wealth than previous GDP per capita estimates. Commenting on the findings, a senior World Bank analyst (Milanovic, 2008, 3) states, based on the release of the December 2007 PPP calculations, which are the most comprehensive to date, that 'the implications for the estimates of global inequality and poverty are enormous. The new numbers show global inequality to be significantly greater than even the most pessimistic authors had thought'. Increasing inequality is experienced not only in developing countries, but also in the industrialised world (Wilkinson, 2005).

The crisis of globalisation

Neoliberal globalisation came to power partly because capitalism had outgrown the Keynesian social-democratic model of development that had existed since the war. The ideological, economic and social hegemony of the new order was legitimised by appeals to the theories of economists like Friedrich Hayek and Milton Friedman. Their ideas were implemented most rigorously in Britain in the 1980s in the form of monetarism. By the end of the decade, however, even the advocates of this initiative had to accept its failure. Since that time British governments have pursued a combination of pseudo-monetarism, 'market fundamentalism' and, more recently, crisis management. A similar trajectory has been followed by many nations, and it is now not clear how governments presume the economy works, except for an unspoken belief that there is some kind of self-correcting mechanism that is activated by markets. This speculative notion rules out the use of interventionist instruments like fiscal policy, and relies instead on interest rate adjustments, which most notably in the US and the UK are now left to the discretion of semi-private institutions: the Federal Reserve and the Bank of England.

It would appear that for the past 20 years, and especially after the euphoria which was generated in the West by the collapse of Communism, the international system has been run on the basis of an unjustified faith in markets. This in turn is supported by an underlying hegemony, fostered since the failure of Keynesianism, which has embedded the market myth and the virtues of individualism into all aspects of economic and social life. In the UK, as in many other countries, government, finance, health provision, the benefits system, academia and many other areas have come to accept the 'laws' of the market as a discourse of the given. Applied at a global level, through the actions of financial markets, it has produced the illusion that the current constraints on capitalist expansion and short-term profit taking can be overcome by the limitless generation of credit, a process which is underpinned by the creation of complex financial instruments and an expectation among the big institutions that they are 'too big to fail' (Lambie, 2009). Now governments are picking up the bill for their belief in the efficacy of financial markets, and the UK is particularly vulnerable because of the size of the City of London's activities in relation to GDP. One of globalisation's advocates, Martin Wolf (2009), the Associate Editor and Chief Economics Commentator of the *Financial Times*, has commented, 'the UK has a strategic nightmare: it has a strong comparative advantage in the world's most irresponsible industry', and now in crisis, 'how should the country manage the cuckoo sitting in its nest'?

High levels of reliance on the City as a generator of economic activity and taxes (largely to the detriment of manufacturing, agriculture and other productive activities), has left Britain with particularly severe financial problems. For instance, the IMF (2009) estimates that write-downs on UK bank assets will be $604 billion, compared to $814 billion for the whole eurozone, and $1.25 trillion for the US, with an economy six times the size of the UK's. This has contributed not only to a large and rising national debt, but also to increasing exposure to the fate of financial institutions. Towards the end of 2009, the official calculation of government debt was £844.5 billion (Office for National Statistics, 2009), with an admission that this would probably rise to £1.4 trillion over the next few years. The Centre for Policy Studies (2009) has, however, calculated that the inclusion of 'hidden' liabilities, such as the costs of the Private Finance Initiative (approximately £139 billion), banking bail-outs (£130 billion), pensions (£1.1 trillion) and other items not included in official calculations, leaves a possible figure of more that £2.2 trillion, which is equivalent to 157% of the total annual output of the UK economy. In early 2010, the then shadow Chancellor George Osborne put forward a Conservative proposal for cuts in public expenditure of £7 billion a year. But taking into consideration the real size of government deficits in the UK, this represents a 'saving' of less than 1%, and has more to do with public relations than any serious attempt to address the problem. Labour argued that such 'drastic' cuts would jeopardise the 'recovery', which it claims to be under way (Woodward, 2010). However, in reality such a miniscule saving is irrelevant. Moreover, there is no substantive evidence to suggest that a 'recovery' can be sustained beyond printing money (quantitative easing). In February 2010 Martin Wolf warned:

> Anybody who looks carefully at the world economy will recognise that a degree of monetary and fiscal stimulus unprecedented in peacetime is all that is prodding it along, not only in high-income countries, but also in big emerging ones. The conventional wisdom is that it will also be possible to manage a smooth exit. Nothing seems less likely.

Failure to make sufficiently large cuts in government borrowing will diminish the creditworthiness of Britain in the eyes of international investors, which could lead to a downgrade of the UK's credit rating and cause higher borrowing costs. Of equal concern are the potential additional costs associated with the banking collapse. Public corporations and major banks such as the Royal Bank of Scotland and the Lloyds Bank Group are being underwritten by the government, but the full extent of their liabilities has not been exposed. The future performance of loans based on property assets, for example, is unknown, meaning that banks may still be vulnerable to losses not yet recognised on collapsing real-estate cash flows. This is all in the context of having probably reached the reasonable limits of 'quantitative easing', which has provided temporary relief by enabling a false rally of the stock market, and a false market for government debt, based on the banks' access to cheap government credit. Once this mechanism becomes unsustainable and any stimulus it has created is exhausted, the true state of the economy will be revealed. It is a sobering thought that in 1976, at the time of the IMF crisis, when the UK was believed to have deep financial problems, the budget deficit was 6% of GDP; in the first part of 2010 it was 12.6% and rising. For the year 2010 the UK government will borrow about £180 billion, which is equivalent to 25% of its total expenditure. The important question therefore arises: how long can this be sustained without profound changes to government tax and spending policies? Added to this worrying prospect, according to the CRESC (2009) report cited above, the government has seriously underestimated the extent to which the British economy is dependent on state funding.

Conclusion

As suggested initially in this chapter and supported with analysis, a fundamental cause of the problems that the UK and other nations face is not so much the technical mismanagement of finance, but the ceding of vital aspects of state power to transnational institutions and actors. Indeed, states themselves have become complicit in facilitating globalisation and the transnationalisation process. This leaves an interesting scenario concerning the outcome of the May 2010 British general election. Despite the upbeat political message that is being presented by the new Conservative–Liberal Democrat alliance, one must ask the question: Today is any party, or combination of parties, able to do more than the bidding of the transnational elites? This seems unlikely, because the UK is so enmeshed in the global financial system that rejection of this role would require even more radical action than that advocated by the Cambridge Group at the time of the AES. In this context, the key variable is not the electoral outcome, but the political response of people in Britain to the forthcoming cuts in public expenditure. Robert Chote, the head of the Institute of Fiscal Studies, has suggested that collapsing tax revenues and the cost of bailing out the banking sector have done 'breathtaking' long-term damage to public finances in the UK (Kirkup, 2009).

While the crisis of the 1980s, precipitated by neoliberal policies, had a negative impact on the organised working class, the forthcoming crisis of the second decade of the 21st century may have a similar effect on the middle class. For the past three decades this class has enjoyed a high level of consumption in the developed world, but its improved living standards have depended heavily on debt, house price inflation and, directly or indirectly, the public sector. By 2006 consumer debt in the UK stood at £1.3 trillion, accounting for a third of all the unsecured debt in Western Europe (Prosser, 2006). In July 2009 (Jamieson, 2009), the IMF predicted a rise in defaults on credit card debt in the UK. With the inevitable cuts in public expenditure that the new government will have to undertake, and possible tax increases and other measures to raise and save revenue, these already existing problems will either exacerbate or precipitate a number of negative trends, including rising unemployment; growing debt and defaults; declining house prices; possible currency devaluation; inflation; and falls in the stock market. This would further undermine the middle class in the UK and elsewhere. In its Global Strategic Trends Programme 2007–2036, the Development Concepts and Doctrine Centre (DCDC) of the British Ministry of Defence stated:

> The middle classes could become a revolutionary class, taking the role envisaged for the proletariat by Marx. The globalization of labour markets and reducing levels of national welfare provision and employment could reduce peoples' attachment to particular states. The growing gap between themselves and a small number of highly

> visible super-rich individuals might fuel disillusion with meritocracy, while the growing urban under-classes are likely to pose an increasing threat to social order and stability, as the burden of acquired debt and the failure of pension provision begins to bite. Faced by these twin challenges, the world's middle-classes might unite, using access to knowledge, resources and skills to shape transnational processes in their own class interest. (DCDC, 2007, 81)

The process described by the Ministry's document could become reality as the debt-driven crisis deepens, and especially if the major industrial nations are obliged to face similar austerity packages to the IMF Structural Adjustment Programmes (SAPs) that were implemented in developing countries after they defaulted on their debts to the banks in the 1980s and 1990s. These measures served to expose fragile economies to unimpeded access by global capital, so that enough wealth could be extracted to pay the creditor banks which had made loans (largely based on Eurodollar market private resources) in the 1970s and 1980s. Indeed the austerity programmes demanded by the international financial markets that are being implemented in Latvia, Greece and elsewhere today are similar to SAPs, and could form the model for other countries as the recession unfolds. In this context it is probable that the powerful global financial institutions and corporations will take advantage of currency devaluations and debt to buy up assets, including much of the existing public sector, leading to an unprecedented wave of privatisations and an increasing transnationalisation of the state. This course may lead to the creation of a global currency and global government in which the power of capital will establish its ultimate hegemony. It is not surprising, given this possible scenario, that the crisis which has been precipitated by the transnational banks and complicit states has been called a 'financial coup d'état' by US Congresswoman Marcy Kaptur (2009).

Alternatively, states may seek to cooperate to contain the debacle in the international banking system by closing down the transnational activities of capital, and bring the failed institutions back into the orbit of the nation, where they can face bankruptcy procedures and be effectively nationalised (Lambie, 2009). This may be the most obvious short-term solution, not only to save the world from potential chaos, but also to restore the functional operations of capitalism. Indeed, states have a long history of changing their institutional form to compensate for the inherent crises to which capitalism is susceptible. Ultimately, however, it is only the conscious rejection of this failed system by the majority of the world's population, and acceptance of the need to rebuild a more sustainable, equitable and democratic alternative, that offers the best chance for the future.

References

Aglietta, M. (1979) *A Theory of Capitalist Regulation: The US Experience*, trans D. Fernbach, London: New Left Books.

Barnevik, P. (2001) 'Growth Spur', *World Link: The Magazine of the World Economic Forum*, September/October, pp 36–9.

Benn, A.W. (1989) *Office Without Power: Diaries, 1968–72*, London: Arrow Books Ltd.

Boggs, C. (2000) *The End of Politics: Corporate Power and the Decline of the Public Sphere*, New York: The Guilford Press.

Braverman, H. (1974) *Labour and Monopoly Capital: The Degradation of Work in the Twentieth Century*, New York: Monthly Review Press.

Brenner, R. (2009) *The Economics of Global Turbulence*, London: Verso.

Brett, E.A. (1985) *The World Economy since the War: The Politics of Uneven Development*, London: Macmillan.

Burk, K. (1994) 'The Americans, the Germans, and the British: The 1976 IMF Crisis', *Twentieth Century British History*, vol 5, no 3, pp 351–69.

Burnham, P. (2003) *Remaking the Postwar World Economy: Robot and British Policy in the 1950s*, London: Palgrave Macmillan.

Cabinet Office (2006) Cabinet Minutes, consulted in 2005/2006. [I am indebted to Mrs Tessa Stirling, The Head of Histories, at the Openness and Records Unit, Cabinet Office Room, Admiralty Arch, The Mall, London, for allowing me access to these documents in advance of their general release.]

Callao, D. (1982) *The Imperious Economy*, Cambridge: Harvard University Press.

Centre for Policy Studies (2009) 'True UK Public Sector Government Debt', www.cps.org.uk/ index.php?option=com_contentandview= cpsarticle andid=261.

Centre for Research on Socio-cultural Change (CRESC), Buchanan, J., Froud, J., Johal, S., Leaver, A. and Williams, K. (2009) 'Undisclosed and unsustainable: problems of the UK business model', Working Paper No 75 (December).

Clarke, S. (1988) *Keynesianism, Monetarism, and the Crisis of the State*, Aldershot: Edward Elgar.

Coates, D. (1980) *Labour in Power? A Study of the Labour Government 1974–79*, London: Longman.

Curtis, A. (dir) (1999) 'The Mayfair Set', four-part documentary examining the rise of business and the decline of political power, BBC2, July–August.

Desai, M. (2002) *Marx's Revenge. The Resurgence of Capitalism and the Death of Statist Socialism*, London: Verso.

DCDC (Development Concepts and Doctrine Centre, Ministry of Defence) (2007), www.mod.uk/NR/rdonlyres/94A1F45E-A830–49DB-B319-DF68C28D561 D/0/strat_trends_17mar07.pdf.

Ellman, M., Rowthorn, B., Smith, R. and Wilkinson, F. (1974) 'Britain's Economic Crisis', *Spokesman Pamphlet*, no 44, pp 1–39.

Engdahl, W. (2004) *A Century of War: Anglo-American Oil Politics and the New World Order*, London: Pluto.

Galbraith, J.K. (1968) *The New Industrial State*, London: Hamish Hamilton.

Glyn, A. and Harrison, J. (1980) *The British Economic Disaster*, London: Pluto.

Gourinchas, P.O. and Rey, H. (2005) *From World Banker to World Venture Capitalist: US External Adjustment and the Exorbitant Privilege*, London: Centre for Economic Policy Research.

Harvey, D. (1990) *The Condition of Postmodernity: An Enquiry into the Origins of Cultural Change*, Oxford: Blackwell.

Healey, D. (1989) *The Time of my Life*, London: Michael Joseph.

Helleiner, E. (1994) *States and the Reemergence of Global Finance*, London: Cornell University Press.

Holland, S. (1975) *The Socialist Challenge*, London: Quartet Books.

Holland, S. (2009) 'Principal designer of the economic proposals contained in Labour's Programme 1973', interviews held in Coimbra, Portugal, 17–19 August.

Horsefield, J. (1969) *The International Monetary Fund, 1945–1965: Twenty Years of International Monetary Cooperation*, 3 vols, vol 1, Washington, DC: IMF.

IMF (2009) *Global Financial Stability Report. Navigating the Financial Challenges Ahead* (October).

Jamieson, A. (2009) 'Credit card crisis to grip Britain, IMF warns', *Daily Telegraph*, 27 July.

Kaptur, M. (2009) Interviewed in 'Bill Moyer's Journal', www.pbs.org/moyers/journal /10092009/watch.html.

Keynes, J.M. (1933) 'National Self-Sufficiency', in *Collected Works of J.M. Keynes*, vol 21, ed D. Moggeridge, London: Macmillan, pp 233–46.

Keynes, J.M. (1980) *The Collected Writings of J.M. Keynes*, vol 26, *Activities 1941–46: Shaping the Postwar World, Bretton Woods and Reparations*, ed D. Moggeridge, Cambridge: Cambridge University Press.

Kirkup, J. (2009) 'Budget 2009: Britain's debt will not be under control until 2032', *Daily Telegraph*, 24 April.

Lambie, G. (2009) 'Nemesis of "market fundamentalism"? The ideology, deregulation and crisis of finance', *Contemporary Politics*, vol 15, no 2, pp 157–77

Milanovic, B. (2008) 'Developing Countries Worse Off Than Once Thought – Part 1', *Yale Global*, 11 February, yaleglobal.yale.edu/display.article?id=10333.

Milward, A. (1984) *The Reconstruction of Western Europe, 1945–51*, London: Methuen.

Moffitt, M. (1983) *The World's Money: International Banking from Bretton Woods to the Brink of Insolvency*, New York: Simon and Schuster.

Nye, J.S. Jr. (2001) 'Globalisation's Democratic Deficit: How to Make International Institutions More Accountable', *Foreign Affairs*, July–August, pp 37–47.

O'Brian, R. (1992) *Global Financial Integration: The End of Geography*, London: Pinter.

O'Toole, F. (2009) *Ship of Fools: How Stupidity and Corruption Sank the Celtic Tiger*, London: Faber and Faber.

Office for National Statistics (2009) www.statistics.gov.uk/cci/nugget.asp?id=206.

Prosser, D. (2006) 'Britain becomes "never, never land" as personal debt runs out of control', *Independent*, 28 September.

Redwood, J. (1994) *The Global Marketplace*, London: Harper Collins.

Reich, R. (1991) *The Work of Nations: Preparing Ourselves for 21st Century Capitalism*, New York: Vintage Books.

Roberts, A. (1984) *The Most Secret Science*, Fort Collins: Betsy Ross Press.

Robinson, W. (1996) *Promoting Polyarchy. Globalisation, US Intervention and Hegemony*, Cambridge: Cambridge University Press.

Robinson, W. (1999) 'Capitalist Globalisation and the Transnationalisation of the State', Paper presented at a workshop entitled 'Historical Materialism and Globalisation', University of Warwick, 15–17 April.

Schenk, C. (1998) 'The Origins of the Eurodollar Market in London: 1955–1963', *Explorations in Economic History*, vol 35, pp 221–38.

Servan-Schreiber, J.J. (1968) *The American Challenge*, London: Hamish Hamilton.

Sklair, L. (2001) *The Transnational Capitalist Class*, London: Blackwell.

Soros, G. (2008) 'Statement before the U.S. House of Representatives Committee on Oversight and Government Reform', 13 November.

Strange, S. (1997) *Mad Money: When Markets Outgrow Governments*, Michigan: University of Michigan Press.

Thomson, M. (1992) 'The Dynamics of Cultural Theory and their Implications for Enterprise Culture', in S.H. Heap and A. Ross (eds) *Understanding the Enterprise Culture: Themes in the Work of Mary Douglas*, Edinburgh: Edinburgh University Press.

Thompson, R. (1998) *Apocalypse Roulette. The Lethal World of Derivatives*, Basingstoke: Macmillan.

UNDP (United Nations Development Programme) (1986–2006) Human Development Reports, UNDP: New York.

Weisbrot, M., et al (2001) 'The Emperor Has No Growth: Declining Economic Growth Rates in the Era of Globalisation', Washington, DC: Center for Economic and Policy Research.

Wilkinson, R. (2005) *The Impact of Inequality: How to Make Sick Societies Healthier*, New York: New Press.

Wolf, M. (2004) *Why Globalisation Works: The Case for the Global Market Economy*, New Haven, CT: Yale University Press.

Wolf, M. (2009) 'Why Britain has to Curb Finance', *Financial Times*, 21 May.

Wolf, M. (2010) 'The world economy has no easy way out of the mire', *Financial Times*, 24 February.

Woodward, W. (2010) 'Tories reject Alistair Darling's "dodgy" claims about their spending plans', *Guardian*, 4 January.

Yaffe, D. (1973) 'The crisis of profitability: a critique of the Glynn-Sutcliffe thesis', *New Left Review*, 80 (July–August).

THREE

Financial crises, governance and cohesion: can governments learn up?

Stuart Holland

The sub-prime crisis of 2007 and the crash of global financial markets in 2008 were caused by a neoliberal apotheosis of markets, as if, god-like, they were all-knowing. Theories of 'efficient markets' and 'rational expectations' premised that investors had perfect information, despite no one knowing for months after the crisis how much had been lost by whom, how or where. US Treasury Secretary Larry Summers had cut the reserve requirements of banks to less than 2% and in 1999 repealed the New Deal Glass–Steagall Act, which had separated commercial banking from speculative finance. Federal Reserve chair Alan Greenspan had cut interest rates to near 1% in reaction to the bursting of the dot. com bubble and the risk of a recession in the US (Tett, 2009). This deregulation and near-costless borrowing turned banks which should have been safe havens for savings into casinos.

But nothing was learned up from the dot.com bubble itself, or the collapse the year before the repeal of Glass–Steagall of the Long Term Capital Management hedge fund, founded by two of the economists who had gained Nobel laureates for their contributions to rational expectations theory. Claims for 'creative financial engineering' continued apace through 'derivatives', which should have been derived from assets but were not, since they were sold through 'structured investment vehicles', which were structured only in name, since they were 'off balance sheet' and not covered even by the minimal assets by then required of banks.

When the sub-prime crisis broke and caused a 'credit crunch' in inter-bank lending this prompted no less than 390 European banks to call for injection of funds from the European Central Bank and the Bank of England, followed by either public shareholdings or outright nationalisations. Their salvage and that of banks in the US was to cost $3 trillion, or more than double the GDP of the US. In August 2008 world stock markets crashed by up to a quarter. After the crash, the

European Commissioner for Competition Policy, Nellie Kroes, held bilateral meetings with the chief executives of major banks and reported that most of them 'were in denial, claiming that "their bank" had no problems – only others did' (Kroes, 2009).

A key role in the crisis has been played by credit-rating agencies, which were not the 'impartial observers' of Adam Smith but clients of the banks and hedge funds which they rated 'triple A' until the day they failed. From October 2009 and the election of a new government in Greece which admitted that its debt and deficits had been understated, the agencies began what, by the spring of 2010, had become a serial downgrading of the creditworthiness of southern European countries, with the prospect also that they could do the same for the UK, whose debt had soared so as to salvage banks which had been hit by the 2007 'credit crunch'. This has relevance not only to the formation of a new government in the UK and whether it can or cannot resolve differences between Conservatives and Liberal Democrats on Europe, but also to whether European governments can 'learn up' from the crisis and draw on financial instruments designed to avoid beggar-my-neighbour cuts in spending, investment and jobs.

The eurozone governments' response to the threat of downgrading national debt by the rating agencies was delayed for months. They did not act decisively until, after an 11-hour meeting, and early in the morning of 10 May 2010, finance ministers announced a package of €440 billion of loans on top of €110 billion agreed only days before for Greece, with the IMF matching this by half, bringing the total available to defend national currencies to €750 billion, or more than five times the annual budget of the European Commission.

There was some euphoria that they had managed so much. The hope underlying the package was that it would not be needed, since it would deter speculation against currencies. It had three parts. One was a €60 billion 'rapid reaction stabilisation fund' to be managed by the European Commission. The second was a 'special purpose vehicle' which would raise up to €440 billion using a mix of loans and loan guarantees from the 16 members of the eurozone. The third was the IMF 'matching funds'. All of this was to be matched in turn by deep cuts in national debt and deficits.

The analogy with deterrence was not missed by the press, such as the mutual defence provision in Article 5 of the NATO treaty that an attack on one of its members is an attack on all (*The Economist*, 2010). Deterrence also includes the MAD theory, that using nuclear weapons would mean 'mutually assured destruction'. But what was missed in the 10 May package was that there also is madness in 'mutually assured deflation'. Its salvage package presumed that there is no alternative to cutting national debt and deficits, which, on the scale envisaged, would lead to a formidable contraction of mutual spending, trade and jobs. Germany is especially exposed. She is mainly dependent on other European countries for her exports. If they cut back demand, she will suffer.

Multipliers compound this. They were drawn on by Keynes and were part of mainstream Keynesian economics until monetarism displaced it. Put simply, if you put a billion into an economy in recession, through public investment or spending, it will multiply. More people will be employed, spending more money and paying tax rather than drawing unemployment benefits. But, inversely, if you reduce public investment or spending, the multipliers go negative.

Milton Friedman denied multipliers because he otherwise would have had to admit that public investment and spending sustains an economy rather than draining it. At the height of Tory monetarism I placed a written parliamentary question to the then Chancellor of the Exchequer, Nigel Lawson, asking what estimates had been made of the private income generated by public expenditure since 1979. His answer was that 'Estimates of this kind are not made' (*Hansard*, 1983), thereby confirming the premise that the government was taking no account of the manner in which its cuts in public investment and spending could have negative multiplier effects, which they did. The cuts doubled unemployment within two years. Those in public housing led to a record number of bankruptcies among construction companies (Holland, 1987).

Recent estimates have indicated that multipliers in public spending for France, Germany and Italy can be up to two, and on investment, for the UK, up to three (Blot et al, 2009). This means that cuts in public spending could doubly cut consumer demand. The negative effects of cuts in investment could triple them. Europe may have saved itself from serial default of eurozone member states, but risks then dying from a thousand cuts. Within days of the 10 May salvage package, markets appeared to be waking up to this (Fletcher, 2010).

This chapter addresses such issues in terms of financial institutions and treaty commitments in Europe which have been displaced, denied or repressed in the recent financial crisis, including the first revision of the Rome Treaty in the Single European Act of 1986, which established economic and social cohesion as the 'twin pillar' with its internal market of the then European Community.

The Single European Act

The case for this had been outlined in 1983 in a report which was supported by Jacques Delors when he was French Finance Minister and of which the drafting committee included economic advisers to him and to François Mitterrand and Felipe Gonzalez, as well as a young Dominique Strauss-Kahn (Holland, 1983). The report was drawn on by both Andreas Papandreou and Mitterrand in calling for a New Messina Conference. The Messina Conference had agreed to establish a European Community, but had also endorsed the principles of the Spaak Report, which had recognised that liberalising capital, labour and trade could aggravate structural, social and regional disparities and that a European Community would need proactive policies to avoid this. With the exception of the Common Agricultural Policy (CAP), which was vital for France, which still had a quarter of its population in farming, and which was structural, social and regional, such policies, in the form of Structural Funds, Social Funds and Regional Funds, only came much later. But Italy, with 24 million people in its Mezzogiorno, or as many as in the three Benelux member states of the Six signing the Rome Treaty, was especially concerned to offset such disparities, and gained a protocol to it establishing a European Investment Bank (EIB) which could finance social and regional projects.

This chapter also draws on a 1993 report on economic and social cohesion written for Delors when he was President of the European Commission (Holland, 1993). This provided the rationale for his White Paper of December 1993, *Growth, Competitiveness, Cohesion*, which was the first to set full employment targets for the EU.

The background was one in which most economists, and central bank, were persuaded that there could be a viable monetary union only if there were also a fiscal union with a supranational European tax base. Proposals for this had been made by MacDougall and others, that it would need to be between 7% and 14% of the GDP of the Union (European Commission, 1977), but no progress was made on them, since the member states of the EC were reluctant to cede general taxation powers. When it was agreed at Maastricht in 1991 to proceed with a common currency, there was no readiness to recognise the scale on which countries that were denied exchange rate changes would need either fiscal transfers from other member states or common European financial instruments to avoid deflation as an alternative to devaluation. The guideline agreed at Maastricht was that national debt should not be more than 60% of GDP, and deficits not more than 3%. No econometric analysis lay behind this, nor the implications of Italy,

Belgium and Greece, with debt levels of over 100% of GDP, meeting it, nor that if they cut public borrowing and expenditure to meet a 60% target, this would have a powerfully deflationary effect on the European economy. For example, Italy would have had either to cut its public spending by half or to double taxes.[1]

The New Deal legitimation

The 1993 report for Delors on economic and social cohesion recognised the deflationary dilemma in the debt and deficit conditions for a single currency and sought to address it. Its key financial proposal was that the European Union should borrow to invest on its own account. The precedent and legitimation for this was drawn from the US New Deal. The Roosevelt administration recovered America from the 1930s Depression not by cuts or raising taxes, which would have deepened it, but by borrowing to invest through issuing US Treasury bonds. But these did not count on the debt of member states of the American Union, such as California, or Delaware. The case, to Delors, was that if the then European Community were to borrow and invest on its own account this need not count on the debt of EU member states. This could offset the deflationary implications of the national debt and deficit criteria for a single currency, and also make it easier for member states to meet them.

The case also centrally addressed the economic and social cohesion to which the European Community had committed itself as its 'twin pillar' in the Single European Act of 1986. For if the investments were in the social domain, in areas such as health, education, urban renewal and the environment, they could lift the cost of this from national budgets and enhance the ability of lower-income member states to align their investment, employment and welfare levels with those of more advanced member states, without recourse to a common fiscal policy.

Delors liked and seized on the proposal, which was included in his December 1993 White Paper as a recommendation that Europe should borrow through Union Bonds. But in the preparation of the White Paper in the autumn of that year, this was strenuously resisted by senior officials in the European Commission's Directorate General for Economy and Finance, who opposed any analogy with the US New Deal on the grounds that this would undermine the Maastricht stability conditions for a single currency. This meant that the White Paper neither carried real credibility nor caught the attention of a wider public, as Delors himself had done. Without the New Deal parallel, the bonds appeared yet another arcane financial instrument, rather than a means to finance the cohesion commitment of the Single European Act. During the following German presidency of the European Council, at Essen, only the Netherlands and Luxembourg supported the proposal for Union Bonds, while Germany and France opposed it.

The social investment focus of the cohesion report to Delors was also displaced by what the Transport Directorate-General of the Commission wished to prioritise but could not find funding for: the so-called TENs, or Trans-European Networks in rail and telecommunications. The difference was crucial. In economic terms, social investments in health, education and urban renewal on a macro scale would have much higher employment, income and fiscal multipliers than transport networks. In political terms, such investments would have touched every member of the Union in terms of better education, health, and the quality of urban life and the environment. The Commission's agenda reflected the interest of the major European construction and transport companies, backed by the employers' federation UNICE, which itself had insisted on introducing 'competitiveness' into the title of the Delors White Paper if it were to support it.

Also, while transport and communications networks may be a necessary condition of competitiveness, they are far from sufficient to achieve either process or product innovation, or to shift economies to higher levels of income and welfare by sustained innovation (Schumpeter [1911] 1949; Freeman and Louçã, 2001). Further, only three of some 10 such transport networks agreed the following spring at the 1994 Essen European Council were completed through the following decade, during which finance ministers at national level axed public investment projects to try to meet the national debt and deficit conditions for a single currency. It was only in 1999 that the Commission's attitude temporarily changed, when Yves-Thibault de Silguy became Commissioner for Economy and Finance and proposed the bonds to support the introduction of the euro that year. Yet still, at the time, without success.

Employment in the social sphere

A second strategic case in the cohesion report to Delors was for more labour-intensive employment in the social sphere, that is, more teachers and smaller class sizes in education, more health workers and shorter waiting lists, more care for the young and the elderly in an aging population. The econometrics showed that this could create up to 5 million or more jobs. But this hinged on the case that the social investments by governments would be co-financed by the issuing of Union Bonds rather than counting against national debt. Again, the resistance of the financial directorate of the Commission to any legitimating cross-reference in the White Paper to the US New Deal precedent for EU borrowing and investment to finance this, and not counting on the debt of member states, meant that it carried no credibility.

The Essen European Council in the spring of 1994 therefore endorsed the ends of the Delors White Paper, but not the financial means. Its Presidency Conclusions prioritised: 'continuing and strengthening the strategy of the White Paper in order to consolidate growth, improve the competitiveness of the European economy and the quality of the environment in the European Union and – given the still intolerably high level of unemployment – create more jobs for our citizens'. It also called for: 'increasing the employment-intensiveness of growth, in particular by more flexible organisation of work in a way which fulfils the wishes of employees and the requirements of competition [and] the promotion of initiatives, particularly at regional and local level, that create jobs which take account of new requirements, for example, in the environmental and social-services spheres'.

This was a direct reflection of the case for more labour-intensive employment in the social sphere, which underlay a third of the 15 million jobs target of the Delors White Paper (Holland, 1993; COM, 1993). The Essen Presidency Conclusions had also started with the case that 'the fight against unemployment and for equality of opportunity for men and women will continue to remain the paramount tasks of the European Union and its member states'. But its later section on Economic and Monetary Union, insisted on by the Economy and Finance Directorate of the Commission, claimed that: 'the first priority is to achieve the consolidation goals announced in the national convergence programmes', then adding that: 'Above all, the structural deficits must decline in order to prevent a further increase in the rate of debt'. Thereby, the Essen Council immediately following the Delors White Paper managed two entirely contradictory 'priorities', a higher and more labour-intensive employment recovery programme and monetarist debt reduction, both at the same time.

Europe's other bank

By 1994 the European Investment Bank had moved from being a statement of intent in a protocol to the Rome Treaty to a major multilateral financial institution which shortly was to overtake, and then dwarf, the borrowing and investment of the World Bank (Robinson,

2009). After the publication of the Delors White Paper and of the cohesion report on which its full employment rationale had been based, one of the Bank's directors, Tom Barrett, read both and then rang me, observing that although the White Paper had not made the analogy with US Treasury bonds of its case for issuing Union Bonds not counting on national debt, I had done so, and then commented:

> Of course the President of the Commission can have any financial instrument he wants or can persuade the European Council to adopt. But I wonder whether he is aware that of the current 15 member states, only two count borrowing from us against national debt, the UK and the Netherlands, and that he therefore already has the equivalent of US Treasury bonds through those issued by the EIB if he would care to take advantage of them.

The EIB had not advertised this to anyone. Nor was it writ in any treaty, since, when the commitment to Europe having its own investment bank had been included in the Rome Treaty, it had not been headlined that while the Union itself could not borrow, the EIB would. By 1994, when Barrett rang me, the fact that only the UK and the Netherlands counted their borrowings from it against national debt was not even known to the Dutch central bank.[2] Several finance ministers did not know. His message nonetheless was clear, and was passed on to Delors. The underlying issues then were seized effectively, after Delors retired from the presidency of the European Commission in 1995, by Antonio Guterres when he became Prime Minister of Portugal. Guterres advocated the case for an extension of investment financing by the EIB at successive European Councils, starting in a minority of one among the then 15 heads of state and government but effectively building consent. This included a Council meeting at which Helmut Kohl, himself under pressure from the Bundesbank, declared that he was opposed to European bonds, since 'the German taxpayer already has paid enough', thereby demonstrating that he did not recognise the difference between a fiscal transfer such as funding the European Commission's 'own resources' and a bond as a means of shifting savings into productive investments.

Towards and after the Lisbon agenda

This was resolved by the brilliant international secretary to Guterres, José de Freitas Ferraz, who, at a meeting thereafter between the three of us, indicated that he had known Kohl's *chef de cabinet*, since they had both been at the OECD years earlier, and suggested drafting a memorandum for the Chancellor which could indicate that, at the forthcoming Amsterdam European Council in the spring of 1997, undoubtedly Prime Minister Guterres would yet again make the case for the EU to issue its own bonds; but that since these were financed by savings rather than taxation, and since they could offer German pension funds a reliable income stream, he should perhaps support the proposal. Kohl then duly did so at Amsterdam, whose 'Special Action Programme' called for measures which could finance investment in health, education, urban renewal and the urban environment. Following this, in the same year the Luxembourg European Council gave the EIB a remit to finance such social investments.

It was due to Guterres' highly effective advocacy that much of the agenda for employment and cohesion underlying the Delors White Paper was endorsed by both the Amsterdam and Luxembourg European Councils in 1997, and in the Lisbon Agenda 2000. Guterres realised that the 1994 Essen European Council had made a commitment to more labour-intensive employment in the social sphere, that is, more teachers, more health workers, and more personalised social services of a kind which are vital to achieving not only fuller but also more useful employment. He also grasped that this could not be financed from the Commission's own resources transferred to it from taxes and levies by member states, but that if the EIB were to finance national investments in health, education, urban renewal and the urban environment, this would release more fiscal resources for them to fund such labour-intensive employment in health, education and social and community services.

Guterres then also gained a further remit to the EIB at Lisbon in 2000 to invest in innovation, including green technology. By 2005 its Innovation 2000 Initiative had already overtaken what the European Commission was funding through its Science and Technology Framework Programmes, many of which are in pure rather than applied research and thousands of which have not created a single new enterprise or even new job. Following the Luxembourg European Council remit of 1997, reinforced by that at Lisbon in 2000, the EIB more than tripled its lending and investments. Its inflation-adjusted annual funding in 1997 was less than €20 billion. By 2007 it was more than €50 billion and by 2010 more than €70 billion (Holliday, 2008). If, by the end of 2011, its venture capital arm – the European Investment Fund – disburses another €35 billion scheduled for small and medium-sized enterprises (SMEs), as agreed by the Nice European finance ministers' meeting of September 2008, the EIB Group – as it now is known – will be investing more than 1% of EU GDP, and nearly as much as European Commission's fiscal 'own resources'.

None of this is impressive in relation to US federal borrowing and spending, which dwarfs it. But nor was federal borrowing and investment in the US before the New Deal, which was as low as 3% of GDP. While just over 1% of European GDP appears small, this is equivalent to the whole of the European Commission's budget on agriculture, structural funds, cohesion funds, regional funds and investment in science and technology. The EIB is also a major global player. By 2008, its financing of investments worldwide in 48 different currencies was the equivalent of €355 billion, or nearly tenfold the lending of the World Bank at the time (EIB, 2008).

The European Investment Fund

The 1993 background report for the Delors White Paper had not intended that the European Investment Bank, rather than a new European Investment Fund (EIF), should issue Union Bonds (Holland, 1993). Delors pushed for this before he retired from the Commission in 1995, and it was established as a financial institution of the EU in Luxembourg, with its capital jointly subscribed by member states, the EIB and the European Commission. But since no headway was being made on the issuing of Union Bonds, its initial design was reduced from a macro financial instrument to equity guarantees for SMEs, with a special remit to support new high-tech start-ups.

The aim behind this still was not modest. One of the reasons why Europe was lagging behind the US in high-tech start-ups in electronics such as flourished in Silicon Valley was that it had no comparable military-industrial complex which could spawn demand for micro technologies for battlefield or anti-missile weapons. But another was that it had no comparable private sector venture-capital market which could sustain innovative small firms from birth through adolescence, while regular interest rate payments on borrowing from banks could suffocate them before they could generate significant income. Also, SMEs are the main employers in the private sector. Even in advanced technology, and certainly in the innovative phase of a product cycle, they tend to be labour intensive.

The scale of the original design for the EIF was ambitious, aiming for 60 billion ECU (the pre-euro European Currency Unit) of venture capital for SMEs, which was more than total spending on the CAP. But this was blocked by the Economy and Financial Affairs Directorate of the Commission, which insisted that it should offer only equity guarantees. The EIB then began to offer loan finance for SMEs and then became the majority shareholder in the EIF, which masked its role even further, although the EIB and EIF have separate institutional frameworks and separate headquarters in Luxembourg. The outcome was that the EIF never gained profile with most SMEs. A decade and a half later, at the September 2008 Nice meeting at which Ecofin finance ministers woke up to the needs for macroeconomic action for SMEs in the face of the fallout from the sub-prime crisis and increased the capital base of the EIB to finance them to €35 billion, most press coverage did not even refer to the fact that this would be through the EIF as its venture-capital arm.

Whether the EIF will be able to gain take-up of this €35 billion is also open to question. Until 2008 it had managed to issue equity guarantees of only €1 billion. One reason for this slow take-up was that guarantees were of less use to SMEs than venture capital. Another was that its initial threshold in applying for them was too high, at more than 10 million ECU. It then raised this to 15 million ECU, which ruled out most small rather than medium-sized firms, and later dropped any applications made directly rather than through national banks or credit institutions. Also, while the original proposal was that it should have 'one-stop shops' in national capitals which any SME could directly access, the national financial intermediaries, being commercial, tended to recommend mixed lending packages, including the fixed- or variable-interest loans which the original design of the EIF had aimed to avoid.

Whether there will be learning up from this remains to be seen. One of the recommendations which Antonio Guterres endorsed and gained in 2000 for the Lisbon Agenda was that the European Council should give the EIB, the EIF and the Commission a remit to coordinate their separate actions for SMEs (Holland, 2000). This was agreed. But what still is needed is the 'one-stop shops' in each member state so that SMEs or their intermediaries and, especially, regional development agencies can directly access all three institutions without having to go to Brussels or Luxembourg for separate meetings with the Commission or the EIB and the EIF.

The Constitution for Europe

The drafting of a 'Constitution for Europe' then missed the chance to raise the profile of either the EIB or the EIF as financial instruments for economic and social cohesion. An invitation had been offered by the European Council to the former French President Valéry Giscard d'Estaing, not to write a Constitution, but to chair a commission to consider the principles that might be embodied in one. This should have been straightforward. It could have been a short document, similar to the Constitution of the United States, affirming principles which should inform citizens of the European Union of their rights and guide both governments and the European Court of Justice in the decisions which they took on implementing them. It also could have stressed that while the European Central Bank (ECB) was the guardian of stability, the European Investment Bank (EIB) was the safeguard of cohesion.

Instead, Giscard presided over the drafting of a text with all the charisma of an out-of-order telephone directory, confusing a constitution with a treaty and embodying every detail of all earlier treaty agreements other than any of the several instruments which had been devised since the Single European Act to finance economic and social cohesion (European Convention, 2003). The draft Constitution left reference to the role of the EIB under 'Other Institutions', some hundred pages after a section stressing the independence of the ECB, and neglected to stress that the European Council can set guidelines for economic policy, which the ECB is treaty-bound to support.

Until a few weeks before its publication, the text on the EIB in the draft Constitution had been lifted, without amendment extant, from the Rome Treaty, even being in the future tense, since in 1957, when the Treaty was signed, a European Investment Bank did not yet exist. No recognition was made that it had a remit, following the Amsterdam Special Action Programme and the Luxembourg and Lisbon European Councils, to invest in health, education, urban renewal and the environment, and to promote new technology and innovation. No reference whatever was made to the EIF. The outcome was unintelligible to anyone other than a dedicated specialist in European constitutional law, and so badly edited that some of its cross-references were to nothing, since the articles or provisions to which they should have referred had already been either rescheduled or deleted. The epitaph was duly delivered in May and June 2005 by the French and Dutch electorates, when they overwhelmingly rejected it.

Who governs?

Polling evidence indicates that most people voted against the Constitution because they want a different, more social, more democratic Europe of and for peoples, rather than for markets and governed by elites.[3] It offered more market and less society. In its later recycling in the Treaty of Lisbon it distanced decision making from national parliaments without a counterpart safeguarding of the institutions of national democracy. Former President of Germany Roman Herzog has claimed that 85% of the legislation now going through the Bundestag is an endorsement of decisions 'made in Brussels', while the European Court of Justice has been overriding the rights of the German Constitutional Court in arbitrary judgments reducing the rights of labour, which are an integral part of the German Constitution (Herzog and Lüder, 2008).

Meanwhile the European Central Bank claimed not only that member states should not run deficits of more than 3%, but also that they should balance their budgets. Well-intended Keynesians have claimed that one of the ways of countering this monetarist bias would be to change its terms of reference, which could be done by the European Council of heads of state and government through a treaty revision, much as the US Congress can change the remit of the Federal Reserve. If modelled on the Hawkins 1978 Full Employment and Balanced Growth Act, these would commit the ECB to 'full employment, balanced growth and reasonable price stability' and signal to European publics that governments not only are concerned to safeguard stability but actually make a reality of a Stability and Growth Pact.

In a series of statements made since the global financial crisis, French President Nicolas Sarkozy has gone further in claiming that Europe needs an economic government to counter the deflationary impact of the ECB. But rather than needing this, which would be supranational and opposed by several governments, since Article 103 of the Maastricht Treaty the European Council has been able to define 'broad economic guidelines' for 'general economic policies' which the ECB is obliged not merely to note, nor simply 'take account of', but 'to support'. The Bank has assiduously neglected this provision in its claims that it is and must remain 'wholly independent'. But it is not, any more than was the Bundesbank, from whose constitution this provision was drawn.[4]

David Marsh, both a journalist and a historian of the Bundesbank, has evidenced that it came under direct pressure from heads of government throughout the postwar period. State secretaries of finance or their deputies regularly attended Bundesbank Council meetings and made their views known. Konrad Adenauer in 1956 denounced the bank for acting like a guillotine, cutting off the *Wirtschaftswunder* by a high interest rate policy. Helmut Schmidt told the Bundestag in 1982 that the Bundesbank was obsessed with inflation and provoking deflation.

Helmut Kohl telephoned the president of the bank in December 1987 to tell him that it should cut interest rates, which it did (Marsh, 1992).

When some media comment on the May 2010 financial package observed that the independence of the ECB now was in question, since it had been obliged to buy up government debt held by financial institutions, it missed the point that the ECB's alleged 'total independence' was a myth. Its first responsibility is to preserve the internal and external stability of the euro, which was under threat from speculation against the bonds of national member states in the spring of 2010, but it otherwise has to support the broad economic guidelines and general economic policies of the Union, which is more than most national central banks are obliged to do in relation to the economic policies of their governments.

Thus, Europe does not have one of the key features of a government, a common fiscal policy, in the sense of a Union tax base, but does not need it to finance its own recovery programme, since it can do so by shifting savings – high in a recession in which the private sector is reluctant or unable to invest – into socially productive investments through its own investment bank – the EIB – rather than its central bank or the ECB. As the 10 May 2010 financial package also showed, it also need not be bound indefinitely by the terms and conditions for a single currency which were agreed at Maastricht in a world which had not yet been hit by the greatest financial crisis and recession since the 1930s.

The EU also had approached this in its March 2005 revision of the Stability and Growth Pact for a single currency to allow an excess deficit over 3% of GDP in exceptional circumstances. After the fallout from the sub-prime crisis in November 2008, with Europe already deep into recession, the EU Commissioner for Economy and Finance, Joachin Almunia, stressed that an 'excessive deficit procedure' would not automatically be invoked when, in such circumstances, deficits were over a 3% nominal limit. Almunia was not a classic central banker committed only to price stability at the cost of growth and employment. He had earlier been the General Secretary of the Spanish UGT trades union and seriously concerned about the level of unemployment which, in Spain after its transition from dictatorship and under the government of Felipe Gonzalez, had soared above 20%, as it again has, following the fallout from the sub-prime crisis.

Before the revision of the Stability and Growth Pact, Almunia addressed a conference convened in Brussels by John Monks, Secretary General of the European Trades Union Confederation. Monks and I made the case to him both at and after the conference that it was vital that a revised Stability and Growth Pact should find a wording that would allow that national co-finance for investments by the EIB need not count on national debt. For there is a key caveat on the potential for the EIB to prove the counterpart of US Treasury borrowing in financing European economic and social cohesion, in that it only co-finances national investments. National governments or other institutions have to finance the counterpart.

This is the reason why only a handful of the Trans-European Transport Networks agreed at Essen in 1994 have been completed. Member states could not match EIB finance because of the debt and deficit conditions of the Stability and Growth Pact. Asking the EIB to fund projects outright is one option, but it clearly would be reluctant to lose the commitment of national partners. Asking it to increase its co-finance from 50% to 60% or more is another, but would not resolve the co-financing constraint. A better option could be to explicitly exempt national co-finance for EIB-agreed projects from the Stability Pact under the terms of its revision in 2005 to allow for 'exceptional circumstances', of which the worst European recession since the 1930s certainly qualifies.

Achieving a European Recovery Programme financed by the EIB therefore does not depend on approval from the ECB. Moreover, unlike the ECB, the institutional culture of the EIB is entrepreneurial rather than monetarist. It wants to 'get things done' (Holliday, 2008), which was the commitment of Roosevelt in the New Deal (Cohen, 2009). Within the revised terms of reference of the EIB since 1997, to finance investment in health, education, urban renewal, the environment, and technology and innovation, the EU already has the means to match the investment-led social and environmental recovery programmes adopted in the US by the Obama administration without this being constrained by either the ECB or the Stability and Growth Pact for the euro. It can already finance a European New Deal through borrowing to invest, as the US Treasury did in the 1930s.

Who finances?

When EU governments realised that cutting national debt to 60% of GDP as a precondition for the euro could mean economies such as Italy, Belgium and Greece cutting public expenditure by up to half or doubling taxes,[5] they simply ignored it, allowing the most generous interpretation of a provision under the Maastricht criteria that they should show 'significant progress' in doing so. But they ignored the counterpart provision in the cohesion report to Delors, that the Union should develop its own financial instruments similar to US Treasury Bonds and thereby enable European financing of investments in a manner which could enable countries such as Italy, Belgium and Greece to reduce their own high debt and deficit levels.

With Nicolas Sarkozy, France has changed its initial stance against the Union issuing its own bonds. German Chancellor Angela Merkel has half learned up, the hard way, initially opposing even a €30 billion salvage package for Greece on the grounds that this could not be paid by German taxpayers, whereas the EU decided on 10 May 2010 on a €450 billion package of loans which would need to be covered by its and other taxpayers if there were a national debt default or serial defaults. This was not a considered reflection on the case for the EU to issue its own bonds on the precedent and with the legitimation of those of the US Treasury, but a panic reaction to speculation against the euro and after reported threats from President Sarkozy to quit it if Merkel did not support the package (Roberts, 2010).

Yet, if Germany had followed the model of the US New Deal and, with France, supported the 1993 Delors proposal that the EU should issue its own equivalent of US Treasury Bonds, there would have been no need for any taxpayer in any country to subsidise another. In a recession savings are high because there are fewer investment outlets in a private sector which is repressed. Public finance can offer them in the social domains, where there is near-unlimited latent demand for better education, health, protection of the environment, shorter working time and enhanced work–life balance, all of which were in the Lisbon Agenda of 2000, even if there has been an assiduous displacement of this by claims that this was about flexible labour markets and reducing, rather than reinforcing, social rights.

What was also missed in this regard by the May 2010 salvage package was that the European Council could declare within 'broad economic guidelines' that a given tranche of the national debt of its most exposed economies should be transferred to the European Central Bank. None of this would imply a debt write-off, even if this is precisely what central banks did for private banks following the sub-prime crisis. The member states still would be servicing the share of their debt now denominated as European Union Bonds, similar to those recommended by Delors in the December 1993 White Paper. But they would be doing so at a lower rate of interest and less cost to other spending programmes.

It then could be possible to gain a balance between monetary stability and higher levels of employment and welfare. Economies still well in excess of the Maastricht debt and deficit criteria for a single currency could be required, as a condition of the transfer of such a tranche of their debt to the Union, to make more significant progress in reducing them than was made following the nominal commitment to this at Maastricht itself. But in parallel, the multipliers from extended investments financed by the EIB, with an exemption of national co-finance for them within the terms of the revised Stability and Growth Pact, would offset the deflationary implications of national debt and deficit reductions.

There is also the issue of what Europe now does in relation to not only its crisis in national debt and deficits but also the agenda of the G20 and the scope and limits for global governance. When Angela Merkel finally agreed to support the May 2010 financial package this followed two phone calls to her from Barack Obama (Roberts, 2010). What he said at the time was not known to a wider public. But its implicit logic was clear. For, if the euro collapsed, the next currency under threat from financial markets would be the dollar.

The issue of Eurobonds by the ECB not only could reactively protect most debt- and deficit-exposed economies of southern and eastern European member states against speculators. It also could proactively contribute to the recovery of the global economy, which has been one of the main commitments in principle of the G20 since its formation in 2008. European bonds could fulfil the aspiration of several of the G20 member states, including Brazil, Russia, India and China, that there should be a more plural global reserve currency system. This in turn would be of more advantage to the US than a collapse of the dollar if there were a double-dip recession in the US caused by one in Europe. A social investment-led recovery financed by bonds would give substance to the formal commitment of the EU since 2009 to a European Economic Recovery Programme. A stronger euro, with bonds financed from a share of surpluses elsewhere in the global economy, and sovereign wealth funds, would counter the casino capitalism which crashed it in 2008, and show the peoples of Europe that governments govern, rather than markets rule.

Notes

[1] Estimates calculated by Alphametrics and passed to Romano Prodi shortly before he formed his first government.

[2] When the *Financial Times* later published a letter by me to this effect, an official of the Dutch Central Bank wrote to tell me that it was not aware of any treaty or other provision that authorised a central bank not to count EIB borrowing against national debt. I replied that he was right, but that other member states had not done so, on the valid enough grounds that bond

borrowings by the EIB were its financial responsibility rather than theirs, and that to include them as a liability on national debt would have been gratuitous double counting. I also passed the message to Gordon Brown, with whom I had been on Labour's shadow Treasury team, but received no acknowledgement.

[3] For instance, a Gallup poll in France in June 2005 found that 83% of those voting 'no' thought that 'EU membership is a good thing'; the same share also thought that voting 'no' would give the 'opportunity for a more social Treaty', while 80% wanted a treaty that would 'better defend national interests'. In the Netherlands the proportions among 'no' voters answering the same questions were 78% for Europe as 'a good thing', 71% for 'a more social Treaty' and 73% for a treaty that would 'better defend national interests' (Manchin, 2005).

[4] The provision in the Constitution of the Bundesbank which this reflects reads that it 'must support the general economic policies of the federal government' – 'die allgemeine Wirtschaftspolitik der Bundesregierung zu unterstützen' – which is far more explicit than a phrase such as 'to support the fundamental laws, or Grundsätze, of the Federal Republic'.

[5] Advice passed both to Romano Prodi and to the Temporary Committee for Employment of the European Parliament. See further Coates and Holland (1995), also Coates and Holland (1996).

References

Blot, C., Creel, J., Rifflart, C. and Schweisguth, D. (2009) *Petit manuel de stratégie de sortie de crise: Comment rebondir pour éviter l'enlisement?* Paris: Observatoire Français des Conjonctures Economiques.

Coates, K. and Holland, S. (1995) *Full Employment for Europe*, Nottingham: Spokesman Press.

Coates, K. and Holland, S. (1996) *Dear Commissioner: Will Unemployment Break Europe?* Nottingham: Spokesman Press.

Cohen, A. (2009) *Nothing to Fear*, New York: The Penguin Press.

Economist, The (2010) 'Europe's 750 billion euro bazooka', 10 May.

EIB (European Investment Bank) (2008) *50 Years of Sustainable Investment*, Luxembourg: EIB.

European Commission (1977) *Study Group on the Role of Public Finance in European Integration*, Brussels: European Commission (MacDougall Report).

European Commission (1993) *Growth, Competitiveness, Employment*, Brussels: EU Commission.

European Convention (2003) *The European Convention. Proposal for a Treaty Establishing a Constitution for Europe*, CONV 850/03, Giscard Constitution, Brussels.

Fletcher, N. (2010) 'Investors fear crisis cure will be worse than debt disease', *Guardian*, 15 May.

Freeman, C. and Louçã, F. (2001) *As Time Goes By: From the Industrial Revolution to the Information Revolution*, Oxford: Oxford University Press.

Hansard (1983) Chancellor of the Exchequer: Answer to Written Parliamentary Question from the Member for Vauxhall, Parliamentary Report, 13 July.

Herzog, R. and Lüder, G. (2008) 'Stop the European Court of Justice', Eurobserver.com, 10 September.

Holland, S. (ed) (1983) *Out of Crisis: A Project for European Recovery*, Nottingham: Spokesman Press.

Holland, S. (1987) *The Global Economy*, London: Weidenfeld and Nicolson.

Holland, S. (1993) *The European Imperative: Economic and Social Cohesion in the 1990s*, Foreword: Jacques Delors, Nottingham: Spokesman Press.

Holland, S. (2000) 'New Financial instruments', Paper for the Portuguese Presidency of the European Council, Lisbon: Office of the Prime Minister.

Holliday, A. (2008) *Promoting Economic and Social Cohesion in the Enlarged EU. In 50 Years of Sustainable Investment*, Luxembourg: European Investment Bank.

Kroes, N. (2009) 'European banks cannot set aside the rules', *Financial Times*, 28 April.

Manchin, R. (2005) *After the Referenda*, Brussels: Gallup Europe.

Marsh, D. (1992) *The Bundesbank*, London: Heineman.

Roberts, D. (2010) 'More than a euro crisis', *Guardian*, 14 May.

Robinson, N. (2009) 'The European Investment Bank: Europe's Neglected Institution', *Journal of Common Market Studies*, vol 47, no 3, pp 651–73.

Schumpeter, J. (1949 [1911]) *The Theory of Economic Development*, Cambridge, MA: Harvard University Press.

Tett, G. (2009) *Fool's Gold*, London: Little, Brown; New York: Simon and Schuster.

Part Two
Policies and issues

Public policy responses to fiscal debt or deficit: is there a difference?

Fred Mear

After the government rescue package for the UK banking sector in 2008–09 the government's fiscal deficit rose substantially and quickly to over 12% pa and there was a consensus that there needed to be an adjustment to reduce the fiscal deficit and the total government debt of the UK. However, there was no consensus over the timing of the reduction, the depth of that reduction or the actions that should be taken to achieve it; as Hunter (2009) pointed out, 'it is not whether the belt gets tightened, but which notch it gets pulled to'. This chapter examines some of the issues behind the arguments about how to view the fiscal deficit and how to respond. The UK election in May 2010 did little to resolve the issues long term, but clarified the position in the short term. The Conservative and Liberal Democratic parties had differing policies in their election manifestos but the coalition government confirmed its intention to adopt the Conservative policy of immediate savings (£6 billion). The political and economic dimensions need to be addressed separately. While these two aspects are usually linked and seen as part of the same problem, in the UK the economic models being used were not called into question, but rather, how to interpret and deal with the factors as applied to those models. This, to a large extent, is part of the consequence of the globalisation of financial markets and hence acceptance of (or more importantly the need to accept) global financial monitoring by the big international financial institutions such as the International Monetary Fund (IMF), World Bank and European Central Bank.

The underlying assumptions

The underlying debate on actions is based on the assumptions of economic models such as those put forward by the IMF, for example, the Mundell-Flemming and Polak models. The workings of the model are not of concern in themselves as they were not questioned by any of the political parties. What is of importance is the assumptions upon which they are based and the consequences of various actions. This chapter is therefore going to take a 'black box' approach to discussing only the input and output elements of the models (for details see Pilbeam, 2006).

The models examine the relationships between various economic variables and predict the implications of various policy actions. The context of the UK is that it has open capital markets. It is assumed in such circumstances that interest rates have little impact on capital flows, impacting, rather, on exchange rates. Assuming perfect mobility of capital, any change in interest rates will then impact on the exchange rate of the pound. If that is the case, then fiscal expansion will normally, over time, lead to higher imports and increased interest rates as the economy finds equilibrium. As such, lower interest rates provide only a temporary stimulus to the UK economy, as reflected in much of the debate about removal of the fiscal stimulus and its timing. The predictive components are made even more unstable, given the 2010 sovereign debt crisis within the eurozone.

Fully functioning capital markets and a stable velocity of cash within the economy are key assumptions of the models. An alternative to fiscal expansion is monetary expansion, which can be a more effective way to stimulate the economy. In 2009–10 we saw £200 billion of quantitative easing (QE) by the Bank of England's MPC (Monetary Policy Committee) in an attempt to increase money supply. QE is an electronic version of 'printing money', thereby increasing the amount of liquidity (cash or near cash) into the economy. M4[1] has increased dramatically (ONS, 2009, 55), which has led to an increased money supply of 6.9% (seasonally adjusted); however, this is more than compensated for by the reduced velocity of circulation of 17.47% (ONS, 2009, 56), giving an overall reduction in economic activity. This is where we see one of the major flaws in the assumptions of established models in dealing with the current exceptional circumstances. There has been an assumption that the velocity of circulation remains constant; the uncertainty, therefore, is whether the reduced velocity is a temporary blip or a more permanent readjustment. The combination of low interest rates, fiscal expansion and monetary expansion is uncharted territory, with significant risks involved.

The economic crises of 2008–09 were exceptional in that capital markets were disrupted. The judgement call was then whether the stimulus of 2009 would allow capital markets to recover. If capital markets resumed normal activity, rising interest rates would return to normal levels and an increased danger would arise of sucking in imports, creating a balance of payments problem. If the capital markets did not recover sufficiently and were not returning to normality, then the risk of a double-dip recession remained if the stimuli were removed too quickly. The impact of the 2010 government debt crisis throughout the eurozone created further turbulence in the capital markets, complicating the position further.

If damage to the functioning of the financial sector reduces monetary circulation, then the lack of lending can still derail any recovery. However, if the financial sector is fully repaired, then the velocity of money within the economy increases and is likely to lead to a need to reverse fiscal and monetary loosening, leading to a second round of fiscal tightening. The pressure is therefore a long-term one that will outlast the initial crisis.

The IMF has a scrutiny and reporting role in ensuring short-term global financial stability and its views on a country's economy are important in how markets react to events. If the IMF is required to support economies (such as Latvia, Iceland and Ukraine have found in Europe), they require structural adjustments similar to those that have been imposed on developing economies needing IMF support. This creates a perverse dilemma. The structural support requires high interest rates, currency devaluations and a reduction of public sector activities and state debt. While the validity of these approaches for economic stability has been well established by the IMF, they are also the requirements for stability within the EU, as Greece and Ireland highlight, in accordance with the Growth and Stability Pact (see below). Economic management is then taken out of domestic hands. It is useful to consider the basis of those models; the responses to the demand of the crises can then be explored. The UK is outside the eurozone and not heading for IMF support – despite recent record levels of deficit, the total debt was still only 59.9% of GDP (ONS, 2009). So the UK had greater flexibility than many other European countries, albeit still being subject to the major influence of market reactions to its public finances. The primary concern for the UK was therefore deficit reduction to a sustainable level. The emphasis changed significantly, following the 2010 election, from deficit reduction to debt reduction.

The political context of any financial and economic reforms to the eurozone and EU countries can also be derailed by democratic forces (such as the Latvian courts overturning pension cuts, Iceland's referendum on meeting its debt obligations, and civil unrest and strike actions in Greece over government spending cuts). If countries fail to achieve the cuts required by the EU/IMF or if the banks are unable to lend sufficiently to replace state spending, then GDP in Europe may reduce further. During May 2010 the political problems facing the eurozone expanded to include Spain and Portugal, and there were fears of a contagion of sovereign debt problems across Europe.

The policy responses: capital markets

Banks had to rebuild their capital reserves and remove liabilities. The improvement in the financial positions of banks could be achieved by increased state investment in the banks; however, the unpopularity of the banks at a time of recession (seen as being caused by poor decisions by banks) and the high levels of state support already given meant that further state investment was never really politically possible. The nationalisation of banks was, in the UK, seen as a last resort, but an option which was used in the case of Northern Rock.

An alternative to outright state control was to support the banks in other ways, such as by stripping out 'toxic' or poorly performing assets. This, in effect, removed liabilities from the banks and placed them under state ownership. The assets may well end up performing adequately, but also have a high risk of failure. The state is therefore taking over the risk element, which reduces the real cost of capital to the banks. An example along the lines of Northern Rock, where the whole bank was nationalised but only 'good' parts of the bank were privatised, shows an area where additional hidden subsidies are being imputed into the system as the riskier debts are taken over by the state. The UK government was in a very difficult position politically in supporting the banking sector during an election year.

The banks were recovering their position slowly by encouraging consumers to repay their debt to the banks (during 2009 and 2010), keeping interest rates to investors very low but lending rates to borrowers high. This allowed the margins between lending and borrowing rates to be used to repair the balance sheets.

The government was therefore looking for ways to repair the banking sector so that it could resume normal operations without additional overt government support. The government could increase the circulation of money supply, but this was difficult at a time when greater restrictions were placed on banks in terms of capital deposit requirements.

The government could also inflate the economy out of the crisis by raising the inflation targets of the MPC; again, politically difficult at a time of wage constraints in the public and private sectors. It is worth noting, however, that in March 2010 the retail prices index had risen to 4.4% (consumer prices index 3.7%) (ONS, 2010b).

Sustainability

At the macro-economic level the major debate on government finance is focused on annual deficits and funding of those deficits, and also of total state debt. There is a broad issue of sustainability: debt level sustainability and deficit sustainability. If we assume that the crisis is a once-in-a-generation shock it could be argued that it is unreasonable to repay the cost of that shock in a short period; rather, the cost should be recovered over a period of time. The deficit is a wholly separate issue and should be sustainable in order to prevent greater problems.

In the December 2009 Pre-Budget Report the Treasury indicated a structural deficit of 8% pa of GDP, with the remainder being due to one-off and cyclical impacts. There was a consensus among all major political parties that significant cuts were needed in annual fiscal deficits, while the precise size and timing of the cuts was less apparent.

There was insufficient liquidity in the UK or global banking systems to ensure liquidity sufficient to meet the needs of the private sector to replace the spending of the state sector if the fiscal and monetary stimuli were removed. The QE had put an additional £200 billion into the system, but stresses on lending were still apparent. The strength of UK bank balance sheets still needed further repair. The ability of the banks to fund the recovery therefore had to be questioned.

So even after any belt tightening there will remain a high degree of uncertainty. Given the level of international contagion there is also potential for non-UK events to damage the banking sector and to impact on global capital movements. The situations in Greece and Ireland in 2009–10 needed to be brought under control quickly because of threats to the stability of the euro and risks of further stresses on European banks. Even how to record information globally failed when the US accounting reforms stalled, with the Securities and Exchange Commission (SEC) commissioner appointed by the Obama administration insisting that reforms to converge with international accounting standards identifying all debts on the balance sheets of banks were not acceptable to the US (Buttell, 2009), again raising doubts over the level of debt. Even the rapid repayment of US government 'bail-out' funding may mean that the banks are recovering more quickly than expected or that the banks are keen to exit the punitive conditions of the bail-out and are exiting early, hoping that the recovery will be sustained. Although the motivation is still unclear, early exit from punitive government conditions has advantages for the management of the banks – after all, the banks are now aware that they will not be allowed to fail, and removal from state interference (especially on executive remuneration) is an attractive option. There are already risks that the asset price has not fully deflated and a new 'prick' of the bubble may occur. This could well be the removal of fiscal stimulus without the private sector having the ability to replace the government's spending, or the sovereign debt crises. It is therefore critical that the banks are in a position to respond, and without additional printing of money (QE) it is difficult to see where this additional funding would be generated, unless China, India and the US expand the global economy rapidly.

The EU

The EU has set targets/limits on annual deficits and overall debt levels for countries to return to growth, along with stability pact targets in the medium term. We could argue about the premise of the sustainability of the EU deficit/debt requirements as a 'one-size-fits-all approach', although breaches of these requirements are allowed on individual, case-by-case considerations. These constraints, in the current circumstances, appear somewhat arbitrary, as the assumptions upon which they are based do not fully reflect the current position. The idea of a 3% GDP annual deficit and 60% GDP total debt is based on an assumed ability of mature economies to grow at 3% pa, making the debt burden sustainable. There is flexibility to meet one-off shocks, such as the current crisis. However, the requirement to be back on track by 2015 may be optimistic. It will also mean that growth will start from a lower base, and hence the impact will be embedded into future economic growth. The need of the EU to rein in deficits may have major social impacts that are not being fully factored into the situation. The arbitrary nature of the limits is illustrated by the position of Estonia, which has faced a 15% reduction in GDP in 2009, has extremely low public debt of less than 8% (7.2% in March 2010) of GDP, but is still limited to a 3% annual deficit.

The previous UK Labour government wished to cut the deficit from 2011. The Conservatives argued that a more dramatic reduction was required, and this was confirmed by announcements from the Conservative–Liberal Democrat Coalition government of cuts of £6 billion in 2010 and an emergency Budget in June 2010.

Does a reduced fiscal deficit improve the economy?

You have read, in the previous two chapters of this book, some of the broader economic arguments. In this chapter some of the individual issues are examined in more depth. In curbing the fiscal deficit and reducing levels of debt we can either raise funds, or reduce expenditure. In either case there is a danger that this will impact most heavily on the most vulnerable in society, when they are the ones most in need during a recession. There is a threat to social cohesion in a multicultural society if the situation is not well managed and any particular social group sees itself being unfairly hit (this issue is examined further in Chapter Five). If we put these together there are major dangers for the future of the economy. There is a high degree of uncertainty as to the future and the actions to be taken.

This unprecedented level of complexity has allowed a variety of political agendas to come to the fore, each selecting various elements of the economic situation to support its arguments. More importantly, it has also allowed an opportunity for a fundamental examination of how public sector and public service provision are made.

If targeting deficits, the emphasis will be on reducing annual expenditure or on raising revenue, from either fees and charges or taxation. The emphasis of the major political parties has appeared to concentrate on the levels of debt; then, in addition to the cutting of costs or raising of revenues, replacing government debt with private debt via privatisations. All parties are committed to reducing the deficit; the debate has been on timing and methods. Those supporting a small government agenda have proposed the reduction of state activity, and those supporting large government have called for increased state intervention in the economy to prevent a repeat of the crisis. The coalition government resulting from the 2010 election meant that while Conservative plans for immediate cuts were still apparent, there was more need for consensus building across political ideologies, rather than a simple battle of 'small' versus 'big' government.

Cutting debt

If debt is targeted, then there is a danger that public investment for future growth may be starved. This may take the form of postponing capital expenditure on infrastructure programmes. The decision to cut UK higher education expenditure illustrates that at a time of greater demand non-priority areas are still at risk. The need for public investment may therefore be forced to undertake approaches that do not impact on the reported levels of debt. Looking at this argument further, we see a number of differing issues coming together. If we see expansion of higher education as a response to the demands of the population, where education and self-advancement are purely beneficial rather than essential, then it could be argued this is a cost the country can ill afford in an economic crisis. If, however, higher education is seen as an investment providing a more highly educated workforce, increasing competitiveness and future growth in the economy, and generating increased future tax revenues through increased earnings, we can see a positive return on the investment. Interestingly, countries such as France and the US are increasing investment in higher education as part of their responses to fiscal problems.

Cutting expenditure

Expenditure cuts have major policy implications. In terms of deficits, there is a danger of cutting services to the most vulnerable, with risks to social cohesion in some areas. This has already been seen in some local authorities where only a legal minimum of provision is to be provided, so that help can no longer be afforded for those with moderate needs, but only for those with severe needs that are covered by legislation. Merrick (2010), reporting on the National Housing Federation's analysis of the December 2009 Pre-Budget Report, stated that the number of affordable homes to be built in the period to 2020 could be halved, adding 1.25 million people to housing waiting lists.

Cutting most or all discretionary service areas may result in reduced support for public transport, for example, thereby reducing provision and increasing car usage. This disadvantages rural communities, making it more likely that they become dormitory towns, dominated by commuters who will use motor vehicles in the absence of adequate public transport and setting back the green agenda.

Closing services in the short term that may be needed in the medium term (such as schools, where there is a drop in demand that may be reversed) is also an issue. One example might be the removal of surplus school places under the Building Schools for the Future programme while other areas of the public sector are planning for increased populations to meet government development targets.

Displacement of services to the charitable sector (at a time when it is itself under severe funding pressures) is a further policy response to the imperative to cut public expenditure. The Conservative–Liberal Democrat government announced 'Big Society' plans which had provision of services by charities and community businesses at their heart.

Tougher capping rules and reduced central government grant settlements are likely to be in force for several years, so as to ensure that local governments do not put at risk the macro-fiscal constraints being imposed. The squeezing of limits, with the enforcement of legal minimum requirements, reduces local discretion. If the capping restrictions are tightened this may lead in some circumstances to local authorities not meeting legal requirements, risking legal action in some cases.

Is there another way, or is it an illusion?

There are strong pressures to resolve reported breaches of international agreements, both within Europe (Growth and Stability Pact) and internationally (IMF Structural Adjustment programmes), in more creative ways. Easterley (1999) identified a number of areas of 'fiscal illusion' which included a range of approaches that, while appearing to reduce the fiscal deficit or debt, left government net worth unchanged. An element of fiscal illusion is inevitable, but the pressure for large-scale adoption of illusionary measures must be guarded against, as the pressure will continue for decades to come. Of the various means to achieve fiscal illusion, probably the most emotive is the use of creative accounting approaches – with the depth of Greece's problems of 2009 being exacerbated by hidden debts in earlier years. The keeping of debts off the records by means of various techniques needs to be guarded against. The increased use of the private sector and partnership working, even when no efficiency gains are achieved, will be particularly attractive when further capital investment is needed. This will be seen by many councils as preferable to more efficient public sector provision if it removes debts from the balance sheets of public sector organisations.

Sale of assets at low prices or when markets are depressed could become expedient. The motivation to sell land and premises is increased in these circumstances, with the reduction of debt levels being prioritised over maximisation of taxpayer welfare. An example of this at the central level would be privatisation of Northern Rock or selling Royal Bank of Scotland shares before they were fully recovered, while providing huge hidden subsidies. If we take the example of 'toxic banks', this provides a significant subsidy to the banks, as the risk is removed from the banks, providing a subsidy that is hidden from the public gaze. The good assets are returned to a depressed market, thereby selling public assets at an undervalued price (due to a poorly performing capital market, and continued risks to banks). Sale of assets and buy-back of services is also an option. This can be done by selling off service provision to the private sector, or by management buy-outs of back-room services. The primary impact is to remove debt from the public sector and replace it with debt in the private sector, but with no cost or efficiency savings. Again, this represents an illusion of benefit, with the associated political image of 'selling off the family silver'.

There is also a risk of the sale of assets at the cost of future revenues. Some services provide surplus revenues. These are obviously beneficial to taxpayers, and can be translated into a capital receipts, discounting future revenues, thus reducing stated debt levels but in the longer term increasing the costs of service provision. An example could be the sale of profitable crematoria, or changes in social housing approaches.

When examining the impacts on local administrations and their responses there will be a clear difference between administrations that philosophically believe in a reduced public sector role, and those that do not. The lack of consensus leaves an almost unique situation in modern times, where increased expenditure and reduced income are being supported by the IMF, which is warning against removal of stimuli too soon because this risks a double-dip recession – while at the same time cautioning against large public sector deficits and debts. It means that political ideological responses can be justified by all. Those administrations that feel that small government is best and that there should be large cutbacks can justify their position. Those that believe in a more interventionist government can point to the risks to economic recovery of removing the fiscal stimulus. This is without the political risks to social cohesion that are common when economies are under stress, with high levels of youth unemployment. The influence of nationalist parties in protecting their own nation's share of public expenditure is likely to be an enduring legacy of the election result of 2010.

Debt or deficit: what is the difference?

Some crucial distinctions need to be made: that is, between deficits and debt. In the previous discussion in this chapter we have concentrated on the issue of debt and the need to reduce debt levels to those within international agreements, that is, to 60% of GDP. As this level was predicted to be exceeded (HM Treasury, 2009, 18), then if we are to return to such levels the deficit must turn into a surplus. There are two different aspects: one is that of deficit sustainability and the other that of debt sustainability. There is a danger that the economic recovery will be delayed, or the speed of recovery be slowed by overshooting what is needed to get the deficit to a sustainable level.

Policy should concentrate on sustainable deficits; examples of fiscal illusion, where deficits increase in the medium to long term in order to meet short-term debt levels, as discussed above, will damage the long-term services delivered. There is also a danger of a 'bounce' effect, where cuts are deeper than needed, with expenditure allowed to bounce back after the debt target has been met.

The fundamental question, then, is whether the real problem is deficits or debt. Cutting the deficit impacts on the broader economy. The fundamental options available are to increase revenue, reduce expenditure or undertake fiscal illusionary techniques concerned with reducing reported expenditure (as opposed to the debt we discussed earlier), or a combination of these.

There will also be major political manoeuvrings to justify actions that may appear counterintuitive. For example, one county council chose a random sample of 6,000 residents to consult on a limited range of options for cuts; this was not based on voting patterns (issues on democratic involvement) and had a clear expenditure element. It demonstrated that some consultation had taken place, albeit limited. The council stated that it would take the views of the randomly selected residents into account. This is a dangerous precedent for the democratic process, and replaces representative democratic principles with 'focus groups' and 'citizens' panels'. The consultation is very limited in such exercises and its accountability is questionable.

Operational decisions

The Treasury identified £15 billion of savings in the 'Operational Efficiency Programme' (Hunter, 2009) and further substantial savings are being looked for. You will note in other areas of this book (particularly in Chapter Seven) major concerns on measurement and accountability. While not directly examining those issues, the techniques applied by many authorities will be aimed at meeting targets, rather than at improving services or making savings. This may create strong pressures to engage in a range of techniques to meet targets, in terms of both recorded outputs and economic targets. The service delivery is then simply replaced by exercises to meet the targets being measured. This will increase the tendency for 'what gets measured gets done', removing the onus of meeting individual needs. Looking at individual care packages in social services, there is a danger that, as individual budgets and user choice are implemented, some authorities may not be able (or willing) to provide support for the most vulnerable to make appropriate decisions to maximise their own welfare support. The protection of communities is examined by Richardson in Chapter Five, and choice and empowerment by Brown and Yates in Chapter Eight.

Examples of operational decisions could be, for example, outsourcing/combining 'back-room' services, the performance levels then being based on contracted measurable outputs only, possibly leaving the non-measurable activities to flounder. But what is the motivation here: service improvements, reduced cost, fiscal illusion or simple ideological beliefs on the size of government? There will be a combination of these, but all will be 'sold' to the public on the basis of improved efficiency.

Increased fees and charges are inevitable. In many senses this may be the simplest response and it may be seen as an opportunity to undertake unpopular actions. Aspects such as congestion charges and workplace parking levies may become an acceptable alternative to funding infrastructure investment (such as trams as in Nottingham). There is also a danger of dysfunctional activities, such as the introduction of fees and charges to encourage use of public transport, while at the same time reducing subsidies and support to public transport.

The use of more targeted benefits, such as providing help only to the most severely in need (ignoring those in moderate need), along with increased means testing for services, is also on the agenda. Clearly, all charges will be reviewed. The impact may well be greatest in those services where the neediest are offered the service for free. In the case of home support, for example, large increases in charges will affect only those who have to pay, but the impact on many activities will continue to be felt for many years, affecting the whole spectrum of services, such as school dinners as well as welfare services and planning applications.

Increased fines could provide a double benefit of discouraging unwanted behaviour and raising income; this in areas such as traffic violations, including greater policing of bus lanes and enforcement of anti-littering legislation. The motivation then needs to be questioned: is this service provision for the public good, or to raise revenue?

Local authorities should be pressing for a broadening of the income base from central government so as to gain greater freedom of local finance. Central government can devolve some of the decision making on cuts in services and increased fee income by reducing central grants to local authorities. While this deterioration of local finance further worsens the financial difficulties of local authorities, it does focus local decisions on where service cuts and fee increases should fall. As identified, there will be significant reductions in service levels. However, the cuts will not be equal across all services; some services will be protected, but not indefinitely – for example, health will be protected in the short term. Education will probably be protected for similar periods. Given that these areas are protected, the axe will fall more heavily in other areas, such as further and higher education. Tactics will be used by vested interest groups trying to protect their particular services, so that even in areas where cuts are being made there will be a great deal of officer manoeuvring to protect individual services.

The bigger question

The combination of these factors could be the most important catalyst for decentralisation since the devolution to national governments of Scotland and Wales, or it may lead to a reduction of local discretion. To control the position there may be greater decentralisation or greater centralisation. For all the rhetoric of devolving power to local councils by the Conservative–Liberal Democrat government, the reality may look very different. Centralising the decision making so as to ensure that the required cuts are achieved, requiring a more direct involvement from central government via the use of directives, will reduce the role of local authorities in policy making, leaving primarily a rump activity of managing local resources to meet legal minimum requirements.

Alternatively, greater autonomy may be devolved to local authorities, the government decentralising in order to pass more of the decisions down to local decision makers. Of course there will be a political dimension in these decisions. If greater control is exercised over the fiscal conditions there is a danger that the role of local government becomes one of simply ensuring that minimum legal requirements are met; or possibly, in some cases, of devolving the decisions as to which laws to break if fiscal rules cannot be complied with, while delivering minimal service levels.

If fiscal decisions are devolved more fully, then the decisions on local services and charges can easily be placed at the feet of local politicians, or those best placed to meet local priorities can put their policies in place. This is probably the most politically opportune time for the devolved governments to push for more autonomy; greater taxing powers, together with law-making powers, could be devolved. The removal of capping legislation would allow local decisions to determine the balance between taxation and service cuts. The first stages may be seen in the call by the Common Home Affairs Select Committee for an end to the capping regime for police forces (Russell, 2010).

Conclusion

We can summarise a number of complex issues in very broad terms. There is an argument that public sector spending is a burden on the private sector, and must be reduced. This is based primarily on the concept of crowding out. The reduced spending in the public sector needs to be taken up by the private sector. The functioning of the commercial banks is key, because if there is no take-up on investment by the private sector of the funds released by the public sector, then the recovery will reverse into a double-dip recession.

The trick, then, is to grow the private sector so as to maintain overall growth, while shrinking state activity. The underwriting of Private Finance Initiatives (PFIs) by the state means that the restricted revenue streams of the private sector banks can be circumvented by the state providing the funds to the private sector. This then means that the government lends money (or offers guarantees) to private sector consortia to build/buy assets to provide public services.

There is an opportunity to develop new approaches, with a greater use of inter-agency and inter-sector activities. This, however, requires greater decentralisation of decision making, allowing greater flexibility in approaches, including greater engagement with the voluntary sector in delivering public policy outcomes. As Leslie (2010) argues, the vague intentions to decentralise declared by central government need to include multi-year financial flexibilities locally as well as nationally.

The state will shrink; that includes education (higher education in particular), welfare (particularly for pensioners, where targeted benefits can be expected, and taxation of other benefits) and security (in particular police and defence, but also fire). The NHS will probably be protected in absolute terms, but will not increase in line with health sector inflation, or the needs of an ageing population. Most areas of discretionary expenditure, such as support for particularly vulnerable groups, above legal minimums, or for the arts and museums, will be seen as expenses that can be cut. Foreign aid is likely to become more tightly controlled and linked more directly to foreign policy, rather than purely humanitarian aid.

The increased use of PPAs/PSAs (Public Partnership Agreements/ Public Service Agreements) that are output driven or contractual deliveries is likely. Increased sales of assets and contracting out of services that can be carried out by the private sector almost regardless of value for money (VFM), but aided by creative accounting techniques and ever more inventive contracting methods, are also possible.

Central government may extend further its lending role to the private sector in areas such as PFIs. The new government agency Infrastructure UK, established in 2009 to coordinate and develop the infrastructure '5–50 year strategy' (Hellowell, 2010), has to find ways of funding the UK's infrastructure programme. The government can be expected to undertake lending in other forms as well. The potential of setting up state funding in return for shares in private companies will be increasingly attractive. Public Private Partnerships are about to have a major resurrection, but with the state providing the lending rather than commercial banks, and there could be greater underwriting by the state of private sector investment for any future development of local infrastructure.

The situation regarding policy responses is distorted by the assumption of a fully functioning banking system, which is yet to be achieved, and so policy decisions will be made by trying to plug each new hole as it appears. The next five years will be the most innovative time in local government; whether future generations will reap the reward or pay the price depends on the extent to which the banking sector has recovered and the level of desperation of local government and the state to meet artificial targets set by external agencies, based on false premises. The increased use of private sector involvement, regardless of VFM, is where there will be much political debate on the motives and benefits of such activities, much along the lines of the PFI debate.

Note
[1] M4 is the broad measure of money supply in the UK; it measures highly liquid assets (which are close substitutes for money).

References

Buttell, A. (2009) 'The hard sell: SEC in a quandary over its push for IFRS', *The Investment Professional*, vol 2, no 1, The New York Society of Security Analysts.

Easterley, W. (1999) 'Fiscal illusion: Taking the bite out of budget cuts', *Economic Policy*, published for the Centre of Economic Policy Research, Oxford: Blackwell Publishing Ltd, pp 56–76.

Hellowell, M. (2010) 'Police forces funding "should not be capped"', *Public Finance*, 29 January–4 February, p 17.

HM Treasury (2009) *Pre-Budget report*, London: HM Treasury.

Hunter, G. (2009) 'At the cutting edge', *Public Finance*, 25 September–1 October, pp 24–5.

Leslie, C. (2010) 'Centre frugal force', *Public Finance*, 29 January–4 February, p 17.

Merrick, N. (2010) 'Social housing targets "likely to be missed"', *Public Finance*, 29 January–4 February, p 13.

ONS (Office for National Statistics) (2009) *Public Sector Finances: Statistical Bulletin* (December).

ONS (2010a) *Public Sector Finances: Statistical Bulletin* (February).

ONS (2010b) *CPI: Statistical Bulletin* (March).

Pilbeam, K. (2006) *International Finance*, 3rd edn, London: Palgrave Macmillan.

Russell, V. (2010) 'Police forces funding "should not be capped"', *Public Finance*, 29 January–4 February, p 12.

FIVE

Protecting the community from the effects of the financial crisis

Joanna Richardson

> An economic slowdown is like a receding tide which reveals the many who are struggling. (Vale et al, 2009, 5)

Local authorities have been implementing cuts to public service budgets since 2008, but the Conservative–Liberal Democrat Coalition government's plans to cut over £6 billion in 2010 added pressure to an already stark situation. While some services have been protected at the centre (such as health), other local budgets are identified as being at severe risk – in particular adult social care services. Other local public services facing pressure include swimming pools, libraries, speed cameras, community centres and other cultural activities. In some areas, warden services in elderly social housing schemes continue to be threatened; and while these are not acute health services, they do comprise a package of public services intended to promote long-term health and well-being, and their reduction or closure will impact heavily on the vulnerable and the elderly.

The New Local Government Network (NLGN) in its (2010) report examined a range of public service areas that faced cuts in order to analyse the options. Individual councils are also undergoing such an exercise, with some, such as East Sussex County Council (2010a), attempting to reconcile the in-year grant reductions with existing local policies and priorities. It is evident that cuts will affect a range of services and groups and that, as stark as the situation is for 2010/11, the challenges will be even greater in future years.

This chapter starts off with a brief overview of the impact of the recession on neighbourhoods and communities, along with ideas on shielding 'places' and neighbourhoods from the effects of the crisis. It then examines issues such as health and housing which, although vital to the whole of society, are difficult to access or maintain in economically difficult times for a range of vulnerable people. It also aims to discuss the impact of the financial crisis on those individuals and communities who may have already been struggling before the recession, and who have been disproportionately affected since the financial crisis started, such as older people, children and Gypsies and Travellers. The challenges of social equality (Wilkinson and Pickett, 2009; Dorling, 2010) and community cohesion should be high on the agenda of a government dealing with the effects of the recession. However, social equality itself seems to be threatened by some of the measures being taken by the Coalition government to reduce public spending. Horton and Reed (2010, 3) state clearly:

> The impact of these cuts will be deeply regressive. All households are hit considerably but the poorest households are hit the hardest.

Neighbourhoods and communities

There are clear links between lack of employment, poverty, access to social networks and overall quality of life. Indeed, the Marmot Review (2010) demonstrated that those in the poorest neighbourhoods in Britain faced up to seven fewer years in life expectancy than those in the richest areas; the Review also reported an even starker figure for those in poor areas, of 17 fewer disability-free years than those in the richest areas. The Review team called for a levelling of this social health gradient. The links between poorer neighbourhoods and poorer life chances are evident, and Leach and Roberts (in Chapter Six) examine community leadership and how neighbourhood working might be used to mitigate the impact of the financial crisis. It is also appropriate to focus more on those poorer areas so as to shield residents from the disproportionate, cumulative effects of the financial crisis.

Parkinson et al (2010) noted the 'real worries' that public sector budget cuts would 'choke' any recovery in the North from previous recessions and initiate a longer period of lower growth. Research from the Centre for Cities (2010) looked at the effect across a number of urban communities, while the Commission for Rural Communities (2009) found financial exclusion of vulnerable groups increasing in rural communities; at the same time, vital networks such as the Post Office have been under threat in some areas.

In more urban areas, problems such as drug dealing and door-step lending have become more prevalent; however, there is evidence of a rapid response from some local authorities. One example was where a loan shark and a drug dealer were creating misery on an estate. In response, the police and Office of Fair Trading took legal remedies against the loan shark. The neighbourhood police inspector appeared to be a key figure in the neighbourhood response to the growing problems (Carter, 2010).

The issue of loan-sharking, for families and communities, is particularly difficult during the financial crisis. Credit was not easily available for inter-banks; for poor individuals credit was even harder to find, and it was this group particularly who turned to loan sharks. Leslie and Hood (2009) suggested that loan-sharking would see a significant increase in numbers as a result of the financial crisis, and estimated over 200,000 people borrowing from these unregulated lenders by the end of 2009. Some of the case studies in their report entailed harrowing accounts of fear, violence, depression and family breakdown. Credit unions were suggested as one way forward, as well as third-sector involvement. The Better Banking Campaign (2010) referred to the interest rates of some loans in the unregulated sector, with examples of 180% APR for home credit lenders, and 1,000% for 'pay-day' lenders. The campaign called for a number of solutions to tackle the problem, including legislative changes to compel financial institutions to fully disclose who they lend to, cap interest rates and incentivise banks to lend to those outside the financial mainstream.

Day (2009) looked at the impact of the recession on communities through four case studies. There were common issues across the case studies, particularly on the fear that the worst was yet to come as public sector cuts impacted on vital community groups and services on poor estates. Tunstall and Fenton (2009) cite the support of community groups through public funding as a way of shifting to 'low-cost but high-impact' methods of renewing neighbourhoods. When there appears to be increasing reliance on the part of government that the charitable sector will pick up provision of services in a number of areas, the financial support of voluntary groups needs to be considered in more depth before cuts are made and decline steepens.

Place shielding

Quirk (2008) talked about the need for a shift from place shaping to place shielding for communities, following the global financial crisis. There has also been recognition from central government that empowering areas to make their own decisions for the benefit of their own neighbourhoods may not only produce the results attuned to the priorities of people in local areas, but also reduce the costs of duplication. The Local Strategic Partnership for Birmingham undertook a mapping study of expenditure and strategic aims (Be

Birmingham, 2009) which examined the total £7.3 billion spent in the country's second-largest city in 2008–09 in terms of meeting stated objectives and understanding how collaborative arrangements might enable more efficient and effective service delivery. The overarching policy idea for this type of approach is 'place-based' budgeting (formerly known as 'Total Place'[1]). Thirteen Total Place pilots submitted their final assessment reports in 2010, and one pilot in the Midlands (Coventry, Solihull and Warwickshire) applied for the removal of ring-fencing on schools budgets, allowing one Total Place budget that promised a lower total spend providing the same services in the region (Illman, 2010). The pilot in this area had attempted to facilitate a more collaborative approach in providing services for young people, particularly children exposed to bullying. It found that collaboration hadn't developed as much as had been hoped for, and there was an imperative, due to reduction in budgets, to work across agencies on a total response to particular issues. The need for such Total Place approaches and the reduction of budget ring-fencing at the centre of government were set out as a way forward for public service delivery by Gordon Brown in early 2009, as part of his plan *Putting the Frontline First*. Total Place/Total Capital approaches were also recommended by Hutton and Jones (2010) in their analysis of economic recovery in the eight core city regions. The LGA (2010a) reinforced the need for place-based budgets in the future governance of local public services, and the NLGN (2010) report also called for the introduction of 'place agreements' as a response to the financial challenges in the public sector.

Place-based budgeting/Total Place concepts are increasingly a part of policy responses to a range of problems, including the effects of the financial crisis on neighbourhoods. One area that has suffered more than many from these effects is Hull, with increases in the Jobseeker's Allowance claimant count, high youth unemployment, a low percentage of 'high skills' in the population and low employment growth (Centre for Cities, 2010). However the city council is responding with a number of initiatives, including a regularly updated 'Place Shielding Action Plan' with measurable targets, and individually named departments taking the lead in specific areas such as business support programmes, supporting local government suppliers, supporting families and individuals through access to housing, finance and facilitation of welfare benefits, tackling unemployment and developing skills, advising the voluntary and community sector and, importantly, providing community leadership and community safety (Hull, 2009). If the holistic aspects of Total Place are considered, rather than just focusing on the savings that might be made, then this approach to delivering local services is potentially a useful development for local government in guiding us out of the financial crisis.

Housing and its importance for communities in crisis

The financial crisis clearly had an impact on home owners and, indeed, on renters of private property whose landlords subsequently faced repossession. The Council for Mortgage Lenders reported in February 2010 (CML, 2010) that there had been 46,000 repossessions in 2009, and while this wasn't as high as predicted, it was an increase on the 40,000 figure in 2008 and a large increase on 2007, which saw 25,900 repossessions (Bowen, 2010). The incoming Secretary of State for Communities and Local Government, Eric Pickles, announced a review of help for homeowners as a priority for the new Conservative–Liberal Democrat government in May 2010.

Local authorities and social housing organisations are providing the lead for neighbourhoods on financial inclusion and housing debt issues. A scheme in Hull was praised by the Legal Aid Minister for having assisted 277 people in the city by providing legal advice and representation in court proceedings for repossession. In the Humber region repossessions fell by 25%, and although there was an increase in the city itself, this was 3% for the third quarter of 2009 (Ministry of Justice, 2009), which was lower than predicted. Another example is RCT Homes; the housing association launched its financial inclusion strategy, Sound as a Pound (RCT Homes, 2009), with training for over 120 staff, and raised awareness of the dangers of door-step lenders through a play for tenants and staff to watch. The East Midlands Housing Group also launched a financial inclusion strategy in 2009 to provide assistance to tenants in budgeting, keeping track of their finances, planning for their future, choosing appropriate financial products and staying informed about financial matters that would affect them – for example, energy prices. Nottingham City Homes' financial inclusion strategy also aimed to support tenants through the crisis and includes the issue of fuel poverty, which was particularly important as crude oil prices rose. Seven Locks Housing Association reported on its work with the local credit union; the Tenancy Support Officer was available to provide advice on a range of money matters to residents. Customer-profiling methods are being employed by some social housing landlords, in order to understand tenants' needs better, provide services and advice, and also to better manage rental income at a time of need for greater efficiency in public sector budgets (see further Richardson, 2010).

The social housing sector aims to house and support those in greatest need. Often this section of the community can also be the most vulnerable, with pockets of low employment and educational attainment, poor social and health outcomes and reduced overall well-being. Providers of social housing will be affected by cuts in public budgets and this will affect not just the housing outcomes of already vulnerable groups, but also health, employment and other measures of well-being, because of the inextricable links between the causes of deprivation and exclusion. There are already increased numbers of homeless people reported in London, of whom almost a quarter are migrants from new EU countries (Ramesh, 2010). Alongside this is the review of housing benefit arrangements and security of tenure for council and housing association tenants, which could ultimately result in more people losing their homes or facing uncertainty over the length of time they will have their home for. The social housing sector is facing huge changes at a time when its service users are depending on it most, and if invested in properly, it could be part of a longer-term solution:

> Just to spell this out for Mr Osborne, every penny spent on housing related support saves more than twice as much on the cost of hospitalisation, prison and other costly and complex interventions. (Duxbury, 2010, 28)

Health outcomes for vulnerable people

Although there was pre-election political consensus on the need to protect the NHS from budget cuts, some have suggested that shielding health is both unnecessary and unwarranted. Health should play a part in economic recovery and there are functions in the service that could perform more efficiently (Bowcott, 2010). The Conservative–Liberal Democrat Coalition government that came to power in May 2010 examined significant back-office savings that could be made in the health service. The International Monetary Fund (IMF) also suggested the need for a more efficient NHS, arguing that rising costs over the long term for an ageing population will exacerbate public deficits, and reiterated its view that more private provision could be part of the solution in Britain (Elliott, 2009). Following the 2009 Budget, the chief executive of the NHS suggested that it would be possible to make up to £20 billion of savings in the period to 2014. When the term 'efficiency savings' is used it is often in relation to 'back-office' systems; however, there was debate in the run-up to the 2010 election as to whether this amount of efficiency could really be found here, and there were suggestions that money would also need to be saved, for example, by the use of generic rather than branded drugs.

Appleby et al (2009) analysed a range of funding scenarios for the health service (from 'arctic' to 'tepid'; cuts in small real-rate rises) post 2011 and up to 2017. Even the most positive scenario suggested 'would just about cover increased demands for healthcare arising from population increases and changes in demographic structure' (p 25). The NHS Confederation (2009) outlined lessons to be learnt for health from previous recessions. Its report outlined 'bad ideas' from history, such as allowing waiting lists to grow, diluting quality, indiscriminate cuts, allowing pay to fall out of line with other sectors (leading to vacancies), cutting training and, finally, cutting preventive care. It also cautioned against automatically reaching for responses such as centralising support functions, mergers, demand management, price competition and staff reductions, and instead suggested a more responsive and sensitive approach 'using quality and process improvement and the adoption of innovative, evidence-based practice' (p 5).

In examining the impact of the financial crisis on health, Whyte (nd) referred to growing unemployment during the recession and cited the many impacts that unemployment has on individual health: increased mortality, cardiovascular disease, lung cancer, suicide, worse psychological health and poorer general health; as well as the impacts of unemployment on neighbourhood health and social well-being: poorer overall health, lower income, lower educational attainment, violence and a range of other socio-economic inequalities. However, in comparing the current climate with previous crises and recessions, Whyte made clear that every recession is different and that health impacts are sensitive to local issues and local responses.

Stuckler et al (2009) examined empirical data in Europe across the last three decades to look at the impact of crises on health. There were a range of findings, such as a 0.79% increase in suicides among under-65s for every 1% rise in unemployment (with a greater level of suicides at 3% unemployment increases). While the rise in suicides was significant, the researchers found that this was short term. The Young Foundation's report (2009) measured the material and psychological needs in Britain's population and found a correlation between worsening debt and mental ill-health. In one county there was debate about the impact of the recession on people in the area. The East Sussex Director of Policy and Communications' *Report to Cabinet* (East Sussex County Council, 2010b) included information from the Hastings Advice and Representation Centre that identified a 28% increase in enquiries about mental health issues, as compared to the preceding year.

Dahlgren and Whitehead's (1991) model of the impact of general socio-economic, cultural and environmental conditions is a useful reminder of the importance of wider factors for health. There are six wider health determinants in the model: agriculture and food production, education, work environment, unemployment, water and sanitation, healthcare services and housing. Wealth and social class also have an effect on health. There have been a variety of studies which have outlined the difference in life expectancy between the social groups. Pantazis and Gordon (2000) found that men in class I lived for up to 5.2 years longer than their counterparts in class V. Van Cleemput and Parry (2001) found even starker contrasts in general health and mortality rates when examining the outcomes for one particularly marginalised group – Gypsies and Travellers. It is the disparity in the impact of the financial crisis on the health of different groups that should be the focus not just of the health service, but of all services working in the areas related to the physical determinants in Dahlgren and Whitehead's model – for example employment, education and housing. So, even within the political discourse of shielding health budgets, cuts in housing and other public service areas will have an impact on the health of vulnerable individuals and neighbourhoods.

Gypsies and Travellers: the impact of the crisis on an already marginalised group

Estimates of the numbers of Gypsies and Travellers in Britain vary, but it is thought that there may be in excess of 300,000, with approximately one-third living in caravan accommodation. However, government figures from bi-annual caravan counts show that a little over 25% of the caravan-dwelling Gypsies and Travellers are on unauthorised sites, effectively homeless and often subject to move-on and eviction, with reduced access to healthcare and education. Certainly, Gypsies and Travellers demonstrate many characteristics associated with marginalised and vulnerable people, and there should be a focus on protecting this community from the multiple and compound effects of the financial crisis. Hills et al (2010), in their report for the National Equality Panel, referred to inequalities for Gypsies and Travellers in education, health and employment issues.

Gypsies and Travellers are already a vulnerable group in relation to health, literacy and other education issues. Distinguishable by their 'otherness' (see further Richardson, 2006, 2007) they are marginalised and discriminated against in discourse which can lead to conflict. In looking at scarce resources such as land for accommodation, the lower density of Gypsy sites, as compared with high-rise blocks, can cause a debate on the 'costliness' of their life-style, which can further delay progress on new site provision, which leads to worse health and education outcomes if accommodation cannot be accessed.

The disparity in a number of socio-economic and health outcomes for Roma, Gypsies and Travellers is not limited to Britain, but occurs across Europe and around the globe. There are proportionally high numbers of Roma living in the least well-off regions in Europe, for example in Romania, and also in regions in Slovakia (Fesus, 2009). There are funding mechanisms to improve such regions in Europe, and in Britain there has been a specific programme of capital grant funding for the development of new sites to meet the shortfall in site accommodation, although this was one of the first grants to be cut by the Coalition Government in the summer of 2010. Funding programmes designed to allow better equality of access to accommodation and other service provision should not be forgotten. The government cuts in site funding will see already disadvantaged communities fall further behind in quality-of-life outcomes.

Government could put pressure on local authorities to deliver sites through the withholding of affordable delivery housing grant until applications for sites grant have been received, in order to provide a balance of affordable housing for both the settled community and the travelling communities. Other solutions might lay in a legal route, through much more efficient use of Section 106 planning gain agreements, or through alternative methods such as co-production and ownership of sites through community land trust and community asset trust initiatives. However, it is becoming increasingly clear that capital funding is no longer available and that planning guidance (Circular 01/06) will be replaced by 'light touch' guidance (CLG, 2010). In the absence of either money or regulation, the government is pinning its hopes on 'incentives' and 'innovation' to deliver much-needed sites. We shall see.

There are already practical innovative solutions to protect Gypsy and Traveller communities from the impact of the financial crisis through voluntary and charitable organisations. In Somerset a charity called the Robert Barton Trust (RBT) offered support and advice to New Travellers in the area for some time. The organisation employed a small number of project workers, one of whom was funded by Somerset Primary Care Trust. RBT was able to supply Travellers with a 'care of' address, which enabled those with no address of their own to access healthcare services. Social networks and skills were enhanced through a knitting group and other support networks; there were also washing facilities, computer and internet access and refreshments available at certain times each week. In addition to this, arrangements were made to secure the free services of a dentist to treat Travellers who otherwise find it impossible to get dentistry services. Additionally, a veterinary surgeon would be available to provide a free service to maintain the basic health of animals. These services are vital to a group that is already on the very margins of society. However, the Robert Barton Trust itself has lost its fight for survival as the agencies on which it depends for pockets of funding are themselves struggling with big budget cuts. Without the work of the Robert Barton Trust, there will undoubtedly be increased pressure on local authority services and budgets to support the Travellers in the area in a time of dwindling resources and capacity.

Older people

The impacts of the financial crisis on older people are varied. For those in their own homes, a combination of the house-price bubble bursting and the reduction in pension values as a result of a period of poor stock market performance, in addition to the rising cost of utilities bills such as for gas and electricity, means that many elderly people have reduced household budgets. Proposals by the previous Labour government for a national care service for the elderly in their own homes met with questions about how such provision could be paid for by the public purse. For the elderly in residential homes, questions have been raised about private care providers, the largest of which in the UK has a 10% market share. With a big recent growth in the elderly care sector, large providers have based their business models on using loans to acquire more market share based on the value of their assets – their homes. This model was undermined by the fall in property values at the outset of the financial crisis, and there were suggestions that these highly leveraged business models affected the ability to update residential homes and to provide the level of care necessary for their elderly residents (Mathiason, 2009).

Responses have varied across different areas, with some concentrating on generic services, rather than on specific needs. In other areas though, the emphasis has been on increasing the understanding of elderly residents and other vulnerable groups of their rights to benefits. A report on the local responses in the North West reported that Lancashire County Council had increased benefit take-up, including Pension Credit and Income Support, by £800,000 over 2008 figures (North West Improvement and Efficiency Partnership, 2009). This response to the needs of vulnerable groups is a better long-term solution than attempting to cut or maintain levels of financial support in a bid to make short-term savings, at the expense of the longer-term sustainability of vulnerable communities. In some areas there is even increased expenditure on care for the elderly, such as through re-ablement services, which include an intensive 6-week period of support to help people learn how to look after themselves in their own homes. Recipients of such services have been positive about the results of re-ablement and councils are able to show that although costs go up in the short term, there are longer-term savings.

The debate surrounding the Labour government's consultation on the National Care Service Green Paper (HM Government, 2009a) demonstrated the underlying arguments on the 'right' to care in old age and the 'right' to pass on saved wealth, often in the form of housing assets, to children. Commentators highlighted the schism in this debate on private wealth and public health: the model of 'big government' in the provision of support and 'small government' in the affairs of taxation or insurance models to pay for the rapidly growing costs of caring for an ageing population is unsustainable, and particularly so during times of large public debt. Increasing discontent between groups fighting for scarce resources became more apparent during the recession – and not just along cultural and racial divisions, as discussed later in this chapter, but also between 'young' and 'old', where the young unemployed were seen to bear the brunt of the luck of the 'baby boomers'; the novelist Martin Amis wrote a contentious article for the *Sunday Times* magazine, suggesting that older people should be able to access 'euthanasia booths', where they would be given a 'martini and a medal' (Chittenden, 2010), which further polarised the debate. In a flip side of this media argument pitting young and old against each other, the *Daily Mail* referred to the phenomenon of 'ageing parents' having to bail out their unemployed children, whom they unhelpfully labelled 'Yuckies' (Young Unwitting Costly Kids) (*Daily Mail*, 2010).

Children and young people

Young people seem to be particularly hard hit by growing unemployment. Vaitilingham (2009) reports the increase in unemployment among 18- to 24-year-olds from 11.9% in July 2008 to 17.3% in July 2009, and refers to the longer-term 'scarring' that can occur for these young people as a result of such a bad experience so early in their interaction with the labour market. Young people across Europe were shown to be badly affected by unemployment following the global financial crisis. There were comparable figures for under-25s' unemployment in Portugal, rates of around 25% in Greece and Italy, and rising sharply to 44% for under 25s in Spain (Smith et al, 2010). News interviews with young people in Greece in February 2010 reflected growing anger among young people at the austerity packages proposed by their government to keep Germany and other eurozone members, as well as international ratings agencies and the IMF, content. The needs of these young people who are not in employment, education or training (NEETs) were examined in a policy briefing by Youth Access (2009). With stark warnings, such as of parasuicidal episodes being 25 times more likely among unemployed young men than those in work, the briefing called for government intervention not just on employment policies, but on services that could help young people to cope with the wider effects of the financial crisis. It was suggested that young people were the hardest-hit group and that this could manifest not just in economic issues, but also on their mental health, well-being and social welfare.

Youth unemployment has risen from 2007, with a disproportionate impact on young people compared with the rest of the population. Shaheen (2009) reports this starkly: one in five people in the population are young, but they represent two in five of the total unemployment figures. The effect and indeed 'scarring' of youth unemployment can be severe and needs separate initiatives to deal with its social and health consequences. There has already been a government response to try to stimulate more jobs or training for young people, and to encourage apprenticeship schemes. £1.2 billion was announced in the 2009 Budget for the Future Jobs Fund for 2009–11. However, this fund was another victim of the Coalition government's early spending cuts. National Indicator 117, which measures 16- to18-year-olds not in employment, education or training, was also prioritised by most local strategic partnerships across the country, demonstrating the importance of this increasingly challenging area. The Public Service Agreement Target from the 2004 spending review was to reduce the percentage of NEETs by 2%, down to 8% by 2010. However, data from the Department for Children, Schools and Families (DCSF, 2009) showed that at the end of 2008 the proportion of NEET 18-year-olds had risen by 2.4% to 16.6%, pushing the overall NEET statistic up by 0.7% to 10.3%.

A £915 million cut in funding announced by the Higher Education Funding Council in early 2010 led to some universities suggesting cuts in teaching staff and, ultimately, cuts in places for students. Applicants in 2009 who were unsuccessful in gaining a place also joined the growing list of applicants in 2010; in addition, young people faced with the rises in unemployment impacting particularly on their age group may have considered higher education when they would not have otherwise done so, leading to a juxtaposition in the number of students applying and places available that was at odds with the political discourse of opening up education and meeting aspiration. Not only does this impact on the current generation's ability to access higher education, which has implications for social and cultural well-being, but there are also longer-term threats to the ability of Britain to compete in the global market if investment in skills and higher education is cut in the short term.

Government ministers suggested that 'efficiency savings' of £1 billion should be possible in schools without affecting front-line staff; however, head teachers responded to this suggestion with concern that the roles of teaching assistants would be affected (Asthana and Syal, 2010). In the short-to-medium term this could have an impact on classroom behaviour and exam results. With universities cutting places, and the remaining places requiring higher exams grades for entrance, there will be a disproportionate effect on the ability of young people who come from already deprived backgrounds to access higher education.

In looking at the impact of public sector cuts on young people, cuts in jobs across local authorities, as on the scale outlined at Birmingham City Council in the first part of 2010, will have an impact on a range of services such as housing and social care. Controversy with public sector unions was initiated by announcements that across the authority there would be 2,000 job cuts and attempts to cut £69 million from the city's budget. Unions reported that children's services would be hardest hit (BBC, 2010) and representatives of the childcare sector reported that £1.45 million would be cut from the city's Early Years budget from April 2010, and a further £2.5 million from April 2011. It was suggested that this would result in all 23 of the city's day nurseries being at risk of closure, with more than 200 staff facing redundancy (Gaunt, 2010).

For some children, there are further disadvantages in the aftermath of the financial crisis. In Iceland, public health experts have suggested that there is evidence of more family breakdown following the recession, with higher incidences of mental health cases and maltreatment of children (Quinn, 2010). Some London boroughs are also reporting higher incidences of family breakdown. In the wake of the Baby Peter case in 2009, more children are being taken into care, but there are also fewer voluntary foster carers to look after these children. The Baby Peter case in London highlighted the already stretched resources in children's services departments, along with poor collaborative arrangements for reporting between agencies; further cuts could mean more failures in social services, unless collaborative models of working improve.

Community cohesion: increased conflict in times of scarcity

Despite government reports that community spirit and civic health are strong (DCLG, 2010), community cohesion is tested in times of scarcity. There are various assumptions about social behaviour in times of economic crisis. Some suggest that there could be violence on the streets, rioting and increased crime. However, Home Office figures for the third quarter of 2009 showed a drop in reported crime as compared to the same quarter of 2008. Police responded to the announcement by referring to better prevention and targeted programmes for reducing crime. Other commentators suggested that a rise in crime may yet come, and they suggested a lagged time effect, following years of families living on little or no earnings (Travis, 2010). There were also fears around revolt among the public against bankers and government institutions. While there were some public demonstrations during the London G20 talks in April 2009, there was not a subsequent long period of social unrest on the streets. Nevertheless, Hutton (2010) warned on the lack of reform to the banking system in 2009 and early 2010:

> But if the elite is allowed to go free while the rest of society suffers, there will be revolt from below. Offend norms of fairness and societies risk disintegration and violence – something British politicians might ponder as they compete with visions of public sector wage freezes while allowing private sector salaries at the top to grow explosively.

There were warnings of unrest from the Metropolitan Police and Scotland Yard in relation to far-right extremist violence and terror attacks; namely, that the recession would increase the possibility of violence (Dodd, 2009). A resurgence of anti-immigration rhetoric and political parties raising tensions while increasing their own political profile on an anti-ethnic-minorities policy platform was part of this concern. An Economist Intelligence Unit (2009) report probed the issue of social unrest a little further and developed a political instability index which showed the areas around the globe that were most at risk of unrest following the global financial crisis. Zimbabwe was seen to be most at risk, the UK being much further down the index with a low-to-moderate risk – further down the risk index than the

US and France, but some way above countries like Germany, Sweden and Denmark, with Norway scoring the lowest potential for social unrest. However, the 'austerity measures' that needed to be taken across Europe have resulted in outbreaks of civil unrest, for example the May riots in Greece by those who thought that public sector workers were being punished by the austerity measures forced upon the government by ratings agencies and eurozone governments, while the bankers, perceived to be the cause of the crisis, walked free.

Conflict in times of scarcity of resources is an issue which government and local community organisations must prepare for. Leadership is needed in areas suffering from poverty, low educational attainment, increasing unemployment and social marginalisation. Fenton et al (2010) examined the impact of the recession on poor communities in Birmingham. In the majority of the press reports following this, the focus was on the impact on white working-class communities; however, the original report discussed four areas – two where the majority of the population was from ethnic minority communities and two suburban areas, predominantly White British. The 'victimhood' of poor White British seems to have key news value in the media and was the focus of discussion. However, in announcing the publication of the report, the Barrow Cadbury Trust strongly cautioned against its findings being used to set different communities in conflict with one another (Stevens, 2010).

The notion of 'poor White working class' is also commented on in the 2009 report of the European Network Against Racism:

> The worsening of the economy and the decline of the political left in part contextualises the subsequent discourse on maximising the economic benefits of migration, controlling borders, and recognising the 'white working class' as the most disadvantaged in society. (Mai Sims and Vanderaa, 2009, 3)

Historically, far right political parties have used this debate to disastrous ends, and similar rhetoric is heard today from groups such as the British National Party (BNP). Unfortunate echoes in mainstream political discourse (Gordon Brown's 'British jobs for British workers') acquiesced to this divisive view of society. This discourse is seen in relation not just to new ethnic minority groups immigrating to Britain, but also to others such as Gypsies and Travellers, who have been resident for centuries but who are often 'othered' in debate, particularly when examining the cost of different life-styles in a time of restricted public spending (Richardson, 2006). Although the BNP had a disastrous election in 2010 in terms of seats in parliament, there was an increase in its overall share of the vote, which perhaps reflects the growing underlying community tensions in times of financial crisis.

This issue of 'fairness' in the allocation of resources was already under debate in the report of the Commission on Integration and Cohesion (2007): 'A new issue that we need to address is that settled communities are worried about the fair allocation of public services – with some thinking immigrants and minorities are getting special treatment' (p 9).

The Local Government Association (LGA, 2010b) asked the House of Lords Economic Affairs Select Committee to look urgently at the collection of data in population movements as the official statistics were 'inadequate nationally and locally', and stated that there was evidence that migration did place demands on local public services which were not reflected in current formulae for funding arrangements. The long-term effects of the financial crisis on community cohesion and on particular ethnic minority groups will not be known for some time, and although the Equalities and Human Rights Commission published a brief report with the Department for Work and Pensions (2009) on the unemployment effects in different sections of the community, there has not been a similar level of introspection by the Commission or others on the deeper-rooted aspects of the crisis for a range of ethnic minority groups and wider societal cohesion.

This discourse of fear and 'unfairness' comes at a time when councils are looking for cuts in public spending. With a need to focus on core services, it is the equalities and support functions that are perhaps most at risk. For example, in the summer of 2009 Nottingham City Council announced significant job cuts; the Gypsy, Roma and Traveller support team and the Black and Minority Ethnic support teams were particularly at risk (*Local Government Chronicle*, 2009). There is also an issue of fairness in areas where local authorities are running a 'You Choose' consultation with local people on which services should be prioritised. There is a danger that extended prejudices could manifest in local decisions on who is most 'deserving' of public services. Cutbacks in services to marginalised communities not only impact on those communities, but also send out a wider message to society that support to vulnerable people, and particularly to ethnic minorities, is expendable in times of financial crisis. This may result in longer-term manifestations of lack of community cohesion and disproportionate hardship for particular ethnic groups. This competition for resources, both in the market-place, and also now for public resources and services, is part of a wider social breakdown. Lawson (2008), in the Joseph Rowntree Foundation's 'social evils' debate, referred to a 'social recession' resulting from global market competition. This social recession may impact doubly on certain vulnerable groups – first, through the impact of the recession and wider global financial crisis on the ability to access homes and jobs in the market, and second, through the withdrawal or reduction of public sector services targeted at specific ethnic groups, in a bid to cut local public sector debt.

Conclusion

The impacts of the financial crisis are many and varied. However, there does appear to be a disproportionate effect on specific vulnerable groups for whom the effects of the crisis are compounded. For example, young people become 'scarred' by long-term unemployment, children may be more at risk in some areas through the cutting of budgets and potential closing of services, and older people may find it harder to access social and health care. Community cohesion is also under threat, with different groups fighting for access to scarcer resources, and with the ascendency of far right political groups who are quick to blame immigrants for the 'victimhood' of White British.

Vale et al (2009) suggest a needs-gap analysis approach to viewing the challenges along the lines of different needs (for example, survival, care, agency and psychological needs) and different need domains (for example, state, market, civil society and individuals) in order to identify the important areas of unmet need. Taking this type of analysis further, it may be possible to see where different needs might be met in different domains where existing mechanisms are failing (market) or facing cuts (state). This issue is discussed a little further in the concluding chapter of this book, in looking for next steps to alleviate the impact of the financial crisis on public services and local government, with a particular eye to protecting the more vulnerable members of society. A range of models – not just state or market – is possible, ranging from cooperative and co-production frameworks to a heightened role for the charitable sector and for 'big society'. However, the importance of government's role in looking after the more vulnerable in society should not be underestimated, or negated by new suggested modes of delivery through community groups and private and charitable sector organisations. There are many and varied groups and areas that are especially vulnerable to the effects of the financial crisis; it is not a marginal issue – a large number of individuals need protection from the effects of the crisis and this is not a time for government to sidestep the responsibility.

Note

[1] Total Place was introduced in the 2009 Budget in an attempt to avoid duplication and waste. Local authorities and agencies worked together to provide more efficient and better services.

References

Appleby, J., Crawford, R. and Emmerson, C. (2009) *How Cold will it Be? Prospects for NHS Funding 2011–2017*, London: The Kings Fund.

Asthana, A. and Syal, R. (2010) 'Headteachers say Labour's £1bn cuts will "decapitate" schools', *Observer*, 7 February, pp 1 and 4.

BBC (2010) 'Unions demand talks over Birmingham Council job cuts', 11 February, http://news.bbc.co.uk.

Be Birmingham (2009) *Public Expenditure and Investment Study, Stage 1 Mapping Report*, Birmingham: Be Birmingham Local Strategic Partnership.

Better Banking Campaign (2010) 'Launch of Better Banking Campaign', 17 February, http://test.acevo.org.uk.

Bowcott, O. (2010) 'Cold Wind of Change', Interview with Sir Robert Naylor, *Society Guardian*, 10 February, p 5.

Bowen, C. (2010) *Repossession Update*, York: Housing Quality Network, www.hqnetwork.co.uk.

Carter, H. (2010) 'Seeing off the predators', *Society Guardian*, 10 February, p 3.

Centre for Cities (2010) *Cities Outlook 2010*, www.centreforcities.org.

Chittenden, M. (2010) 'Martin Amis calls for euthanasia booths on street corners', *Sunday Times*, 24 January, www.timesonline.co.uk.

CML (Council of Mortgage Lenders) (2010) 'Mortgage arrears and possessions declined in fourth quarter of 2009', 11 February, www.cml.org.uk.

Commission on Integration and Cohesion (2007) *Our Shared Future*, www.integrationandcohesion.org.uk.

Commission for Rural Communities (2009) *Rural Economies Recession Intelligence*, www.ruralcommunities.gov.uk.

Communities and Local Government (2010) *Planning, Building and the Environment – Travellers*, www.communities.gov.uk.

Dahlgren, G. and Whitehead, M. (1991) *Policies and Strategies to Promote Equity in Health*, Stockholm: Institute for Futures Studies.

Daily Mail (2010) '£30,000 bill for "Yuckie" generation who can't afford to become independent', 17 February, www.dailymail.co.uk.

Day, K. (2009) *Communities in Recession: The Reality in Four Neighbourhoods*, York: Joseph Rowntree Foundation.

DCLG (Department for Communities and Local Government) (2010) *Our Nation's Civic Health*, London: CLG.

DCSF (Department for Children, Schools and Families) (2009) '16–18 year olds NEET', 15 December, www.dcsf.gov.uk.

Dodd, V. (2009) 'Police fear far-right terror attack', *Guardian*, 6 July, www.guardian.co.uk.

Dorling, D. (2010) *Injustice: Why Social Inequality Persists*, Bristol: Policy Press.

Duxbury, N. (2010) 'Coming in to land', *Inside Housing*, 16 July, pp 28-32.

East Sussex County Council (2010a) *Report to Cabinet, Reconciling Policy and Resources – In-Year Grant Reduction*, 5 July, www.eastsussex.gov.uk.

East Sussex County Council (2010b) *Report to Cabinet, Recession: Update on Impacts and Action*, East Sussex Council website, www.eastsussex.gov.uk/yourcouncil/about/committees/meetingpapers/cabinet/2010/26january.htm.

Economist Intelligence Unit (2009) *Manning the Barricades: Who's at Risk as Deepening Economic Distress Foments Social Unrest*, London: Economist Intelligence Unit.

Elliott, L. (2009) 'Cut NHS costs to pay off debt, IMF warns Britain', *Guardian*, 2 October 2009, p 1.

Equality and Human Rights Commission and Department for Work and Pensions (2009) *Monitoring the Impact of the Recession on Various Demographic Groups*, London: Government Equalities Office.

Fenton, A., Tyler, P., Markkanen, S., Clarke, A. and Whitehead, C. (2010) *Why do Neighbourhoods stay Poor? Deprivation, Place and People in Birmingham*, Barrow: Cadbury Trust.

Fesus, G. (2009) 'The Effectiveness of Health Policies and Programmes in Support of Roma Communities: Does location matter?', Conference paper, Regional Studies Association Winter conference, December.

Gaunt, C. (2010) 'Cuts threaten all Birmingham council's nurseries', *Nursery World*, 27 January, www.nurseryworld.co.uk.

Hills, J., Brewer, M., Jenkins, S., Lister, R., Lupton, R., Machin, S., Mills, C., Modood, T., Rees, T. and Riddell, S. (2010) *An Anatomy of Economic Inequality in the UK: Report of the National Equality Panel*, London: Government Equalities Office.

HM Government (2009) *Putting the Frontline First: Smarter Government*, London: The Stationery Office.

Horton, T. and Reed, H. (2010) 'Don't forget the spending cuts! The real impact of Budget 2010', www.unison.org.

Hull City Council (2009) *Place Shielding Action Plan*, Hull: Hull City Council.

Hutton, W. (2010) 'Don't laugh at Europe's woes. The travails facing Greece are also ours', *The Observer*, 14 February, p 38.

Hutton, W. and Jones, A. (2010) *Driving Economic Recovery: Core Cities – a New Partnership with Government*, Manchester: Core Cities/Tenant Services Authority.

Illman, J. (2010) 'Pilot in pioneering £2bn schools bid', *Local Government Chronicle*, 4 February, www.lgcplus.com.

Lawson, N. (2008) *A Wrong Turn in the Search for Freedom?*, York: Joseph Rowntree Foundation, www.jrf.org.uk.

Leslie, C. and Hood, A. (2009) *Circling the Loan Sharks,: Predatory Lending in the Recession and the Emerging Role for Local Government*, London: New Local Government Network.

LGA (Local Government Association) (2010a) *Place-based Budgets: The Future Governance of Local Public Services*, London; LGA.

LGA (2010b) Local Government Association submission to the House of Lords Economic Affairs Select Committee Inquiry on the Economic Impact of Immigration, www.parliament.uk/documents.

Local Government Chronicle (2009) 'Nottingham job loss details emerge', 12 June, www.lgc.org.uk.

Mai Sims, J. and Vanderaa, K. (2009) *European Network Against Racism Shadow Report 2008: Racism in the United Kingdom*, www.enar-eu.org.

Marmot, M. (2010) *Fair Society, Healthy Lives* (the Marmot Review), London: LSE.

Mathiason, N. (2009) 'Debts that threaten the elderly and vulnerable', *The Observer*, 17 May, www.guardian.co.uk/business.

Ministry of Justice (2009) 'People at risk of home repossession and eviction in Hull offered a lifeline', 16 November, www.justice.gov.uk.

NHS Confederation (2009) 'Commissioning in a cold climate', www.nhsconfed.org/leadership.

NLGN (New Local Government Network) (2010) *Scanning Financial Horizons: Modelling the Local Consequences of Fiscal Consolidation*, www.nlgn.org.uk.

Northwest Improvement and Efficiency Partnership (2009) 'Local responses to the economic downturn in the NW', Northwest Improvement and Efficiency Partnership.

Pantazis, C. and Gordon, D. (eds) (2000) *Tackling Inequalities: Where are we now and What can be Done?* Bristol: The Policy Press.

Parkinson, M., Evans, R., Jones, G., Karecha, J. and Meegan, R. (2010) 'The Credit Crunch, Recession and Regeneration in the North: What's happening, what's working, what's next?', *The Northern Way*, www.thenorthernway.co.uk.

Quinn, B. (2010) 'Iceland's children paying for slump', *Observer*, 24 January, p 44.

Quirk, B. (2008) 'Barry Quirk, Analysis', *Local Government Chronicle*, 21 October, www.lgcplus.com.

Ramesh, R. (2010) 'Migrants from new EU states increase London homeless tally', *Guardian*, 5 July, www.guardian.co.uk.

RCT Homes (2009) Financial Inclusion Strategy, www.rcthomes.co.uk.

Richardson, J. (2007) *Contentious Spaces: The Gypsy/Traveller Site Issue*, Coventry: CIH/JRF.

Richardson, J. (2006) *The Gypsy Debate,: Can Discourse Control?*, Exeter: Imprint Academic.

Richardson, J. (ed) (2010) *Housing and the Customer: Understanding Needs and Delivering Services*, Coventry: Chartered Institute of Housing.

Shaheen, F. (2009) *Sticking Plaster or Stepping Stone? Tackling Urban Youth Unemployment*, London: Centre for Cities.

Smith, H., Tremlett, G., Kington, T. and Coman, J. (2010) 'Europe's south refuses to downsize without a fight', *The Observer*, 14 February, pp 42–3.

Stevens, J. (2010) 'Recession creating "sense of victimhood" among white working class', *Guardian*, 22 January, www.guardian.co.uk/society.

Stuckler, D., Basu, S., Suhrcke, M., Coutts, A. and McKee, M. (2009) 'The public health effect of economic crises and alternative policy responses in Europe: an empirical analysis', *The Lancet*, vol 374, no 9686, pp 315–23.

Travis, A. (2010) 'Murder, burglary, robbery and car thefts fall as crime figures defy financial crisis', *Guardian*, 22 January, p 11.

Tunstall, R. and Fenton, A. (2009) *Communities in Recession: The Impact on Deprived Neighbourhoods*, York: Joseph Rowntree Foundation.

Vaitilingham, R. (2009) *Recession Britain*, www.esrc.ac.uk.

Vale, D., Watts, B. and Franklin, J. (2009) *The Receding Tide: Understanding Unmet Needs in a Harsher Economic Climate*, London: The Young Foundation.

Van Cleemput, P. and Parry, G. (2001) 'Health status of Gypsy Travellers', *Journal of Public Health Medicine*, vol 23, no 2, pp 129–34.

Whyte, B. (nd) 'The potential health and social impact of the financial crisis ("credit crunch") in the West of Scotland', Presentation: Glasgow Centre for Population Health.

Wilkinson, R. and Pickett, K. (2009) *The Spirit Level: Why More Equal Societies almost always do Better,* London: Allen Lane.

Young Foundation (2009) *Sinking and Swimming, Understanding Britain's Unmet Needs*, London: The Young Foundation www.youngfoundation.org.

Youth Access (2009) 'The impact of the recession on young people and on their needs for advice and counselling services', Youth Access, www.youthaccess.org.uk.

SIX

Exploring the local political context of the recession

Steve Leach and Mark Roberts

Introduction

Local authorities across the country have been dealing with the first budget process in which the impact of the recession has played a major influence. Not that previous years have been easy; there has since 2004 been an expectation, following Sir Peter Gershon's report, that authorities would be able to identify considerable economies on a year-by-year basis, primarily through increasing use of IT, especially in back-office functions. For the past few years, grant settlements have built in this expectation and, given the problems of raising additional revenue from council tax (a 1% increase in revenue expenditure typically requires a 4% increase in council tax), it is not surprising that authorities have had to focus on identifying savings rather than funding new initiatives. However, the challenges facing them in setting budgets for 2010–11 have been on a different scale. Furthermore, whereas in the past council actors have been able to use their room for manoeuvre in the local context to protect at least one of the holy trinity of staffing, services and council tax, many now are already bringing forward proposals for a 'triple whammy'.

It is clear that the situation is going to get much worse before it gets better. Even if Britain avoids a 'double-dip' recession following cuts in 2010, a prospect which seems at best uncertain, it is hard to see a plausible scenario in which public expenditure, including that of local authorities, is not cut every year, primarily to respond to the costs incurred by the government in bailing out the banks in 2009. Four or five increasingly lean years, probably up to 2014–15, is a widespread expectation.

How will local councils respond to this gloomy prospect? In the national media and the political discourse of Westminster the focus is on cuts to public services, with a widespread assumption that local authorities will follow central government's lead in terms of protecting 'front-line' services and wielding the axe to every other department and function. This in turn would imply that the resources previously committed to so-called 'soft' initiatives such as community leadership will be one of the first targets for local councillors and, as a result, may all but disappear.

In this chapter we bring together our understanding of how the local government and local governance agendas have developed with a conceptual framework based on institutional theory. From this locus we show how the patterns of response by councils to critical financial pressures are likely to show a great deal more variation than this basic slash-and-burn scenario suggests. In particular we seek to illustrate how many local authorities might employ the potentials embedded in their governance role to mitigate some of the worst impacts of the recession. Since the conceptual scope of community leadership and local governance is extensive, we focus our analysis through the lens of one particular aspect of this agenda, neighbourhood working, which has been developed in the vast majority of local authorities in the UK and, as such, represents the most widespread manifestation of these ideas in council activity.

The chapter is structured as follows. Firstly, we show how local government and local governance, two analytically separate concepts used to define the functions of local authorities, have emerged over time and how in practice they are intertwined. We go on to show how the concept of community leadership has been developed from an increasing emphasis on governance and how this trend has, in turn, encouraged a focus on the concept of neighbourhood. Following on from this, we use our knowledge of the course of events in previous recessions to briefly set out some of the likely consequences of the current recession for local government. We then outline an institutional perspective on change and stability as a conceptual framework which facilitates our understanding of how local councils might respond to the challenges of recession. In the final section of the chapter we bring together our analysis with our institutional perspective on stability and change to show how the existing ways of neighbourhood working might be used by council actors to mitigate some of the worst impacts of the recession.

Combining government and governance in service provision and community leadership

In this section we briefly outline how two analytically separate concepts used to define the functions of local authorities – local government on the one hand, and local governance on the other – have emerged over time and how, in practice, they are intertwined.

The familiar, traditional and most publicly recognisable role of local government is that of providing a range of services, which it is either required or permitted to do by law, and which cannot be provided by the private sector. The services that fall into this category have varied over time, depending upon the ideology of the government in power, but have typically included education, child protection, adult social care, public housing, leisure and recreation facilities, highways and transportation, and regulatory services such as planning control and licensing. Since the mid-1980s the term 'provider' has become reinterpreted by successive governments to encompass the technologies of commissioning as well as direct provision. By this account, when in 'steering' rather than 'rowing' mode, local authorities do not necessarily have to provide directly a service for which they have responsibility; they can commission another agency to provide the service on terms specified by the local authority. Nevertheless, many key services are still provided by councils, and the 'control freakery' (Stoker, 2002) of central government, on the one hand, and the institutionalised perceptions of service users, on the other, continue from above and below to hold local *government* responsible for the quantity and quality of services in their area, whether these are provided directly or by an external contractor.

However, alongside service provision, local councils have a long history of playing the more broadly based civic role which has recently been 'remembered' as local *governance* (John, 1998; Lowndes, 2005). For example, in the late 19th century, councils such as Birmingham developed a role of civic entrepreneurship, providing gas, electricity and water facilities for residents at a time when they were not legally required to do so. Although this role was never wholly lost, it fell into abeyance after the Second World War, but was revived by Labour authorities in the 1980s, who sought to revive their local economies during a period of recession, and then by the 1997 Labour government, which coined the term 'community leadership' for this type of activity. Basically, the idea of community leadership embraces a *governance* role which goes well beyond the provision of statutory services, to encompass a responsibility for facilitating a response to social, economic and environmental problems in an area, even where the local authority does not possess exclusive (or in some cases any) powers to deal with them. Examples of such issues have included economic regeneration, environmental sustainability, anti-social behaviour and community health.

Although the capacity to respond to these issues has been hampered by resource constraints, in terms both of government grant and the problems since 1990 of raising extra finance through the council tax, many authorities have taken this community leadership role seriously, recognising a responsibility to respond to local problems even where statutory powers are limited. Furthermore, although analytically separate, in terms of government as service provision and governance as community leadership, we can see from a historical perspective how, in practice, the two functions have been intertwined. Hence local governance is characterised by council actors reaching out to potential partners within that political space to tackle 'wicked issues' cooperatively. However, the product of partnership working has often been intended to enhance the scope of services available to the local population (for example, anti-social behaviour teams of youth workers, housing providers and police officers). Similarly, while government has traditionally been about delivering services from discrete departments from the top down, the networking of council actors across the local business and community sectors has operated beneath the surface of local government long before the ubiquitous partnership sought to codify cooperation (Friend et al, 1974; Thompson et al, 1991; Sullivan and Skelcher, 2002).

Community leadership and the neighbourhood

We will now show how the concept of community leadership has been developed at local and sub-local levels and how this trend has in turn coincided with a reactivation of the concept of neighbourhood. Having established earlier that the concepts of governance and community leadership go back at least as far as Chamberlain's Birmingham, we now focus in on developments since 1997 and the advent of New Labour. True to our line of argument in the previous section, as we review our experience of these developments, we detect aspects of service delivery, and hence government, mixed in with the emergence of neighbourhood working as a template for most local authorities in the UK.

Under New Labour a focus on community empowerment and co-production of services has been developed by local authorities since the early 2000s. Put at its simplest, the central idea is that local communities should be given more say in the future of their areas (participation) and more scope to play a part in the way services are provided and problems dealt with (empowerment). As more local residents are drawn into structures developed to enhance participation and empowerment, so the representatives of the public, private and third sector organisations in the area are pulled into co-production mode. In this respect, therefore, the horizontal pattern of local governance is clear for all to see, coexisting with the vertical, largely top-down channels of local government. In formal legislative terms the 2000 Local Government Act placed considerable emphasis on the importance of public participation, but also little in the way of legal requirements on local authorities to pursue this agenda. Equally the 2007 Local Government Act contains a host of 'good ideas' such as asset management, local budgeting and an enhanced role for local petitions, but again there is little in the way of binding legal provisions.

Actors at local authority level have a long track record of responding selectively to central government initiatives, whether these be 'fully funded' and set down as requirements in legislation, or arrive as guidance without any substantial resources for implementation (Cochrane, 1993; Lowndes, 2004). So with the aspects of community leadership which focus on empowerment and participation, a systematic review of the evidence, commissioned by the Department for Communities and Local Government from De Montfort University and the University of Southampton (DCLG, 2008), shows that while some authorities have failed to respond to the agenda, a significant number of councils have specialised in one or more aspects of the six key mechanisms for empowerment – asset transfer, citizen governance, electronic participation, participatory budgeting, petitions, redress – and in many of these cases have developed their chosen specialisms some way beyond the initial expectations of central government.

The emergence of neighbourhood working in local authorities as one aspect of the community leadership agenda follows this pattern of local discretion and specialisation. And so the majority of councils are now engaged in some variation of neighbourhood working (APSE, 2009) and this trend confirms the tendency observed above of local actors to selectively create a momentum behind some ideas from government, which eventually escapes the centre's control.

Indeed, Leach (2004, 80) suggests that the 'values of localism' have been employed by all three major parties in British politics over the last 30 years to enable them to innovate in policy terms and 'try things out at the local level', but many of the policies which appear to have been initiated at central government level have drawn on initiatives and practices first developed in local government. In this way both central and local government can be said to be rediscovering an appetite for neighbourhood working, rather than inventing a new dish.

When New Labour came to power in 1997 it became clear that its policy makers had 'remembered and borrowed' (Lowndes, 2005) the concept of neighbourhood as a site for an initial assault on inequality and social exclusion. In the course of the administration this focus on the regeneration of the most deprived urban areas became somewhat blurred as the concept was redeployed in an effort to stimulate a more participative, decentralised form of local governance in a much wider range of neighbourhood types (Durose et al, 2009). As a policy initiative, therefore, neighbourhood governance has emerged alongside, but may be usefully distinguished from, local government's efforts at regeneration per se.

And so bringing together our analysis so far in this chapter, we conclude that expectations of both government and governance from local councils have been around for a long time and the service delivery and community leadership functions of these two concepts have become intertwined in practice. This inherent 'messiness' has been compounded in the last 10 years as New Labour rediscovered the concept of neighbourhood, and actors have produced their own specific mixes of government and governance, service delivery and community leadership at the local level. At one end of the spectrum, a few local authorities have moved rapidly to place neighbourhood working at the centre of their interlaced service delivery and community leadership agendas. At the other end, a small number have paid lip service to the community leadership role post 2000 and, if they have embraced neighbourhood working at all, have done so simply to communicate service delivery developments from the top down. Most councils lie between these two extremes. Each has produced its own distinctive mix, with some attempting ambitiously to bridge across all four Lowndes and Sullivan (2008) rationales, while others have consciously specialised in a particular technique for engaging citizens and partners in government and governance.

In the next two sections we set out the rather bleak context in which councils will take forward their individual government–governance mixes in the wake of the 2010 general election, and we deploy theoretical concepts from institutionalism to explain what this might mean for the development of neighbourhood working in particular.

The local–central relationship and the recession

In this section we use our knowledge of the course of events in previous recessions to briefly set out some of the likely consequences of the current recession for local government. First we outline the impacts on local politics of spending cuts imposed from Westminster, then we look more generally the influence of the 2010 general election on local–central relationships, and more particularly on the leadership offered to councils as they attempt to implement cuts in a politically acceptable manner at local and sub-local levels.

In the build-up to the election, all three major political parties indicated that large cuts in central government's financial support to councils over the next few years were as certain as death and taxes. Following the Chancellor of the Exchequer's Pre-Budget Report in December 2009, the Institute of Fiscal Studies (IFS) attempted to put a figure on these warnings: 'The IFS says whichever party wins the next general election will have to cut 6.4% per year between 2011 and 2014 if they want to protect schools, hospitals and increase overseas aid, as both Labour and the Conservatives say they do' (BBC, 2009). The experience of previous recessions indicates two likely consequences from such a deep retrenchment. Firstly, recent political history tells us that cost-cutting administrations quickly lose support in local elections (namely during the 1981–83 period, following the Conservative election victory of 1979, and during the 1967–70 period after the Labour election victory in 1966). Hence relationships between central and local politicians quickly become fraught with conflict, even when most of them belong to the same political party, and consequently some councils become openly rebellious, while others work ever more furiously to subvert central policy to their own strategic intent.

Secondly, recessions tend to highlight the gap between rich and poor in a more obvious way than is apparent during times of relative prosperity. In these circumstances increased polarisation between the parties at local level often results in radicalisation of both left- and right-wing politics (namely in the early 1980s with the rise of the so-called 'loony left', and in the 1976–79 period with the rise of the more doctrinaire Conservative administrations in London boroughs such as Wandsworth and Westminster). With this polarisation came an increased danger of the British National Party (BNP) (and its predecessor the National Front) winning seats in more local councils by capitalising on the sense of insecurity among the white working class which tends to develop during periods of recession (there are parallels in the rise of the National Front in the early 1930s). Although the results of the 2010 election did not show the expected gain in seats for the BNP, there was an overall increase in its share of the vote. In this way the rise of radical actors in local government in response to public spending cuts further weakens the link between councils and Westminster.

But in addition to and beyond its formal powers to allocate or withhold financial support to local government, the more general tenor of relationships between local authorities and the administration in Westminster also gains significance in straitened times, as experienced in the consistency and predictability of central government's response to attempts by individual councils to 'square the circle' as they implement cuts. In this sense, in a country where the practice of government is as centralised as it is in the UK, the quality of leadership from central government in a recession is a factor in the relationship between central and local political actors which goes beyond transparent grievance over cuts in public spending. In short, local politicians ask themselves: 'Is this government going to see this through?', and an answer in the negative fuels the tendency to view local political context as of exclusive significance and the determination to 'go it alone'.

We can now bring together these reflections on impacts of the recession on councils beyond the 2010 election with our analysis earlier in the chapter of the existing pattern of messy mixes. What we envisage, in brief, is a scenario in which individual councils take on the responsibility for reducing their levels of activity without strong leadership from Westminster driving them to uniform solutions. Hence, the differentiated pattern which is already in evidence on the local government terrain will be overlaid with an additional set of the products of specific context and agency as cuts are implemented. To understand how the rules of government and governance may be changed in this classic dialectic between structure and agency we need to employ a conceptual framework from a well-established body of theory. It is for this reason that in the next section we turn to an institutional perspective on change, stability and path dependence.

An institutional perspective on change, stability and path dependence

Contrary to the more common use of the term, in which institutions are synonymous with organisations, institutionalists are concerned with institutions specifically as rules (Lowndes, 2002, 97–8). As applied to public policy analysis and research, Lowndes (2002, 103) states a preference for Hall's (1986, 7) original definition of institutions as: 'the formal rules, compliance procedures, and standard operating procedures that structure the relationships between people in various units of the polity and economy'.

This definition offers the advantage of capturing in a sentence the multilayered nature of the different types of rules which constitute institutions and their extension into wider economic and political conduct. However, the brevity of any such definition is also a disadvantage in that it requires substantial unpacking and interpretation to deliver its full significance. Many scholars work around this problem by describing institutions in terms of their characteristics in relation to a particular set of contextualising factors: Peters (2005, 29), for example, recalls the characteristics which feature in the original March and Olsen (1984; 1989) texts which are commonly credited with 'rediscovering institutions'; while Goodin's (1996, 19–20) analysis of the characteristics of institutions is particularly significant in that it emphasises the relationships between institutions and the actors, as well as the 'historical roots' of institutions and their capacity to 'embody, preserve and impart differential power resources to individuals and groups'. Other scholars lay more explicit emphasis on the developing and incomplete nature of the perspective: Lowndes (2002, 97–101), for example, proposes a schema of 'analytic continua' which identify common directions of travel as the new institutionalism absorbs and modifies the 'old' body of theory.

Here we offer three interrelated characteristics of institutions which are derived from the work of these scholars and hold particular significance for the development of the concept of institutions as applied to the local political context of the recession.

Firstly, institutions embody ideas and, in public policy and political analysis, ideas are powerful weapons in the hands of political and managerial actors. Institutions express a particularly potent set of ideas which not only constrain but also empower actors. Institutions limit the choices available to actors but, in freeing them from infinite choice, also free them to act. Furthermore, the ways in which institutions are designed, applied and interpreted in the public policy arena define who is included and excluded, and who has a say and who does not.

Secondly, institutions are the rules which shape the everyday behaviour of political and managerial actors. They take on various forms as, for example, the formal rules which first spring to mind when the term 'rule' is used, but they also appear as the informal rules of conduct in any given context, which are usually unwritten, but exert a strong influence on actors' thinking and action. In their wider manifestations, institutions take the form of stories which tell actors about 'the way we do things around here'. In these narrative accounts which relate details of the local political context, the expression of the rule usually comes at the end of the story as a normative conclusion, or moral, which tells actors how things have been done in the past and how they should be done in the future.

Finally, institutions appear to be stable and durable. This appearance of stasis is created by the interlinkages made and maintained by actors between these formal, informal and narrative layers which preserve their general shape over long periods. But beneath this veneer institutions are only 'relatively' stable. This tension between stability and change is caused by a dialectic relationship with actors in which 'the rules of the game' both influence and are themselves influenced by the conduct of those actors.

This third characteristic regarding the relative stability of institutions raises the question of how institutions change and begins to address Hay's (2002, 15) observation that institutional theory 'is rather better at explaining stability than change'. The use of the comparative is important here because it is clear that institutionalists have produced a number of different explanations for institutional change over the years. Indeed, there are well-developed models of 'punctuated equilibrium' (PE) which found a home some time ago within several strands of the new institutionalism by theorising that periods of 'normal' political time are punctuated by periods of fast tempo, when significant institutional change is more likely to take place (for example, Krasner, 1984; Baumgartner and Jones, 1993; True et al, 1999; John and Margetts, 2003). However, as Gorges (2001), among others, points out, these explanations of institutional change call on external, or 'exogenous', forces to produce the motive forces for change, rather than explaining what part actors within the local political space, or 'endogenous' forces, have played in institutional dynamics.

In recent years theorists across the several schools of institutionalism have responded to these challenges by producing conceptual frameworks for change which are consciously set apart from models of punctuated equilibrium. Streek and Thelen (2005, 6), for example, critique the 'highly static conception of institutions as "frozen" residues, or "crystallisations" of previous political conflict'. They draw attention to the fact that, by contrast, 'a growing body of work has begun to conceive of institutional reproduction as a dynamic political process'.

For our purposes we can identify three specific ways in which this body of work departs from the former orthodoxy. Firstly, these scholars argue that institutional change is taking place gradually but significantly in normal time (Pierson, 2004). Therefore we need to be 'on the look out for models of change which do not conform to the classic breakdown or replacement model' (Thelen, 2003, 233). Secondly, rather than the privileged few possessing the ability to generate change, as theorised in some adaptations of PE (for example Blyth, 2002), a multitude of 'ordinary' actors contribute to institutional dynamics and institutional stability over time. In this 'dynamic political process' institutions are '*continuously* established, restored, redefined and defended against all sorts of disorganising forces' (Streek, 2001, 31; our emphasis). Thirdly, when change does occur, actors tend to employ tried and trusted templates rather than creating new ones in the form of 'institutional materials that were to hand' (Crouch and Keune, 2005, 84–5). Hence even 'in times of crisis or deep uncertainty, actors often specifically eschew experimentation and fall back on familiar formulas – resulting in institutional reproduction not change' (Thelen, 2004, 292).

In turn this theorisation casts a different light on path dependence as a concept central to institutionalism. Whereas traditional approaches based on punctuated equilibrium have portrayed path dependence as a stop-start process which is, at its inception, unconvincingly contingent, and then equally unconvincingly deterministic thereafter (Pierson, 2004, 50–3), these opposing theorisations promote a more consistent ontology in which elements of agency, contingency and constraint are privileged to similar extent throughout. Hence path dependence takes place in a contested multilateral environment and incorporates agency as a collective and continuous process. And so actors remain on the same policy path both because they choose to do so in pursuit of their perceived group and individual interests, and because they believe they are constrained by prior commitments. Equally, in reusing the materials to hand, those who seek to defend existing ways of doing things must be at least as creative as those who wish to promote institutional change, lacking as they do the benefit of recourse to the 'new'.

While most strands of institutionalism do not lay any claim to a locus within predictive science, the centrality of path dependence to the perspective must alone imply that some general regularities in actors' conduct flow forward into the future. This tension between agency and structure, contingency and determinism, is central to institutional theory. Looking back, institutionalism helps us to understand how the concepts of governance and government have become intertwined over time and how different mixes have developed in different councils. Looking forward, we can see both how local actors will commonly defend their existing ways of working in imaginative ways and how, in the absence of a strong central lead, in its specifics this differentiation will increase and existing trajectories will continue to diverge.

Hence, if we return to the spectrum of existing responses that we outlined earlier, then we can reasonably suggest that those few local authorities who have moved rapidly to place neighbourhood working at the centre of their interlaced service delivery and community leadership agendas will not only remain on that path but will find increasingly creative ways of defending this position. At the other end of the spectrum, the small number who have paid lip service to the community leadership role post 2000 may take this opportunity to withdraw, as far as the intertwining of roles will allow them. Between these two extremes, local actors in the majority of councils will find ways of defending their own distinctive mix of government and governance, including pointing out the intertwined nature of the projects in practice and emphasising the 'lock-in' caused by the raised expectations of engaged citizens and partners.

Not all will be successful in their defence, and in the final section of this chapter we address our concerns to those who could be said to be already halfway down the path to neighbourhood working and beyond. We examine how these actors who are already substantially committed to defending their particular government–governance mix might go about the task of using the materials at hand to fight the worst consequences of the recession.

Exploiting the potential of a neighbourhood approach

From our work in Derby, Nottingham, Leicester, Birmingham and elsewhere, it is clear that for a neighbourhood approach to prove effective – particularly as a serious response to the local fall-out from a major recession – there are a number of conditions which have to be met. These are listed in Box 6.1 and then discussed in sequence.

Box 6.1: Conditions for successful neighbourhood working

- The approach has to be council-led and to incorporate an infrastructure for decision making and resource allocation at a local (ideally 'neighbourhood') level.
- It has to build upon definitions of neighbourhood which residents identify with and regard as a focus for action. The neighbourhood arrangements must involve a serious level of commitment from other key agencies, in particular police, health authorities and the voluntary sector.
- A critical mass of 'movers and shakers' has to be involved at two different levels: the various public agencies involved *and* local residents.

- There needs to be a flexible attitude to the use of public resources – for example, schools, leisure centres, council buildings – to facilitate their use of a wider agenda of neighbourhood objectives.

A council-led approach

Because the local council (or councils, in the remaining areas of two-tier local government) provides a wider range of services than any other local public agency, and because it is the only directly elected and hence democratically representative local agency, it is essential that it play a lead role in the development of a neighbourhood approach. To do so signals to local people that the council is committed to the project, and establishes an important two-way link between the neighbourhood and the council whereby the priorities of the former can be identified and resources (albeit limited in a time of recession) can be provided by the latter. Local councillors have been at the heart of the more ambitious and effective neighbourhood schemes. In any event, if decisions are to be made and resources allocated in relation to council responsibilities, they can only at present be taken by elected councillors (or officers to whom powers have been delegated). Hence there is a need for an infrastructure to underpin neighbourhood working, typically involving some form of neighbourhood committee linked to a neighbourhood forum with a wider membership.

The need for council leadership does not imply council dominance; indeed the hope would be, as the project developed, that ways could be found of transferring power to a wider representative group of local leaders and activists. But at its current state of development (with a few notable exceptions) the need for council leadership to 'kick start' this kind of project is paramount.

In the context of a major recession it is important that the approach cover the whole of the local authority area. There may well be a case for prioritisation of neighbourhoods which have been particularly hard hit. But to prioritise such areas should not imply the exclusion of others, as was the case in the recent 'New Deal for Communities' initiative. The recession will cause problems in middle-class as well as deprived areas.

A basis in neighbourhoods with which local people identify and a commitment from key partners

The use of the term 'neighbourhood' has become distorted in recent years, not least by the government in its response to bids for unitary status, where the concept of neighbourhoods as large as 40,000 has been taken seriously. A population of 40,000 implies a sizeable town, not a sub-area within a town or city with which local people identify. There is a long-term sociological interest in the neighbourhood concept, with a population size of 5,000–10,000 typically having been identified in studies of neighbourhoods 'on the ground'. Interestingly, this scale of neighbourhood proved congruent with the perceptions of local councillors in Derby and Norwich (and elsewhere) who, in several cases, claimed that they could identify viable neighbourhoods of this size in the parts of the city with which they were familiar. This kind of size criterion is also congruent with the typical catchment area of a primary school, and the recent definition of 'community policing' areas. The implication is that there would be around 50 such units in a city the size of Derby or Norwich (200,000–250,000).

The importance of using neighbourhoods which have a real local significance is that residents' potential capacity for involvement is more likely to be realised in relation to an area with which they feel some affinity. In rural areas, small towns and villages will typically operate as neighbourhood equivalents.

To use real neighbourhoods as a building block does not necessarily imply that decision making (including resource allocation) should be organised at neighbourhood level. Indeed there would be major logistical problems in doing so. In Derby and Norwich, average ward size is around 17,000, which would typically be associated with three or four individual neighbourhoods. If local authority decisions have to be taken by elected members, it is difficult to see how a system of 50 such decision-making bodies would be feasible. It would involve either a group of three ward councillors operating in each of three or four neighbourhoods *or* a single councillor allocated delegated power in each neighbourhood. Both options are problematical. A way has to be found of linking a neighbourhood-based priority-setting and action programme with a decision-making process carried out across larger sub-areas.

It is of course not just local authorities whose local agendas will be challenged by the resource restrictions and social and economic problems associated with a recession. Other public agencies, in particular health and police authorities, will be similarly affected. In many councils which have developed some form of neighbourhood approach, there is already acknowledgement that many local partners will require action from other public agencies, but with a good deal of overlap between the responsibilities (and potential contributions) of such authorities and those of the local council. In response to this awareness, de facto local partnerships have developed at sub-authority level in many cases, with police, health and voluntary sector representatives working together with local representatives to tackle the (interrelated) problems of the locality. There are potential benefits to all these agencies, particularly given the expectations regarding crime prevention and health education, which are high on the agenda of police and health authorities respectively.

This kind of infrastructure is an essential prerequisite to the development and implantation of a coherent action plan to tackle the local impact of the recession (which, although it will have some common features, will also generate different local impacts, depending upon the socio-economic characteristics of the sub-area). In several authorities, the infrastructure is already there; in others it would need to be established. As with decision making, individual neighbourhoods are almost certainly too small in population size to provide the basis for local partnerships, particularly in cities and larger towns. The challenge is to provide an effective two-way channel between the neighbourhood and a set of wider areas (possibly at ward level) where such arrangements are feasible.

A critical mass of movers and shakers

This is the most critical ingredient. A group of committed councillors (and partner representatives) and a locality-based infrastructure with decision-making and (limited) resource-allocation powers will not by themselves generate a requisite level of voluntary commitment and input from residents. Experience from the Derby research demonstrates the difficulty of generating this kind of commitment and input, particularly in some working-class areas with little in the way of a tradition of community action.

But even in such areas there were individuals who, if encouraged and supported, could form the nucleus of a developing network of such activists. Here are two examples.

- A mother of three on a deprived council estate, who was aware of the lack of after-school facilities for children on her part of the estate and with some friends set up a facility of this nature.
- An Anglican priest who recognised the role his church could play as a community facility, and has developed this role (irrespective of the faith – or lack of it – of local residents) and also acted as an advocate on their behalf.

The challenge in relation to the recession is to harness and extend this kind of community activism. There are a number of possibilities here. A movement called 'Transition' has developed over the past few years. Its focus is on climate change and on generating local community action to respond to it. But the way in which it has developed local networks to take local action (for example, local vegetable growing) in relation to a global problem provides a useful model in relation to the recession.

The important thing is to identify and utilise whatever opportunities are available locally for strengthening community involvement and action. It may be a local 'Transition' group, an active local community association, an outward-looking local church, a Neighbourhood Watch group or a number of individuals with a track record of stimulating community action. The particular challenge in the more deprived and/or apathetic areas is to strive to ensure that the groups/individuals identified are not dominated by unrepresentative (typically middle-class) residents.

The same point about 'movers and shakers' applies to the representatives of the public agencies who are part of the local neighbourhood machinery. Neighbourhood working will become effective only if enough of these representatives are prepared to act in a proactive and flexible way, which typically goes beyond their job descriptions. Again, some illustrations from the Derby research may be helpful.

- In one ward, a local PCT (Primary Care Trust) official recognised the impact on the level of community activity in the area of the fact that the local annual carnival had become defunct. She set in motion and facilitated a process whereby the carnival was reintroduced (with a strong public health theme). This had the effect of raising the level of community involvement and directing it towards activities which would in due course improve levels of health in the area.
- In another ward, a schools/community liaison officer saw it as part of her role to stimulate interest and involvement in the recently established neighbourhood forum and board, which had so far generated little interest. This role, which was beginning to prove effective, went well beyond her official job description.
- In a third ward, a local resident who was a member of the neighbourhood board had a job which involved visiting older residents of the ward in their homes. She used the job as a two-way communication mechanism, making older people aware of what the neighbourhood ward was doing, and channelling their concerns and priorities to the board.

What these examples show is that de facto community development activities can stem from a variety of sources. One of the key tasks of the neighbourhood managers in Derby is to identify and support the people involved. There is also an onus on the partners involved (including local authority departments, such as children and young persons' services) to be prepared to permit scope for those kinds of developmental activities to be pursued.

Making use of existing public/voluntary resources: a flexible approach

In most neighbourhoods (certainly in most wards) there will exist a range of public facilities – schools, leisure centres, community centres, libraries, churches with community facilities, local medical centres. Although each of these will have specific purposes, there is often scope for extending the use of such facilities in a way which contributes to a wider 'community involvement' role. Dual use of school leisure facilities is one familiar option, use of libraries for meetings of community groups is another. In addition, some churches have been prepared to provide a range of valuable outreach community facilities – for example, pre-school play groups, mother–and–toddler groups – without requiring church membership or even evidence of religious belief.

In a move to open up opportunities for local action at a time of recession, these resources can make a valuable contribution. It should be part of any local action plan to survey the range of facilities of this nature which are available and to seek to extend the way in which they are used to contribute to mitigating the impact of the recession.

Summary and conclusion

In a situation of budgetary constraint, there will be strong pressure for local authorities to concentrate on protecting key services and to retract from a broader community governance agenda. We have argued that there will be a great deal more discretion available to local actors than a uniform slash-and-burn scenario would predict. Firstly, we have shown that separating out the intertwined strands of activity in service delivery and community leadership will be more difficult than the rhetoric implies. Secondly, we have shown in relation to the example of neighbourhood working how very context-specific these individual government–governance mixes have become at council level and below. Thirdly, we have argued that a strong lead from central government against 'localism' and locally based initiatives is unlikely.

Finally, in the sections immediately above we have suggested from our empirical research that some local (and perhaps even national) actors will recognise that community governance is precisely what is needed at a time when social and economic problems are certain to increase. To complete this chapter we consider how a best-case scenario might evolve from recent developments and future trajectory of neighbourhood policy.

In principle, one way of moving the best-case scenario forward would be to stimulate and harness a greater commitment from local people, on a collective basis, to safeguarding (or enhancing) the social, economic and environmental well-being of their local areas, in order to augment the inevitably more limited contribution which local authorities (and other public agencies) will be capable of making. If this outcome proves possible there will also be a positive spin-off for service quality, because, as we have shown, service quality and community governance are inextricably intertwined.

If the energies and commitment of local people are to be harnessed in this way, they will have to be focused at a spatial level with which local people identify – the neighbourhood (or small town/large village) sociological evidence suggests an average population size of around 5,000–10,000 fits the popular conception of the local neighbourhood.

For this kind of collective response on a neighbourhood basis to develop, there would need to be a facilitatory infrastructure in place which could be used to organise and stimulate community activity. We have used the concept of path dependence to demonstrate that local authorities have made varying degrees of progress in relation to neighbourhood governance. Some have hardly started along the path; some have introduced elaborate systems of service delivery and decision making at the neighbourhood level; many are at various stages in between these two extremes.

We have also suggested in the previous sections that the concept of path dependence can be used in the sort of scenario building undertaken in this chapter to 'predict' in the most general sense that actors who have made substantial investments in certain policy goals will defend these when they are threatened in the future and will thereby increase their investment further, and the likelihood of their continuing down that policy path.

Realistically, it is only those authorities which have made significant progress along this particular path who could hope, within the next four to five years, to achieve the outcomes we have indicated. We identified a series of four conditions which would need to be met for the project to have a good chance of succeeding (see Box 6.1). For authorities in which neighbourhood arrangements have already met some of these conditions, there is a real possibility of developing the structures and processes further, to make real progress along the path we have identified. For those authorities that have hardly started, it is difficult to see how the resources that would be needed to 'kick start' such an approach could be found in the next year or so.

The focus of this chapter has been on what could be done by local authorities (and local people) within the existing legislative framework. There are a number of other measures which, if introduced as part of a legislative programme, could contribute further to safeguarding (or enhancing) the well-being of neighbourhoods through collective action. Firstly, for example, if those on unemployment benefit (but seeking work) were required to contribute a specified number of hours each week to community work (using the term in the broadest sense, and ensuring that a wide range of choice of activity was available to the individuals concerned), that would provide a major resource for 'filling the gaps' left by local authority financial cutbacks (we are aware of the counter arguments to this proposal). Secondly, if local public institutions – in particular schools, leisure centres and libraries – could be used much more flexibly as a resource to facilitate a much wider range of (community-led) activities than is currently the case, that too could be of real benefit. Thirdly, there is the possibility to 'levering in' external resources. The People's Lottery (part of the National Lottery) is one possibility. There is also scope for drawing in professional expertise, provided on a voluntary or low-cost basis by local residents with such skills who are prepared to apply them for the greater (local) good.

Finally, as councils respond to the demands of the financial crisis and adjust to a change of central government, how do we interpret developments which have emerged in the last six months as they shape the trajectory of neighbourhood policy? At the national level the localism espoused for some time by all three major parties developed into 'a proxy war' between Labour and the Conservatives in the run-up to the general election, in which each party used a London council to 'play out key general election battle issues on the ground', and the future of neighbourhood working in particular (Travers, 2010).

In late summer of 2009 the Conservative leadership presented the London Borough of Barnet's 'easyCouncil' as its 'flagship' for local government and localism in the future. Barnet is making arrangements to sell off its planning function to managers and staff or establish a joint venture with the private sector in an attempt to find savings of £25 million a year. The council will retain a controlling share in the venture, and just as budget airline customers can pay extra for priority boarding, residents will also be able to pay more for access to a 'customer relationship officer', which means they can speak to the same person each time they telephone. The council's stated aims are to 'facilitate self-help through behaviour change' and provide 'more services delivered by organisations other than the council'. The interpretation of localism here, and its application to neighbourhood working, is very much in terms of a modern, behaviourist approach to a 'nudging' rather than 'nannying' state, and towards 'selling off' services to local people, an approach which replicates the privatisation model familiar in local government since the Conservative administrations of the 1980s (Booth, 2010).

On 31 March 2010 Labour announced its 'Mutual Manifesto', which included measures to allow users to take over the running of their local services, including health and social care, council housing and SureStart projects. The Cabinet Office minister, Tessa Jowell, also announced that 115 Labour groups or councils were committed to becoming 'co-operative councils' along the lines of the London borough of Lambeth, which is currently consulting on plans to make all its services part-run by its users. In this vein, Lambeth's first response to Barnet's initiative has been to hire a group of local residents to create 50 green co-operative organisations, growing and selling a variety of vegetables and foodstuffs. Presented as the 'John Lewis' council in opposition to Barnet's 'easyCouncil', Lambeth is also committed to handing over community centres, housing associations, primary schools and SureStart projects to local community groups, subject to a ballot result in favour of the transfer (Stratton, 2010). The interpretation of localism here and its application to neighbourhood working is very much is terms of reviving the Old Labour idea of the co-operative moment at neighbourhood level through existing arrangements for asset transfer, and melding this with the John Lewis reputation for quality production in partnership working. The incoming Conservative-Liberal Democrat government in May 2010 did not diverge from such co-production ideas in its ideas and announcements on 'big society'.

In terms of our application of the institutionalist concept of path dependence above, we now have a better idea of how those councils that have hardly started along the road to neighbourhood governance will conduct themselves in the recessionary aftermath and how, by contrast, those that are a long way along that road will respond. Nevertheless, we should emphasise that, in keeping with institutionalist theory, these two templates will be adapted to meet local demands, and we already see some unease and protest from local actors around both models, which will accelerate the tendency towards differentiation. In

Barnet the 'easyCouncil' has already suffered repeated setbacks from the High Court and a council taxpayers' challenge, while in Lambeth, Burgess and Rogers (2010), as local union representatives, suggest that 'There is a danger that this could lead to the same attempts to offload responsibility that we see in Barnet'.

In this chapter we have departed somewhat from the conventional 'critical' approach to public policy in two respects. Firstly, we have not only looked backwards in our analysis of neighbourhood working, but have also tried to 'predict' a little of its future. Secondly, we have not only adopted a sceptical approach to some the claims associated with the policy, but have also taken an optimistic view of its capacity to harness the hidden resources within communities during a recession. At the conclusion of this chapter we see still see many reasons to be cheerful about the future of neighbourhood working.

References

APSE (Association for Public Service Excellence) (2009) *The Ensuring Council: A New Model for Governance, Neighbourhoods and Service Delivery*, Manchester: APSE.

Baumgartner, F.R. and Jones, B.D. (1993) *Agendas and instability in American politics*, Chicago: University of Chicago Press.

BBC (2009) '"Darling must cut £36bn", IFS think tank says', http://news.bbc.co.uk/1/hi/uk_politics/8406670.stm, accessed 13 May 2010.

Blyth, M. (2002) *Great Transformations: Economic Ideas and Political Change in the Twentieth Century*, Cambridge: Cambridge University Press.

Booth, R. (2010) 'High court bars "easyCouncil" from removing live-in wardens', *Guardian*, 15 December.

Burgess, J. and Rogers, J. (2010) 'Co-operative councils must not be used as a cover for privatisation', *Guardian*, 27 February.

Cochrane, A. (1993) *Whatever Happened to Local Government?*, Buckingham: Open University Press.

Crouch, C. and Keune, M. (2005) 'Changing institutional practice: making use of institutional diversity in Hungary and the United Kingdom', in W. Streek and K. Thelen (eds) *Beyond Continuity: Institutional Change in Advanced Political Economies*, Oxford: Oxford University Press.

DCLG (Department for Communities and Local Government) (2008) *Empowering Communities to Influence Local Decision Making: Evidence-based Lessons for Policy Makers and Practitioners*, London: DCLG.

Durose, C., Rees, J. and Lowndes, V. (2009) *Where Now for 'Neighbourhood'?*, School for Environment and Development seminar series, March, Manchester: University of Manchester.

Friend J., Power, J. and Yewlett, C. (1974) *Public Planning: The Intercorporate Dimension*, London: Tavistock.

Goodin, R.E. (ed) (1996) *The Theory of Institutional Design*, Cambridge: Cambridge University Press.

Gorges, M.J. (2001) 'New Institutionalist Explanations for Institutional Change: A Note of Caution', *Politics*, vol 21, no 2, pp 137–45.

Hall, P. (1986) *Governing the Economy: The Politics of Intervention in Britain and France*, Cambridge: Polity Press.

Hay, C. (2002) *Political Analysis: A Critical Introduction*, Basingstoke: Palgrave.

John, P. (1998) *Analysing Public Policy*, London: Continuum.

John, P. and Margetts, H. (2003) 'Policy Punctuations in the UK: Fluctuations and Equilibria in Central Government Expenditure Since 1951', *Public Administration*, vol 81, no 3, pp 411–32.

Krasner, S.D. (1984) 'Approaches to the State: Alternative Conceptions and Historical Dynamics', *Comparative Politics*, vol 16, pp 223–46.

Leach, S. (2004) 'Political parties at the local level', in G. Stoker, and D. Wilson (eds) *British Local Government into the 21st Century*, Basingstoke: Macmillan.

Lowndes, V. (2002) 'Institutionalism', in D. Marsh and G. Stoker (eds) *Theory and Methods in Political Science*, Basingstoke: Palgrave Macmillan.

Lowndes, V. (2004) 'Reformers or Recidivists? Has Local Government Really Changed?', in G. Stoker and D. Wilson (eds) *British Local Government into the 21st Century*, Basingstoke: Palgrave Macmillan.

Lowndes, V. (2005) 'Something Old, Something New, Something Borrowed ... How Institutions Change (and Stay the Same) in Local Governance', *Policy Studies*, vol 26, pp 291–309.

Lowndes, V. and Sullivan, H. (2008) 'How low can you go? Rationales and challenges for neighbourhood governance', *Public Administration*, vol 86, no 1, pp 53–74.

March, J.G. and Olsen, J.P. (1984) 'The New Institutionalism: Organisational Factors in Political Life', *American Political Science Review*, vol 78, no 3, pp 734–49.

March, J.G. and Olsen, J.P. (1989) *Rediscovering Institutions*, New York: Free Press.

Peters, B.G. (2005) *Institutional Theory in Political Science: The 'New Institutionalism'*, 2nd edn, London: Continuum.

Pierson, P. (2004) *Politics in Time*, Princeton, NJ: Princeton University Press.

Stoker, G. (2002) 'Life is a Lottery: New Labour's Strategy for the Reform of Devolved Governance', *Public Administration*, vol 80, no 3, pp 417–34.

Stratton, A. (2010) 'The future for local authorities: is it John Lewis or easyCouncil?', *Guardian*, 18 February.

Streek, W. (2001) 'Introduction: Explorations into the Origins of Nonliberal Capitalism in Germany and Japan', in W. Streek and K. Yamamura (eds) *The Origins of Nonliberal Capitalism: Germany and Japan*, New York: Cornell University Press.

Streek, W. and Thelen, K. (eds) (2005) *Beyond Continuity: Institutional Change In Advanced Political Economies*, Oxford: Oxford University Press.

Sullivan, H. and Skelcher, C. (2002) *Working across Boundaries: Collaboration in Public Services*, Basingstoke: Palgrave Macmillan.

Thelen, K. (2003) 'How Institutions Evolve: Insights from Comparative Historical Analysis', in J. Mahoney and D. Rueschemeyer (eds) *Comparative Historical Analysis in the Social Sciences*, Cambridge: Cambridge University Press.

Thelen, K. (2004) *How Institutions Evolve: The Political Economy of Skills in Germany, Britain, the United States and Japan*, Cambridge: Cambridge University Press.

Thompson, G., Frances, J., Levačić, R. and Mitchell, J. (eds) (1991) *Markets, Hierarchies and Networks: The Coordination of Social Life*, London: Sage.

Travers, T. (2010) 'Lambeth v Barnet: Local councils fighting a proxy war', *Guardian*, 17 February.

True, J.L., Jones, B.D. and Baumgartner, F.R. (1999) 'Punctuated-Equilibrium Theory: Explaining Stability and Change in Public Policymaking', in P. Sabatier (ed) *Theories of the Policy Process*, Boulder, CO: Westview Press.

SEVEN

Efficiencies in public service delivery

John Seddon and Brendan O'Donovan

Introduction

The 'efficiencies' debate in political discourse, alluded to already in this book, imagines there to be a number of 'back-office' activities that can be cut without impacting on 'front-line' services. Perhaps what is needed, though, is a more radical overhaul of the design and delivery of public services. The aim of this chapter is to show how an ideological approach to managing the public sector has driven it in the wrong direction. Between 1999 and 2009, public services received a 55% real-terms funding increase, as financed by an increase of 5% of GDP in public expenditure. This investment was not matched by improvement: public sector productivity fell by 3.4%, compared to the private sector's 27.9% productivity gain over the same period (Blond, 2009). At the same time, the instruments of 'deliverology' (Barber, 2007) were invented and forced upon the public sector with the aim of reforming public services and delivering improved results. The financial crisis and the consequent fiscal deficit inherited by the Conservative-Liberal coalition government of 2010 made the levels of public service expenditure of the last decade no longer affordable: indeed, within days of coming to power, the new government announced plans to implement £6 billion of cuts by 2011. However, the waste created by the government's public sector reform regime now offers an unexpected opportunity for improvement. Not only has the reform programme not delivered improved services, it has actually made performance worse: a bureaucracy of specifications and inspection has driven public services in the wrong direction and sapped public sector morale. At present, the public sector is so full of non-value-adding activity that there is huge potential for improvement in both service delivery and improved efficiency. In light of the failure of 'deliverology', it is clearly time to experiment with new approaches to managing the public sector. The widespread adoption of a different way of managing and delivering services, based on systems principles, already has a strong track record in individual public sector services, in spite of its inherent antithesis to the ideology of the reform regime (ODPM, 2005; Jackson et al, 2007; McQuade, 2008; Middleton, 2010; Zokaei et al, 2010). There are now many examples of dramatically better services with significantly lower costs. Nevertheless, before the wider potential for success can be realised, the current ideology must be discarded and the reform regime must be dismantled.

'Targets and terror': the product of an ideology

For the last 30 years, public sector reform has been derived from an ideological approach imported into politics and management from economic theory. 'Quasi-markets', choice and incentives have been assumed to be the means for stimulating improvement in services. These ideas were derived from a field of study called 'public choice theory'. This took the assumptions and mathematical models of 'game theory' and applied them to the world of political science. Public choice theory is concerned with the behaviour of voters, politicians and government officials. It posits their actions on a narrow model of human behaviour where people are expected to act as totally self-interested agents. The ideal organisation for human interaction is held to be a notional perfectly competitive market, where individuals are able to contract and compete with others to earn precisely what the market believes them to be worth. The 'human as a businessman' (as one game theorist[1] labelled the radical individualist at the heart of the model) is able to exercise his/her choices, preferences and appetites in this perfect market-place and the 'invisible hand' ensures that each is allocated what he/she is objectively worth.

These ideas were seen as the principal alternative to the corporatist approach to managing all aspects of the economy which had prevailed in the UK after the Second World War. Successive Conservative and Labour governments had employed Keynesian economic policies in what became known as the postwar consensus: incomes policies, maintaining the welfare state and nationalised industries helped to keep high levels of employment and steady growth. However, by the late 1970s, economic instability and fractious industrial relations led many to believe in what became known as the 'state overload' thesis: the state was seen as having extended beyond its reach until it had grown too big (Hudson and Lowe, 2004). The public choice theorists had by this time gained influence with many right-wing UK think-tanks and proposed radical free-market policies to unburden the state: public sector bureaucracies would become subjected to markets and competition. Public choice theory modelled the state bureaucracies as being too 'producer-focused', readily exploiting their monopoly position as state service providers and as a result delivering poor-quality, standardised services to taxpayers who were expected to passively take what they were given. Civil servants were caricatured as 'Sir Humphrey' in the BBC satirical comedy 'Yes, Minister'[2] and labelled as 'budget-maximisers' by the public choice theorists (Buchanan, 1978; Niskanen, 1994). They were thought to be acting in their own self-interest by ensuring that they increased their own sphere of influence within ever more expensive departments. The theorists believed that if the state could be opened up to competition, then these public sector organisations would be forced to react to the requirements of the needs and wants of their 'consumers', and would therefore become both more effective and efficient.

After the election of the neoliberal Thatcher administration in 1979, government followed these prescriptions wherever it was feasible to do so and opened up large parts of the state to competition. Many of the old nationalised industries and public utilities were privatised. Citizens were encouraged to act as consumers exercising choice in the market, purchasing stakes in the newly privatised companies or buying their council houses through the 'right to buy' schemes. Where the remaining parts of the public sector were seen as unsuitable for privatisation, politicians required another way to make them more competitive. The government and its advisers took to the idea of 'quasi-markets': the simulation of the competitive market within the public sector. In place of the profit motive which drove action in the private sector, it was thought that an artificially constructed market would provide an equivalent means to drive change into public service delivery.

Public choice theory spawned the mantras of 'new public management' (NPM): disaggregation, competition and incentivisation were the new ways of managing the public sector (Dunleavy et al, 2006). There would no longer be any presumption of the existence of such an old-fashioned concept as public duty in this rational, self-interested world. The bureaucrats, who had for a long time been trusted as 'knights' presumed to be doing their professional best for the public, were now to be treated as 'knaves' who were interested only in personal gain (Le Grand, 2003). Newly constructed objective targets were to be deployed which would set these knavish managers free, unburdened from their old roles as knights. They would now be expected to innovate in the manner of their private sector counterparts: numbers and rationality would replace the 'invisible hand' of the competitive market. NPM reforms encouraged managers to show entrepreneurship in achieving their targets: so long as the numbers were aligned in the quasi-market, this system was assumed to be working to the benefit of taxpayers and the politicians. For public sector managers, targets would act as their surrogate profit motive, and their pay and career progression was likely to be directly linked to the achievement of their personal targets. Through alignment of these incentives and mimicry of the market, it was believed that the public sector could be guided to private sector levels of productivity and efficiency.

By the time that New Labour came to power, these conceptual models of public sector reform had been adopted into the political mainstream. When the first Blair government was elected in 1997, its victory owed much to the feeling among voters that public services had been run down by Conservative neglect and consequently required higher levels of investment. However, when New Labour duly raised levels of public expenditure, the investment was accompanied by a requirement for those services to earn their taxpayers' money. A science of 'deliverology' was invented by the newly formed Prime Minister's Delivery Unit (Barber, 2007). Performance measures and targets supposedly offered a way of guaranteeing that money was producing results for the public. With an even greater zeal than before, targets and expenditure levels (in the form of 'public service agreements') were thrashed out between Gordon Brown's all-powerful Treasury and individual government departments. These targets were then cascaded down through the hierarchies across the public sector. At the same time, inspection and regulatory bodies were beefed up to inspect and publish performance data on all public sector bodies (Cope and Goodship, 2002). This 'targets and terror' approach became compared with Soviet-style systems for its severity, with some targets becoming known in the bureaucratic vernacular as 'P45' or 'hanging' offences if they were missed (Hood, 2006). Meeting the targets became all important. In response to this pressure, public sector expenditure on reporting against targets and inspection began to increase: by 2006, it was estimated that, on average, each local authority spent £1.8 million on reporting its performance measures upwards to government (DCLG, 2006). Collectively in Leicestershire, it was estimated that public sector bodies had spent £3.6 million on preparing for inspections (LGA, 2009). In addition, a new phenomenon called 'gaming' began to be observed, where managers were seen to have 'hit the target but missed the point'. One example involved hospital patients being offered a date which the hospital staff knew the patient could not attend, in order to then class these patients as having refused treatment, and thus remove them from hospital waiting lists and improve performance rankings (Bevan and Hood, 2006). Ministers were quick to dismiss these instances as exceptional and as the actions of a few bad apples.[3] Separately, a debate emerged around the perceived failure of NPM techniques to deliver. One set of commentators said:

> The intellectually and practically dominant set of managerial and governance ideas of the last two decades, new public management (NPM), has essentially died in the water. (Dunleavy et al, 2006, 468)

Undeterred, the regime moved on to what it called the next step in its reform journey, delivering 'citizen empowerment'. David Miliband, when he was the Local Government Minister, called it 'double devolution' (*Guardian*, 2006). This was a reflection of government's fear of giving control to those who were delivering public services: instead, government believed it could replace the lever of the centre with the lever of the customer.

> In local government, we are increasing the power of citizens to shape their communities and the services they receive. With local councils, we are delivering personalized services, establishing rights to minimum levels of entitlement and giving people new ways to shape their local services – from citizens' panels to participatory budgeting – complementing the role of elected local councillors. (HM Government, 2009, 17)

In the summer of 2009, the Labour government announced legally binding 'entitlements' of standards in education, healthcare and policing. Entitlements of this type were targets with added legal redress. This represents, in systems pioneer Russell Ackoff's terms, an attempt to 'do the wrong thing righter' (Ackoff, 2004). Labour's move from its early promise of 'education, education, education' to a legally enshrined right to educational standards demonstrated the 'deliverology' regime's failure to deliver, or to recognise that it was the underlying ideological beliefs behind the methods which were at fault. In the face of mounting evidence to the contrary, the regime persisted with its ideology.

> If both common sense and empirical evidence suggest the contrary, why does the pessimistic model of people as

> purely self-interested beings still so dominate management-related theories? The answer lies not in evidence but in ideology. Theories of social phenomena are, and have to be, ideologically motivated. Despite the pretence to be values-free, no social theory can be values-free. And, while no social science discipline makes a stronger claim to objectivity than economics, no domain of the social sciences is more values-laden in both its assumptions and its language than economics and all its derivatives. (Ghoshal, 2005, 83)

The damage caused by the reform regime has become apparent to all bar its architects. The political and economic ideology which informed the reform regime's approach only served to reinforce a pre-existing set of 'command and control' conventional management beliefs about how best to design and manage efficient services. These ideas can be traced back to F.W. Taylor's 'scientific management' (Taylor [1911], 1998) and then Henry Ford and Alfred Sloan's mass-production techniques (Ford [1926], 2003; Chandler, 1977). The practical manifestations of these managerial ideas can be summarised as three commonly held core beliefs (Seddon et al, 2010). As has been discussed, politicians commonly think that managers can be incentivised by the need to meet centrally imposed targets, which are in turn translated into myriad local performance indicators further down the hierarchy. Influenced by economic and managerial models developed in early 20th-century mass-production manufacturing, the ministers also believed that the creation of public service factories (through 'economies of scale') would generate greater efficiency. Finally, they were led to believe that the imposition of standardised specifications for the delivery of services would enable them to simultaneously guarantee service standards to the public and control the costs of their delivery. Through these means, politicians aimed to deliver what they considered to be the noblest yet most elusive of political ends: the optimisation of taxpayers' resources in efficient public services. The potency of their prescriptive and damaging methods was all the greater when filtered through the 'deliverology' regime: resistance was rewarded with low inspection scores and attention from central government.

An example of these ideas in action came in the 2009 Budget. The potential for £15 billion of public sector efficiency savings was announced as part of the Treasury's Operational Efficiency Programme (HM Treasury, 2009). To achieve £7 billion of these savings, the report recommended the creation of more shared 'back-office' services such as HR, IT and finance. The idea of separating front and back offices in services was first proposed by Robert Chase of Cornell University (Chase, 1978). In essence, his argument for 'back-office' service production was that creating a back office allowed a decoupling of the service from the customer and could thus offer greater potential to operate at peak efficiency. The back office could then be run as a factory, optimising efficiency through operations management techniques such as inventory control and work measurement. In line with Chase's ideas about efficiency, public sector managers are therefore encouraged to think of services as being organised for economies of scale. The focus of management is on how best to manage resources. The managers become preoccupied with solving such problems as 'how much work is coming in?', 'how many people have I got?' and 'how long do they take to do things?'.

Systems thinking: a challenge to convention

Systems thinking offers a different perspective to managers. Systems thinking as a general theory has developed in many forms since the Second World War, and has been applied in a variety of ways to solving managerial problems (Jackson, 2000, 2003; ODPM, 2005). Whereas conventional approaches to the design and management of work concentrate on optimising the performance of the separate individual functions of an organisation, often without reference to one another, systems thinking adopts a fundamentally different analysis, focusing on the inter-relationship between the various parts of a system. In particular, systems thinking encourages managers to closely examine 'what is the problem I am trying to solve?'. Often examination reveals that management's problems are not those they thought they had.

Systems thinking, as applied to the design and management of work, has its origins with W. Edwards Deming, the renowned management advisor to the Japanese during the American postwar reconstruction of their economy. Deming argued that our organisations, and thus our economies, were in crisis because of our beliefs in flawed management assumptions:

> Most people imagine that the present style of management has always existed, and is a fixture. Actually, it is a modern invention – a prison created by the way in which people interact. (Deming, 1994, xv)

His point was simple: we (mankind) invented management, we should reinvent it. His book (*Out of the Crisis*, 1982) included a scathing and detailed critique of Western management assumptions. His main targets for criticism were the use of arbitrary measures to govern the way we manage work, the management of separated functions independently within an organisation and the separation of decision making from the worker. The better alternative, he argued, was that we should understand and manage our organisations as systems.

At the same time as Deming was advising Japanese industry, Toyota's production genius, Taiichi Ohno, was the first person to break the mould of Western management thinking. He learned to manage Toyota as a system, developing the now fabled Toyota Production System (TPS). In his development of the TPS, Ohno made a series of startling counter-intuitive discoveries which represented challenges to management conventions. Ohno knew that Toyota could not gain competitive advantage by taking on its mass-producing US competitors (such as Ford and General Motors) at their own game – by attempting to achieve economies of scale. Through experimenting firstly with simple die-change techniques (ways of stamping metal sheets), Ohno was able to perfect the whole process until it could be reduced from taking one day down to three minutes. In doing so, he discovered that it cost less per part to make small batches of stampings than to produce in large batches: fewer units and greater variety actually meant lower costs. He found that true costs of production were end to end (from the start to the beginning of a process), and that more variation in his line left fewer parts tied up in inventories and work in progress. While the unit cost for each product was higher, the total production costs were considerably lower (Womack et al, 2007).

As Ohno demonstrated, systems thinking requires beginning with the study of work as a system. To echo Ohno, the first step has to be concerned with understanding. It was Ohno's favourite word:

> I believe it [understanding] has a specific meaning – to approach an objective positively and comprehend its nature. Careful inspection of any production area reveals waste and room for improvement. No one can understand manufacturing by just walking through the work area and looking at it. We have to see each area's role and function in the overall picture. (Ohno, 1988, 57)

To obtain understanding of a system, it is necessary to study the way it is designed and managed. Taking this different perspective surfaces any flaws in the management's current assumptions. To illustrate, we will describe briefly what is learned from studying one service – housing benefits – as a system.

Housing benefits service – viewed as a system

In the early years of the New Labour government, Gordon Brown, then Chancellor of the Exchequer, famously asserted that there would be no investment in public sector services without reform. The Department for Work and Pensions (DWP) persuaded him to invest £200 million in promulgating a new design for the delivery of housing benefits, a service provided to those in need by local authorities. It was one of the earliest attempts to impose a separate front/back-office design; the front being the means of access and the back being the place where claims are processed, with the two being connected via document image processing – documents received in the front office are scanned and sent electronically to the back office.

Included in the promulgated design were targets for the front office (how quickly people were seen, how quickly phones were picked up, how quickly documents were scanned and sent to the back office) and the back office (how quickly correspondence was responded to, how many work activities were done and the time it took to process a claim) (Figure 7.1).

Figure 7.1: The DWP-promulgated design for housing benefits

Targets
How quickly people are seen
How quickly phone calls are taken

Targets
Speed of response to correspondence
Time to calculate claims

Front office

Back office

Document image processor

When housing benefits services were studied as systems,[4] the flaws in the design became apparent. Studying demand revealed something that is intuitively obvious: no one arrives with all of the documentation one would need to establish eligibility and entitlement. But to conform to the targets, whatever is brought in is processed and sent off to the back office. The design led to backlogs in housing benefit offices all over the country. On the advice of the DWP, local authorities employed 'backlog-busting' services from the private sector, costing tens of millions of pounds. Much of this work was concerned with finding the various electronic 'work objects' belonging to a single case to create one 'work object' that could now be used to actually do the work (establish eligibility and entitlement). This activity was exacerbated by the problems associated with electronic identification ('work objects' are frequently lost) and thus people were often asked to bring in things that they had brought in before. To meet their activity targets, back-office workers were more inclined to send out letters of further forms requesting more information than to try to resolve the request. The consequence was that people turned up at the front office repeatedly in order to get their problems solved. It should be no surprise that managers felt compelled to put up posters announcing that any rudeness to staff would result in action by management.

The systems approach also reveals the true end-to-end time it takes for claimants to receive a service. It is typically an average of 50 days and it can take as long as six months. It is the design that is the cause of poor performance, and at the heart of the design is management by targets. It reveals a paradox: working to targets actually makes performance worse. But meeting targets is the way to win approval from inspectors.

The systems approach reveals what is going on in the system, with the biggest clue coming from studying demand – the demands claimants place on the system. There are two types of demand that interest a systems thinker: value demand and failure demand. Value demand is 'demand we want': demand that the service is there to provide for. In the case of housing benefits there are only two value demands: 'Can I make a claim?' and 'I have had a change in my circumstances'.

Failure demand is 'demand caused by a failure to do something or do something right for the customer' (Seddon, 2003). Progress chasing ('What has happened to my claim?', 'I don't understand how to fill in your form'), having to bring in things that have been brought in before, having to visit repeatedly – all of these represent demands, and therefore more work, caused by a failure of the service to work from the claimant's point of view. Typically, failure demand accounts for as much as 70% of the total demand in housing benefits services.

Studying demand reveals what a terrible service this is from the claimant's point of view. In a typical queue at a benefits front office it will be possible to find people who are turning up for the fifth, sixth and up to the tenth time. Often they have been told to bring something they have already provided, because it has been lost or is stuck in an electronic queue, waiting to be processed. It is typical to learn that as many as 20% of the documents held in the electronic system are duplicates. Greater diligence on the part of the workers providing the service will make no difference, as losing things is a system (design) problem.

The service standards in the front office lead to a preoccupation with seeing people quickly, meaning that claimants have to be processed as speedily as possible. If the quickest way to deal with the claimant is to send them off with a form or send them off home to get something else, that will be done. Meanwhile the back office becomes a repository of electronic 'work objects' and the job of the workers is to process a number of work objects each day. Much of this work is 're-work'; for example, finding the seven 'work objects' that belong to one claimant and bringing them together such that the proper work (systems thinkers call it 'value work') can begin. Each time a new piece of information comes in people have to start a case all over again, as there is no continuity or case ownership, so the worker has to ask: 'does this complete the picture?'. Most often the case is incomplete and so the back office workers send out requests for more information. As a consequence, the amount of work to be done in the 'back office' grows and the volume of failure demand in the front office also grows.

While the workers may be meeting their activity targets, the claimant is being bounced from pillar to post, time is going on and their problems are not being solved. The same phenomenon has been witnessed in local authorities all over the country; compliance with this design has created massive backlogs in the back offices. As well as employing private sector 'backlog busters' (solving the wrong problem), local authorities have been encouraged by the Audit Commission (an inspector turned specifier) and the Gershon (2004)[5] efficiency review to share and/or outsource back-office housing benefits services. It reflects the regime's belief in economies of scale. The systems approach reveals that sharing back offices will lead to high costs and poor service; having a back office is itself a design mistake.

The systems approach is to design against demand. It is a simple but profound idea; in practice, it means the customer should be able to 'pull value' (get what they want) from the system. Knowing the type and frequency of demands – why citizens make demands on the housing benefits service from their point of view – puts people in a position where they can design a service that works.

As already discussed, there are only two value demands in a housing benefits service: 'I want to make a claim' and 'my circumstances have changed'. The former will be used to illustrate the systems approach: 'I want to make a claim'. The claimant demand dictates the value work

– the things that need to be done to satisfy that demand. In this case the value work is:

- obtain 'clean' information (which fully completes the picture of the claimant's circumstances)
- make a decision
- notify the claimant
- pay (if entitled) the claimant.

Knowing the type and frequency of demands for claims, it makes practical sense to equip the people at the first point of contact with the necessary expertise to respond to the high-frequency predictable demands – demands which the organisation knows it can expect. That is to say, it makes no sense to train everybody in everything; but it does make sense to ensure that people are trained to deal with the bulk of the predictable work. When less frequent demands hit the system, people working at the point of contact 'pull' expertise from others in the organisation to help them provide service to what are, in effect, more unusual cases, for example self-employed people. This design principle keeps the ownership with the person providing the service and, consequently, speeds up their rate of learning – as they meet more 'less frequent' demands in their work they learn the skills and knowledge required to deal with them.

In practice many claims for benefits are tied up with people's council tax obligations; it follows that the expertise required to deal with the council tax implications must be designed into the roles of people who work with the claimant at the point of transaction.

Finally, to understand how well a service is working it is necessary to measure achievement of purpose from the claimant's point of view. It means measuring end-to-end time accurately, from when the claimant first presents to the point where they have received the correct money or been told they do not qualify. Typically, the result, when taking the systems approach, is that all benefits are processed in an average of three to six days. It is a result far beyond current targets (28 days); so far beyond that it would not be considered achievable if it had been set as a target.

Those that have followed the systems approach find themselves in difficulty with their inspectors. The inspectors inspect against their requirements, and in a systems design they cannot see the things they expect to see (target monitoring, plans for sharing services, etc). It should be no surprise that inspectors coerce managers to do what systems thinkers know to be the wrong things, the things they have been sent to monitor; to fail inspection does not look good in the 'targets and terror' regime.

The cost of failure

The failure demand found in housing benefits services is only part of the extraordinarily costly failure of services for the most vulnerable in society. A study conducted by Advice UK (Advice UK, 2008; 2009) shows that the failure of the DWP and Her Majesty's Revenue and Customs (HMRC) to provide their primary services leads to failure demand into advice agencies, local authorities, social landlords, legal services and the courts. The majority of the poor souls who are dragged through this experience are not penalised, because the judge can see the failure of the process. The most vulnerable people in society are treated in the most uncivilised way.

DWP and HMRC are flagship 'service factories': they represent, in the Treasury's view, the best of what is to come. These organisations have been industrialised, and industrialisation is creating distant, alienating and unresponsive services as well as unhappy, demoralised public service workers (*The Times*, 2007). Both DWP and HMRC have adopted 'lean management' techniques, wrongly being persuaded that the tools developed in the Toyota system, while solving problems associated with making cars at the rate of demand, have universal applicability (Seddon et al, 2010).

Chasing economy of scale is the wrong thing to do

> Contradicting what is said in virtually all operations management textbooks used in American universities, Toyota has demonstrated that it is possible to produce small quantities of product in high varieties at mass production costs. There is no longer any reason to rule out localization of economic activity on the grounds of scale economies. Scale economy, beyond very small volumes, is a concept that should be discarded. (Johnson, 2008, 102)

In industrialised designs, managers worry about the volume of work to be done, the number of people they have and how long people take to do things. Managers seek to reduce transaction costs by moving work to call centres and/or the internet; they seek to reduce training costs through specialising the workers and they use any means at their disposal to reduce activity times (scripts for workers, standardised routings for customers through their systems, putting services into IT systems, and so on). Managers are focused on costs and, as a consequence, they drive costs up. Studying these designs as systems reveals counter-intuitive truths.

Cost is in flow, not activity

At the heart of industrialisation is the management of workers' activity on the assumption that activity equals cost. Moving work to call centres, the separation of front office from back office, the specialisation of tasks and the standardisation of work are all management activities driven by this basic belief in the need to manage activity as cost. Paradoxically, managing costs drives costs up. The cost of a service is made up of all the transactions it takes for a customer to get a service.

Demand is the greatest lever for improvement

The industrialisation of services creates failure demand; often failure demand into public services runs as high as 80% or more of the total demand. It is an easy concept to understand and thus, unsurprisingly, it got the attention of the regime and, ironically, became the subject of a government target (National Indicator number 14) in itself. The regime made the mistake of believing that forcing public service managers to report failure demand (renamed 'avoidable contact') would encourage them to do something about it, when all it did was encourage them to under-report it. The target was unceremoniously dropped in April 2010, less than two years after its introduction.

To a systems thinker, demand is a temporary measure, something you measure to understand a problem rather than something you measure to control operations. Things always go wrong; understanding what is going wrong predictably leads to productive action, and only predictable failure demand is preventable (Seddon, 2009).

Studying value demand enables services to be designed from the user's point of view, enabling the user to 'pull value' – to get what they want. In that way, service improves as costs fall.

It is the system that accounts for performance

It is as Deming taught: 95% of variation in performance is due to the system (Deming, 1982). It shows the futility of managing workers' activity and refocuses management on their responsibility to design a system that delivers what customers need.

Any failure to absorb variety will drive up costs

An important feature of transactional services is the variety of demands they experience from their customers. Front-office/back-office splits, specialisation of work and standardisation of work prevent services from absorbing variety and thus these measures drive up costs (Middleton, 2010).

Systems thinkers set out to design a system to absorb the variety of customer demands. As discussed with the housing benefits example, the approach is to train workers against demand, to put them in control of their work – doing it as well as improving it – and to design management roles that are complementary to the work, where action is required on the system.

Reforming the regime

David Cameron has talked of a shift to redistribute power and control from regulation and bureaucracy to local communities, engendering greater 'responsibility' (Cameron, 2009). To reignite such responsibility would require recognition that the current regime fosters compliance rather than innovation. For innovation to flourish, it is necessary to change the locus of control away from the specifiers and inspectors, to those who have responsibility for providing the services. The very thing the reform regime has feared most (giving control to those they distrust) is the only productive way forward. Getting rid of the specifiers will lead to two types of savings: the cost of those jobs and the cost of adhering to the specifications (a much greater cost).

Seddon (2008) has argued that the Audit Commission should be reined back[6] to 'following the money' and that any inspection on matters of management should be limited to the inspector asking one question: 'What measures are you using to help you understand and improve the work?'. This would increase the reliability and validity of inspection, would rid the public sector of the costs of preparing for inspection (estimated, for example, at £2 million per local authority) and would actually make it harder for the incompetent to hide – whereas the reform regime has made it easier to just comply with the specifications and keep one's head down.

Adopting a systems approach is not about 'giving up control', as politicians at first fear. The fact of the matter is that public services are currently out of control, as every case of systems analysis has revealed across the public sector. For example, the reason Baby P was seen by so many people on so many occasions can be linked directly to compliance with the 'Integrated Children's System', an IT system to which services were obliged to comply and which dictated the way the service was designed and managed (Munro, 2005; White et al, 2009).

The design of Adult Social Care services is, like the design of children's services, an inhumane example of industrialisation. Adult Social Care (ASC) consists of services aimed at helping people to live as independently as possible. More than 1.5 million people use social care services in England. While the largest group of users for publicly funded social care are the over 65s, other groups of people in receipt of social care can include those with sensory impairments, physical or learning disabilities, terminal or mental illness, problems connected to ageing, alcohol or drug dependencies. Types of ASC services can include home care, day care, residential care, meals in the community (commonly known as 'meals on wheels'), car 'blue badges' for people with a permanent disability, equipment, and adaptations to help people live independently at home.

ASC services have been mandated to install call centres as a means of contact. Behind the call centres the separate functional services – occupational therapy, social work, home care, domiciliary care, meals on wheels, and so on – operate to their functional activity targets. Managers believe their main task to be to control the workers' caseloads. While a service may be meeting all of its activity targets, the experience of the user reveals a completely different story: many assessments covering much the same ground, extraordinarily long end-to-end times to receive a service and, as a consequence, many people deteriorate and are pushed into care homes (O'Donovan, 2010; Zokaei et al, 2010). When services are delivered at people's homes, they are often provided by outsourced means, with the service prescribed by the 'package' as contracted. What ought to be the thermostat in care provision does not function as such. Instead the contracting out of care delivers care in an arbitrary, time-based manner – for example, two baths a week, 30 minutes each – and will inevitably drive costs up as the service delivered fails to match the variety of need. Less activity time – as the adult becomes more independent – is not in the interests of the provider. More time – when needed – is beyond the control of the provider and will risk deterioration of the cared for and further (failure) demand on the care service. Redesigning care services using the systems approach both maintains people's independence in their communities and prevents the higher costs associated with (unwanted) residential care (Zokaei et al, 2010). The potential for improvement is huge – if only the wrong-headed ideas enforced by the reform regime's army of specifiers and inspectors can be removed.

Economy through flow – the relevance of localism

The economic improvements achieved by pioneers of systems thinking in the public sector are equivalent to those achieved by the Toyota system. By both learning to design services against demand and learning how to manage value to service users, managers have been able to drive out costs while improving their services. They recognise that demand is local, not national; it is also high variety, and thus can only be accommodated by people using their professional judgement, informed by data to take responsibility for improving their work. Local service delivered by local people using real measures of achievement of purpose from the user's point of view will give all in the system the freedom to innovate, and will also provide transparency to the served, the taxpayer and central government. Disciplined pluralism should replace central planning. Pioneering, systems-thinking councils have witnessed unintended consequences in the behaviour and engagement of local citizens, suggesting that better service design has the potential to lead to the greater involvement of communities in their local services (Seddon, 2008). The approach also has the advantage of being much cheaper. The savings accrued from no longer needing to pay for both the thousands of specifiers and the upward-reporting bureaucracy will provide an immediate and significant cost reduction. These savings, however, will be dwarfed by the benefits of ceasing to comply with the ideologically driven command-and-control ideas.

Conclusion: managing public services in austerity requires study of our systems

In the face of high public debt and with a political consensus on the need for cuts, systems thinking offers a fairer and more intelligent way of using resources. Significant efficiency savings have been achieved by those who have followed the systems approach. Local authority housing repairs, planning, housing benefits and road repairs departments have all made savings of between 20% and 40%: remarkable amounts when compared with official government efficiency targets (Seddon, 2008). This is without considering the aforementioned sizeable returns from dismantling the inspection regime itself. However, if the government opts for a crude approach to cost cutting, it is likely to find that its costs go up elsewhere: to drive costs out from a system, one needs to first understand the causes of costs. The starting point for any systems success must be to study the demands being placed on services. It is the duty of politicians and public sector managers to study their own systems so that they can establish for themselves the scope for improvement and the challenges to their thinking. Following citizens' demands through the various service providers illustrates powerfully how services are fragmented and brings into clear view the ways in which central requirements impede service delivery and create costs. From this position a constructive change can occur. Those who seek cost reductions will fail, yet, paradoxically, cost reductions are a by-product of a better systems design for work. For the politicians who are far sighted and courageous enough to break free of over 30 years of ideological assumptions about public management, the rewards on offer promise to be substantial.

Notes

[1] John Nash, quoted in the *Guardian*, 3 March 2007.

[2] Sir Anthony Jay, one of the writers, was an avowed fan of public choice economics and has admitted that it lay at the root of nearly every episode of the comedy (Tullock et al, 2000).

[3] Although a systems thinker would recognise gaming to be endemic and ubiquitous – see Seddon (2008).

[4] For more detail on the analysis of housing benefits as a system see Seddon (2008).

[5] Blond (2010) has adopted some of these systems concepts further, combining the necessary reintroduction of responsibility of a systems design with the idea that there should be mutual ownership of organisations based around sound knowledge of local demand as part of his vision for 'Red Toryism'.

[6] Eric Pickles, the Coalition's Community Secretary, announced in August 2010 that the Audit Commission will close in 2012 – a move Seddon had long called for as a major step towards the required dismantling of the inspection regime.

References

Ackoff, R. (2004) 'Transforming the Systems Movement', paper (downloadable from www.acasa.upenn.edu/RLAConfPaper.pdf accessed 9 December 2009).

Advice UK (2008) *It's the System, Stupid! Radically Rethinking Advice*, London: AdviceUK (downloadable from www.adviceuk.org.uk, accessed 7 April 2009).

Advice UK (2009) *Interim Report: Radically Rethinking Advice Services in Nottingham*, London: AdviceUK.

Barber, M. (2007) *Instruction to Deliver*, London: Portico's Publishing.

Bevan, G. and Hood, C. (2006) 'Have targets improved performance in the English NHS?', *British Medical Journal*, vol 332, 18 February.

Blond, P. (2009) *The Ownership State*, London: ResPublica/NESTA.

Blond, P. (2010) *Red Tory*, London: Faber and Faber.

Buchanan, J.M. (1978) *From Private Preferences to Public Philosophy: The Development of Public Choice*, Institute of Economic Affairs Readings 18, London: IEA.

Cameron, D. (2009) 'The Big Society', Hugo Young Lecture, 10 November.

Chandler, A.D. (1977) *The Visible Hand*, London: Belknap Press.

Chase, R.B. (1978), 'Where does the customer fit in a service operation?', *Harvard Business Review*, vol 56, no 4, pp. 137–42.

Cope, S. and Goodship, J. (2002) 'The Audit Commission: Delivering for Whom?', *Public Money and Management*, October–December, pp 33–40.

DCLG (Department for Communities and Local Government) (2006) *Mapping the Local Government Performance Reporting Landscape*, Wetherby: CLG Publications.

Deming, W.E. (1982) *Out of the Crisis*, Cambridge, MA: MIT Press.

Deming, W.E. (1994) *The New Economics: For Industry, Government, Education*, Cambridge, MA: MIT Press.

Dunleavy, P., Margetts, H., Bastow, S. and Tinkler, J. (2006) 'New Public Management Is Dead – Long Live Digital-Era Governance', *Journal of Public Administration Research and Theory*, vol 16, pp 467–94.

Ford, H. ([1926] 2003) *Today and Tomorrow*, Oxford: CRC Press.

Gershon, P. (2004) *Releasing Resources to the Front Line: Independent Review of Public Sector Efficiency*, London: HM Treasury, www.hm-treasury.gov.uk/media/C/A/efficiency_review120704.pdf, accessed 9 December 2009.

Ghoshal, S. (2005) 'Bad management theories are destroying good management practices', *Academy of Management Learning and Education*, vol 4, no 1, pp 75–91.

Guardian (2006) 'More Power to the People Urges Miliband', 21 February.

Guardian (2007) 'Cry Freedom', 3 March.

HM Government (2009) *Building Britain's Future*, London: HM Government.

HM Treasury (2009) *Operational Efficiency Programme: Final Report*, London: HM Treasury.

Hood, C. (2006) 'Gaming in Targetworld: The Targets Approach to Managing British Public Services' *Public Administration Review*, July–August, pp 419-22.

Hudson, J. and Lowe, S. (2004) *Understanding the Policy Process: Analysing Welfare Policy and Practice*, Bristol: The Policy Press.

Jackson, M. (2000) *Systems Approaches to Management*, New York: Kluwer/Plenum.

Jackson, M. (2003) *Systems Thinking: Creative Holism for Managers*, Chichester: Wiley and Sons.

Jackson, M., Johnstone, N. and Seddon, J. (2007) 'Evaluating Systems Thinking in Housing', *Journal of the Operational Research Society*, no 59, pp 186–97.

Johnson, H.T. (2008) 'Lean Management and True Sustainability', in *The Lean Manufacturing Yearbook*, Michigan: Society of Manufacturing Engineers.

Le Grand, J. (2003) *Motivation, Agency and Public Policy: Of Knights and Knaves, Pawns and Queens*, Oxford: Oxford University Press.

LGA (Local Government Association) (2009) *Delivering More for Less: Maximising Value in the Public Sector*, London: LGA Publications.

McQuade, D. (2008) 'Leading Lean Action to Transform Housing Services', *Public Money and Management*, vol 28, no 1.

Middleton, P. (2010) *Delivering Public Services that Work*, Volume 1, *Systems Thinking in the Public Sector*, Axminster: Triarchy Press.

Munro, E. (2005) 'A Systems Approach to Investigating Children Abuse Deaths', *British Journal of Social Work*, vol 35, pp 531–46.

Niskanen, W. (1994) *Bureaucracy and Public Economics*, Cheltenham: Edward Elgar.

O'Donovan, B. (2010, forthcoming) 'Systems Thinking in Adult Social Care', in Z. Zokaei, J. Seddon and B. O'Donovan (eds) *Systems Thinking: From Theory to Practice*, Basingstoke: Palgrave Macmillan.

ODPM (Office of the Deputy Prime Minister) (2005) *A Systematic Approach to Service Improvement: Evaluating Systems Thinking in Housing*, London: ODPM.

Ohno, T. (1988) *Toyota Production System*, Portland, OR: Productivity Press. (Translated from Japanese, first published 1978.)

Seddon, J. (2003) *Freedom from Command and Control*, Buckingham: Vanguard Press.

Seddon, J. (2008) *Systems Thinking and the Public Sector,* Axminster: Triarchy.

Seddon, J. (2009) 'Failure Demand – from the horse's mouth', *Customer Strategy*, vol 2, no 1, pp 33–4.

Seddon, J., O'Donovan, B. and Zokaei, K. (2010, forthcoming) *Rethinking Lean Service*, London: Springer.

Taylor, F.W. ([1911] 1998) *The Principles of Scientific Management*, New York: Dover Publications.

The Times (2007) 'Is this banana active?', 5 January.

Tullock, G., Seldon, A. and Brady, G.L. (2000) 'Government: Whose Obedient Servant? A Primer in Public Choice', The Institute of Economic Affairs, Readings 51, London: IEA.

White, S., Wastell, D., Broadhurst, K., Peckover, S., Davey, D. and Pithouse, A. (2010) 'Children's services and the iron cage of performance management: street-level bureaucracy and the spectre of Svejkism', *International Journal of Social Welfare*, vol 19, no 3, July, pp 310–20.

Womack, J.P., Jones, D.T. and Roos, D. ([1990] 2007) *The Machine that Changed the World*, New York: Macmillan.

Zokaei, Z., Elias, S., O'Donovan, B., Samuel, D., Evans, B. and Goodfellow, J. (2010) 'Lean and Systems Thinking in the Public Sector in Wales', Lean Enterprise Research Centre report for the Wales Audit Office, Cardiff University.

EIGHT

Choice, empowerment, personalisation: taking forward public services in a recession?

Tim Brown and Nicola Yates

Introduction

There is a political consensus. The three main parties in England support the principles of choice, empowerment and personalisation for users of public services. They also recognise that there is a growing need for these services. At the same time, there is an acceptance that there must be severe public expenditure controls over the next decade to deal with the impact of the financial crisis and to plan for the upturn. The Conservative–Liberal Democrat coalition agreement in May 2010 prioritised deficit reduction and a commitment to £6 billion cuts in non-front-line services in 2010–11. Nevertheless, they contend that front-line services can be protected, if not enhanced (Conservative Liberal Democrat Coalition, 2010).

Choice, empowerment and personalisation are embedded in the public sector. Simmons et al (2009) illustrate their central role in health, social housing, education and social care. In relation to the health sector, it includes choice of GP and appointment times. In social housing, the government set a target in 2002 that all local authority allocations systems should be using choice-based lettings by the end of 2010 (although the 'terror' of targets in systems has been discussed in the Chapter Seven). In education, the focus has centred on choice and type of school. From a social care viewpoint, personalisation through individual budgets has become a mainstream policy. 'Choice', 'empowerment' and 'personalisation' are, however, terms that are often used in an unsatisfactory, interchangeable way. For the purpose of clarity, we use 'choice' to refer to the opportunities for users to choose the content and level of service, the provider and form of access. 'Empowerment' relates to the provision of information so that the user has knowledge of what is on offer, by whom and how. The state has a major role in performing this enabling function. 'Personalisation' refers to the ability of the user to actively make informed decisions, that is, operationalising the concept of choice.

Nevertheless, the implementation of choice, empowerment and personalisation has not been straightforward over the last decade, during a period of relative economic prosperity. There will, thus, be further challenges during the recession. There is already compelling evidence that it has and will continue to generate additional need for public services over and above long-term trends created, for example, by the demographic time bomb of an increasing ageing population. Cut-backs in public expenditure are likely to be severe. Budgets for some services face a reduction of 20–30% over the next few years (CIPFA and SOLACE, 2009). This poses a major issue for the belief that a customer-orientated approach to services can be protected – a conviction that was, nevertheless, reiterated in the Conservative–Liberal Democrat coalition agreement (2010). Back- and front-office services are not independent but are fundamentally interrelated. Customer relationship management is a topical subject in the public sector, as it has the potential to deliver services that the consumer wants at a time and place when demanded (Richardson, 2010). However, it requires substantial investment in back-office information and communications technology and staff training. There are significant upfront costs that are only likely to be recuperated in the long term.

This chapter draws on the research and experiences of the two authors in taking forward the choice, empowerment and personalisation agenda over the previous decade. This has focused, in particular, on choice-based lettings and social care. It also draws on work in Kingston-upon-Hull, which is a port city of 250,000 population in the Yorkshire and Humber Region. The chapter begins by critically outlining the development of the agenda, including an analysis of the issues. This is followed by a review of the existing state of play on choice, empowerment and personalisation. The explicit implications of the financial crisis are then considered. The prospects for taking forward this agenda during and after the recession are analysed. We argue that there is and should be a future for choice, empowerment and personalisation. But it must be aligned with new ideas and thinking on public services that are most likely to emerge at the local level.

Development of choice, empowerment and personalisation

There are a number of books and articles that have critically explored developments in choice, empowerment and personalisation over the last few decades. There are also specific studies on particular services. An example of the former is the work associated with the Economic and Social Research Council programme on the cultures of consumption. Simmons et al (2009) argue that customer choice is a gross oversimplification of a much more complex set of developments associated with consumerism. They point out that public services must recognise the differentiated customer and community. People are customers, citizens and members of communities. They demand and need services in different ways and for a multiplicity of reasons. At the same time, there is a well-established perspective that the public expect better services at less cost. Cole and Parston (2006) argue that a citizen-centric approach has fundamental implications for elected officials, senior managers and front-line staff. The demand for better services equates with a greater degree of choice, empowerment and personalisation in the way they are accessed and delivered as well as in their substantive content. Think-tanks frequently promote the benefits of these ideas. For example, authors contributing to a publication by Demos on liberation welfare recommend an extension of individual budgets and personalisation from social care to include health, education and employment (Gregg and Cooke, 2010)

In relation to the latter, there has been a continuing programme of research on, for instance, social care and individual budgets (see, for example, Glasby and Littlechild, 2002; 2009). This initiative started on a small scale in the early 1970s through the Independent Living Movement, driven in part by customers and their advocates who were dissatisfied with the shortcomings of directly provided services for vulnerable people. Its principles include, firstly, that anyone, whatever the nature of their impairment, is capable of exercising choice; secondly, people with disabilities have the right to participate fully in society; and thirdly, the rejection of the medical model of disability and its replacement by the social model. In England this resulted in the government moving forward on this issue. In relation to adult social care, councils have been set a target that those receiving services should be entitled to a personalised individual budget (Department of Health, 2009a). This has led to challenges for professionals and managers faced with a culture change in service provision. It is exemplified by the frequently quoted example of Gavin Croft, who spent part of his personal budget for season tickets to Rochdale Football Club for himself and a friend (Hunt, 2009). It proved to be a cost-effective form of respite care for his wife, despite cynics suggesting that this type of activity would discredit the personal budget system.

This is not to suggest that choice, empowerment and personalisation is an uncontested area of public policy. Clarke (2010) argues that while a lack of choice can be frustrating, its constant extension is overwhelming. Le Grand (2007) has identified a diverse range of criticisms, which include that people don't want choice. Drawing on the work of Schwartz (2004), he noted that consumers in the private sector find excessive choice demotivating. He further pointed out that there is a widely held view that choice is a middle-class issue, even though there is considerable empirical evidence to the contrary. Finally, Le Grand suggested that there is an intellectual tradition associated with left-of-centre politics that is suspicious of choice. This, in part, stems from a belief that this programme has been engineered by right-wing politicians who have coupled it with competition and quasi-markets. A variant on this perspective is the assumption that it is a hidden agenda which leads to the transfer of costs from the state to the individual. These viewpoints can be countered. For example, there is a neglected tradition within the labour movement of ethical and Christian socialism based on the independence of and choice for individuals (Brown, 1999).

There are three interrelated messages that emerge from the literature on choice, empowerment and personalisation. Firstly, it is important to avoid a simplistic interpretation. There is little merit in debating, as Le Grand (2007) notes, the assertion that 'the users of public services do not in fact want choice, they require instead a good service'. The reality is that quality of service is influenced by three factors, including elements of choice. These are whether it is 'fit for purpose', such as a housing repair completed so that it functions satisfactorily. There is the process of empowerment, that is, the customer is able to choose a time that is suitable for the work to be undertaken. There is the perception of the organisation, that is, it is regarded as customer friendly. A service can only be good or high quality if all three elements are achieved. A more pertinent focus is, therefore, the extent to which the Labour government's policy between 1997 and 2010 on public services was achievable. John Hutton, a former Cabinet Office minister, stated:

> Greater personal choice, individually tailored services, stronger local accountability, greater efficiency – these are all central to the new direction of travel that we have set for our public services. (Hutton, 2005)

A key issue is the degree to which these objectives, especially choice, empowerment and personalisation, can be delivered during a recession.

Secondly, there is the policy development and innovation dimension. In England, there has been an emphasis on government and regulatory targets – a command-and-control approach (see Seddon and O'Donovan, Chapter Seven). All councils are required to be operating a choice-based lettings system in social housing allocations by the end of 2010, and the Department for Communities and Local Government (2009) has issued prescriptive guidance. This reduces the opportunities for local innovation. But choice-based lettings did not suddenly and mysteriously appear in the government Housing Green Paper in April 2000. Instead, they emerged through a complex process of policy transfer from the Netherlands, linked with innovative schemes in England and Wales that were initiated by councils and housing associations (Brown et al, 2000). Public expenditure cuts could result in top-down prescriptive agendas on choice, empowerment and personalisation or lead to local innovation.

Finally, choice, empowerment and personalisation need to be located within the modernisation of government agenda, especially breaking down departmental silos (see Sullivan, Chapter Nine). The experience of the authors on choice-based lettings is illustrative of this issue (Brown and Yates, 2005). Greater choice during the lettings process is generally welcomed by customers because of its transparency as compared with traditional allocations systems. But it is highly circumscribed because of the lack of affordable housing of the right type in a suitable location. One way of addressing this issue is by aligning choice-based lettings with advice services that are run by public, private and voluntary sector agencies, that is, empowering customers with information to make informed decisions. A person's housing problems may be able to be resolved more effectively through, say, tenancy support and/or housing adaptations than by exercising choice through bidding on a limited number of advertised properties. More radically, housing difficulties may be a symptom rather than a cause. There may be underlying challenges faced by a household because of multiple debts or the need for social care. Joined-up thinking is needed, for instance, to link choice-based lettings with individual budgets in social care. This requires collaboration and partnership working between many organisations, which is a mantra of the modernisation of government agenda. But it often remains an ideal rather than a reality. The public expenditure cut-backs are resulting in two different outcomes: (1) a retreat back into silo thinking, or (2) effective collaboration leading to innovative solutions. Prescriptive guidance and targets set by the government will lead to the former.

Existing state of play

As has already been pointed out, the three main political parties in England support the principles of choice, empowerment and personalisation. The Labour government pledged to protect front-line services during the recession (HM Government, 2009). Principles included guaranteeing high-quality public services, using technology to ensure personalisation of services and empowering people to take an active role in improving their own life chances. The Conservative Party in its 'vision for Britain' emphasised that people expect to be able to make more decisions for themselves. 'Advancing opportunity means shifting power from the state to individuals and civic institutions, in order to open up this new world of freedom to everyone' (Conservative Party, 2009). The Liberal Democrats, in a policy paper, set down the principles for a mandatory universal service code to ensure high-quality standards for both the public and private sectors (Policy Projects Team, 2009). It included a commitment to 'ensure that people are able to make informed choices'. These ideas were re-emphasised during the general election in 2010. The Labour Party (2010) stressed the 'right to choose your own GP', 'more personal care with the right in law to choose from any provider ...', and a 'choice of good schools in every area'. The Conservative Party (2010, 45–6) in its general election manifesto stated:

> So we will give every patient the power to choose any healthcare provider that meets NHS standards, within NHS prices ... We will make patients' choices meaningful by:
>
> - Putting patients in charge of making decisions about their care, including control of their health records;
> - Spreading the use of the NHS tariff, so funding follows patients' choices.

The Liberal Democrat Manifesto (Liberal Democrats, 2010) included commitments to 'giving every patient the right to choose to register with the GP they want ...', and to 'introduce a universal service code to secure high quality customer service in the private and public sectors, for example, by requiring that the customer service phone number is free from mobiles and landlines'.

This consensus on choice, empowerment and personalisation derives, in part, from the findings of evaluation studies (see, for example, Glasby and Littlechild, 2002; 2009). Although few, if any, studies have explicitly addressed the implications of the recession, it is possible to draw out emerging issues. In the case of choice-based lettings, there have been two government-commissioned evaluations as well as a significant number of studies on individual schemes. Customers value the transparency and straightforwardness of the process as compared to the previous traditional approach, which involved customers waiting to be allocated a property that was deemed by officers to be suitable. They have been empowered through the provision of information on the lettings process and on the properties that are available. It has not been uncommon for over 70% of households that are able to compare the two approaches to state a preference for choice-based lettings (Brown and Yates, 2005). However, customers are less satisfied with the outcomes of making choices through individual decision making. This is because of the growing imbalance in the social housing market. Households on housing registers increased from 1 million in 1997 to over 1.8 million in 2009. This has created an unprecedented demand for affordable housing. Even in a city such as Hull, which had been regarded as having a low-demand housing market with a number of difficult-to-let council estates, the average number of responses to adverts in the first half of 2009 through its choice-based lettings scheme was 40. In the case of houses, the average figure was over 55 bids for each advertised property. This is not surprising, as the housing register comprised 10,300 households, which represented over 10% of all households in the city. As Brown and King (2005) have argued, the reality of operationalising choice is extremely limited.

The situation of need outstripping supply and the resultant limitation of choice in social housing has been exacerbated during the financial crisis. Brown and Murphy (2009) point out that nearly 60% of councils in a survey in 2009 were experiencing a rise in the need for social housing, while a further 30% expected to do so. In such circumstances, the appropriateness and relevance of choice-based lettings is further called into question. This has resulted in seven local authorities in England deciding not to implement a scheme, despite the national target (see above). Portsmouth City Council argued that encouraging households to actively participate in the bidding process was inappropriate, as the majority were unlikely to be successful in the foreseeable future. Instead, the local authority has focused on enhancing its advice and options service to provide households with support in making better-informed decisions to address their housing problems. A useful contrast can be drawn between choice-based lettings schemes that merely enable customers to make bids on advertised properties and those that are aligned with housing advice services that provide opportunities for households to operationalise choice through information, personalisation and individual decision making. Nevertheless, in both cases outcomes are heavily circumscribed because demand for service outstrips supply, especially as a result of the recession and public expenditure cuts.

Implications of the financial crisis

So far, this chapter has highlighted the political consensus in moving forward on choice, empowerment and personalisation. National policies, targets and pilot programmes are well established and have been implemented despite the recession and the financial crisis. For instance, individual budgets are a core theme in social care policy, with a target that people in receipt of council welfare services will have this option (Department of Health, 2009a). At the local level, there are innovative empowerment initiatives to enable vulnerable people to make decisions about their health and social care needs, that is, personalisation. In 2009 Hull City Council and NHS Hull (formerly Hull Teaching Primary Care Trust) jointly launched a three-year telecare and e-health programme. There has been an emphasis on information and education so that customers and their formal and informal carers can make decisions. Specific projects include a 'safe and sound' programme that involves life-style monitoring for people with dementia so that they have the confidence to live independently if they wish to do so. Similarly, vulnerable people can use their existing television to access bespoke information on health and social care, such as advice on fall prevention and staying well in cold weather. Empowerment and personalisation through information enables people to make choices about their quality of life and take responsibility for their life-style.

But the financial crisis has brought into stark relief the challenges of choice, empowerment and personalisation. The individual is a consumer, a citizen and a member of a community and wishes to exercise choice in different ways and by a range of mechanisms. Empowerment is facilitated through the provision of information and advice. Personalisation involves making informed decisions on the choices available. But will a range of choices exist? For instance, will telecare and e-health services be available to an older person wishing to be discharged from hospital and return home to a safe, secure and homely environment rather than being transferred to institutional accommodation? Will information and advice on these services be on hand to empower an older person to make informed personal decisions? If the answer to these questions is 'no', then the relevance of choice, empowerment and personalisation becomes marginalised. There would be a retreat back towards providers retaining power, firstly, by limiting the range of services available and, secondly, through the control of knowledge at the expense of the customer, that is, a gatekeeping function. The challenge is whether a cost-driven (referred to by Leach and Roberts in Chapter Six as 'slash and burn') or customer-centric system will prevail.

Recessions also result in an increased need for public services, while the demand for private sector services decreases (see Richardson, Chapter Five). Yet it is the public sector that faces expenditure cuts. Reference has been made to the growth in size of housing registers. There is also an increased need for other public services, such as debt advice, help in tackling mortgage arrears and repossessions, and support for maximising welfare benefits. The Commission for Rural Communities' study on financial exclusion found that the Citizens Advice Bureau reported a 3.1% increase in debt cases in rural areas as compared to 1.4% in urban areas in the second half of 2008. In sparsely populated rural areas the increase was over 20% (Commission for Rural Communities, 2009). It also pointed out that the nature of the debt problem had changed, as affluent middle-income households were increasingly seeking advice because of negative equity and problems over mortgage payments. The Equality and Human Rights Commission (2009) highlighted that people from ethnic minority groups have disproportionately been affected by unemployment since the start of the recession. The Caribbean and African community has seen unemployment levels rise from 13.2% in the first quarter of 2008, to 20.1% in the third quarter of 2009. This compares with a 2.8% rise in white unemployment, from 4.8% to 7.6%, over the same period. The Work Foundation has emphasised that it is low-skill cities and neighbourhoods that are struggling most with the recession (Jones et al, 2009). The Audit Commission (2009) similarly concluded that low-skilled jobs have been most affected and these are often concentrated in deprived neighbourhoods. From a geographical perspective, it pointed out that councils in the West Midlands and Yorkshire and the Humber regions have been most affected. Not only is there an aggregate need for more public services, but also provision has to be differentiated to reflect continued and new demands, as well as taking account of the geography of the recession. At the same time, there is an expectation among the main political parties that front-line services can at least be maintained if not improved through choice, empowerment and personalisation.

The crisis in public expenditure is well known. It is estimated by CIPFA and SOLACE (2009) that some services face a cut of 20–30% over the next 5 years. To this, however, has to be added the challenges in funding transformations in, for instance, social care. The Department of Health (2009b) labelled this as the 'big debate' in its Green Paper on Shaping the Future of Care Together. It is estimated that 1.7 million adults will require care services by 2026. Attention has been paid to ideas such as a national care service, a greater role for the NHS and merging commissioning functions. A more effective balance between national and local funding has also been stressed. On the one hand, there is the option of a fully funded national system to provide universal assessments and avoid a postcode lottery. Alternatively, there are possibilities of developing a part-national and part-local funding approach, so enabling councils and their partners to decide resource allocation on delivering agreed levels of care. A former director of social services, and now professor of social work, is quoted as stating 'with the perils of the current recession, the timing could not be worse for an informed debate about the future of social care' (see Dunton, 2009). This comment applies equally to discussions on taking forward the choice, empowerment and personalisation agenda in other public service areas.

Lastly, there is the capacity of the public sector to respond to the twin challenges of the recession and the choice, empowerment and personalisation agenda. The Audit Commission (2009) commented that councils have taken low-risk steps to provide services to support vulnerable households during the recession. It noted, however, that considerable variation existed over the appropriateness and quality of these interventions. It was not optimistic over future initiatives, as there was a failure to understand the trajectory of the recession. The Audit Commission considered that the multiplicity of national schemes created confusion and uncertainty, as well as failing to reflect and acknowledge local circumstances. It concluded that local interventions can be quicker and more effective, but are often difficult to design. This can be illustrated in relation to tackling mortgage repossessions. There were a number of government schemes set up during 2008 and 2009. However, an analysis of repossession data and cases in Hull indicated that the majority of affected households would not benefit (Brown, 2008). The number of repossession cases increased from 360 to 815 per year between 2003 and 2008. The characteristics of mortgagees affected by possible repossession in Hull were diverse. They included households that were dissolving through divorce/separation and were unable to sell a property at a sufficient price to pay off the existing mortgage, households that have had to borrow additional money (often from a different lender to the main mortgagor) to fund urgent repair work, and people struggling with multiple debts, including credit cards. There was anecdotal evidence of households voluntarily 'handing back the keys' to the lender, and, in extreme cases, abandoning their home. Because of the scale of the problem, Hull was one of 20 local authority areas where the government targeted additional funding on advice. The council and its partners responded through the Hull Community Legal Advice Centre, which provides a housing repossession court duty scheme. In its first year of operation it helped 277 households at risk of repossession and eviction. From a choice, empowerment and personalisation perspective, the scheme enabled the Community Legal Advice Centre to provide advice to households so that they could make more informed decisions on the most appropriate choice of actions. Even so, these choices are heavily constrained because of the reactive nature of this 'last-ditch' advice. A more proactive advice service is required so as to empower households early in their housing careers to make informed decisions on the choices that are available, such as owner occupation, shared ownership, private renting or social housing.

Prospects for choice, empowerment and personalisation

The recession has generated a passionate debate on the future direction for public services. This caught the media's attention in the latter part of 2009, with the contrast drawn between an 'easyBorough' model loosely based on Easyjet and Ryanair and a 'John Lewis' approach centred on mutuality. The former espouses a basic low-cost set of public services with an opportunity for the consumer to pay more for additional services. The latter focuses on the customer and the provider working together to design and deliver services. Although there is merit in popularising what can appear to be turgid debates on public service reform, there is danger of gross simplification, as well as of a failure to explore the similarities as well as the differences. It is, of course, not the function of this section to provide an overview of alternative models for public services. Instead, the objective is to consider the implications of five different but not mutually exclusive ideas for the prospects for choice, empowerment and personalisation. These are:

- service retrenchment
- a return to the traditional welfare model of delivery
- libertarian paternalism
- a two-tier approach (including the easyBorough model) and
- mutualism and co-production.

In each case, the idea is outlined along with its application and implications for choice, empowerment and personalisation.

Retrenchment

Much of the debate on the future of public services ignores possible retrenchment by reducing eligibility for services. This should not be dismissed out of hand as it was commonplace in previous recessions. It is associated with departmentalism and a silo mentality. The reasonable preference categories used in social housing allocations could be tightened, as could be the criteria for access to social care services. The option of a national care service funded centrally, highlighted in the Social Care Green Paper (Department of Health, 2009b), could pave the way for this type of approach by introducing strict eligibility criteria. A variant of this theme is retrenchment between (as well as within) services. As has already been pointed out, there is a consensus among the three main political parties in England on a degree of financial protection to education and schools, the NHS and the police. The corollary is that other services, such as housing and social care, face more drastic cut-backs in public expenditure (CIPFA and SOLACE, 2009) (Rosewell et al, 2009) and even tighter constraints for customers on access to services.

From the choice, empowerment and personalisation perspectives, it would be too simplistic to argue that it would represent their nemesis. Choice would exist for those deemed eligible, but its scope would be restricted to a limited number of people. Empowerment through advice and information would be available only to those entitled to receive services, who would then be able to make informed decisions. The agenda would, thus, be highly differentiated. For example, many health service customers would continue to be able to select GPs and hospitals, as well as having individual budgets. But opportunities for choice, empowerment and personalisation in social care and through choice-based lettings would be reduced.

Retrenchment would represent a victory for a cost-driven approach to tackling the public expenditure crisis at the expense of a customer-centric viewpoint. The possibilities of pooled budgets and holistic thinking between health, housing and social care provision, for instance, would be reduced. The ability of a vulnerable person leaving hospital to be empowered to make individual decisions on a range of choices on care in the community would be reduced. Extra-care housing and a return to a former home with support are less liable to be available, compared to institutional accommodation.

Return to welfare

The era of large public sector bureaucracies implementing common universal policies was a characteristic feature of the 1960s and 1970s, but it could make a comeback with the recession. A return to the traditional welfare model of delivery poses a challenge for choice, empowerment and personalisation. It is based on managers, administrators and professionals allocating scarce resources by determining eligibility for a specific service. Of course, aspects of this approach have continued to be present during the last decade, despite the rise of a customer orientation in public services. Eligibility for social care is strongly influenced by administrative decisions on the degree of need. In an environment of public expenditure cuts, the gate-keeping function potentially becomes even more paramount. The availability of a range of service options would be drastically reduced, as would information and advice services. Empowerment leading to personalisation would be replaced by a model based on professional and managerial expertise in assessing the degree of need and identifying the most appropriate service from a limited short-list.

A return to this earlier model of service delivery addresses an issue raised by Le Grand (2007), who argued that traditional left-of-centre politics often expresses concerns over the choice agenda because of its association with Thatcherism. However, a return to the traditional welfare approach would recreate the well-researched problems associated with the postwar bureaucratic model of an undifferentiated service managed in a paternalistic manner by officers and professionals, that is, 'a one-size-fits-all' approach, irrespective of individual needs and desires. Deference rather than choice, empowerment and personalisation would characterise the user experience. The New Economics Foundation (2009) has referred to this model as the 'supplicant state'. Again, this type of approach is cost driven rather than customer-centric.

Libertarian paternalism

This has received prominence through the work of Halpern (2010) and Thaler and Sunstein (2009). They argue that the state has a significant role in influencing customer and citizen behaviour. Thaler and Sunstein highlight that it is a legitimate role for governments to try to influence individual behaviour while, at the same time, maintaining or extending freedom of choice. Halpern cites the importance of using the principles of behavioural economics in shaping the actions of individuals. He suggests that the state has a significant role in influencing citizens, firstly, where behaviour adversely affects the community (for example anti-social behaviour) and, secondly, where the costs fall on the individual (for example obesity). In each local authority area there are a relatively small number of households that face a multiplicity of problems such as poor health outcomes, low educational attainment, persistent unemployment and difficult conduct. This has been highlighted in a number of the government's 'total place' pilots, which have investigated the potential for aligning different funding streams to provide better services. The Birmingham case study showed that a small number of people incur high costs, for example, 6% of children are permanently excluded from schools and this costs, on an individual basis, £12,250 in additional services (Be Birmingham, 2010).

Traditionally, the emphasis has been direct state intervention, but an alternative is to try to change behaviour through imperceptible nudges. These principles can be translated into action by 'nudging' the customer through setting the context for individual decision making. This is sometimes referred to as 'choice architecture', which is defined as a user-friendly policy that improves the quality of decisions made by individuals. Officers and professionals move from being gatekeepers to 'choice architects' in the way, for example, that they make information and advice available to customers. Unlike the traditional paternalistic approach of the postwar welfare state, Thaler and Sunstein emphasise, choices are not blocked off or constrained. Instead, the focus is on empowering individuals to make decisions to improve their lives without adversely affecting the rest of the community. There are, thus, strong links between libertarian paternalism and choice, empowerment and personalisation.

At a practical level, Thaler and Sunstein (2009) highlight the importance of 'nudges' as a set of tools to encourage individual decision making. They can take the form of information and advice, that is, empowerment. An example of the growth of this type of action is social marketing (Kotler and Lee, 2008). In England, a National Social

Marketing Centre has been set up as a strategic partnership between the Department of Health and Consumer Focus (formerly the National Consumer Council). At a local level, NHS Hull has initiated a series of social marketing campaigns to raise individual awareness of health issues to 'nudge' people to make informed decisions. The Director of Public Health commented:

> It was important for us to gain insight into people's understanding and opinions on health, such as why they act as they do and what services they need, before communicating with them ... Using the results of our research we have created engaging and stimulating campaigns that will appeal directly to people who actively want a healthier lifestyle, as well as those who haven't previously thought about changing their habits. (Richardson, 2009)

From a choice, personalisation and empowerment perspective, libertarian paternalism attempts to influence individual behaviour and decision making by the provision of information rather than by directing customer conduct. But there is a tension between nudging and dictating behaviour and choices. Where, for example, does one end and the other begin? To what extent is 'nudge' a cost-driven or a customer-centric approach?

Two-tier approach

During 2009, there was extensive media coverage of developments in service provision in the Conservative-controlled London boroughs of Barnet and Hammersmith and Fulham. These have been parodied as representing a Ryanair or Easyjet model for public services. The basic principle is that there are two levels of service. Firstly, there is a minimum level to which the public is entitled. Secondly, there are areas where residents can opt for differing levels of service. Examples of the latter might include waste collection and the development control part of the planning service. But there are legal issues over whether some of these types of change are possible. The London Borough of Barnet referred to this overall approach as 'personalisation options' (Drillsma-Milgrom, 2009). It would involve working with customers to identify the value of additional services and the extent to which there would be opportunities to charge. It could also be linked to personal budgets for vulnerable households.

It is important, however, to appreciate that a two-tier service approach is not new. In the housing sector, Irwell Valley Housing Association in Greater Manchester initiated a gold service standard in 1998 (Brown, 1999). Membership criteria included paying rent on time and abiding by tenancy agreements. Benefits comprised a faster repairs service, access to education and training grants, and service guarantees. This was taken forward and adopted by a number of housing associations.

There are, thus, a number of approaches for two-tier systems for public services. The approach might centre on providing the basic minimum statutory requirements, with customers paying for enhanced or additional services. Alternatively, it might centre on a loyalty-and-reward package for customers.

From a choice, empowerment and personalisation perspective, these models represent contrasting approaches. The 'Barnet system' focuses on customers being empowered to make decisions on paying for levels of services over and above a basic standard. The gold service system entitles 'good' customers to make decisions on whether they wish to access a wider range and/or a higher level of services. The former is cost driven, while the latter is customer-centric.

Mutuality and co-production

There has been considerable coverage of these concepts, including by Boyle and Harris (2009), Boyle et al (2010), Cabinet Office (2010), John et al (2009) and Jowell (2009). The focus is on governments supporting and creating organisations that give a greater degree of control to customers, communities and staff. Customers work with providers through making use of their resources and skills to improve public services at less cost by designing out failure demand, that is, consumers contacting providers because of the inability to deliver 'a quality service first time and every time' (see further Seddon and O'Donovan, Chapter Seven). It is argued that employees and customers become 'more intolerant of waste and bureaucracy and significant savings can be made' (Stratton, 2010). Rewards for customers in getting involved in co-production might include council tax rebates.

There are already a number of examples, including some social enterprises, the Co-operative Group and John Lewis. As has already been noted, media coverage has portrayed co-production as an alternative to the 'easyBorough' model for the future direction of public services. At John Lewis, all permanent staff are 'partners' and share in the benefits and profits. They also have a voice in the running of the organisation. Tessa Jowell, the former Cabinet Office minister, commented in 2009 that the Labour government was examining the potential of mutuals to run services in social care, housing and children's trusts. She argued that mutualism would help to deliver accountability, individual empowerment and community responsibility (Jowell, 2009). Both the Conservative Party and the Liberal Democrats also espoused versions of mutuality. The former, in its general election manifesto, stated as part of its 'big society' pledge:

> We will use the state to help stimulate social action, helping social enterprises to deliver public services and training new community organisers to help achieve our ambition of every adult citizen being a member of an active neighbourhood group. (Conservative Party, 2010, 37)

Similarly, the Liberal Democrats emphasised their commitment to 'handing power back to local communities' by supporting the voluntary sector (Liberal Democrats, 2010), and the Conservative–Liberal Democrat Coalition government published ideas on these concepts in its 'Big Society' announcements at the end of May 2010.

Mutuality and co-production are, however, not new concepts. They were highlighted by Moore (1995) as a basis for improving public services through engaging with employees. Moreover, co-operatives, local development trusts, social enterprises and community asset trusts have extensive histories but have frequently been on the margins of debates on public services. Nevertheless, there are numerous examples, including:

- Goodwin Development Trust in Hull, which was set up as a charitable trust on the Thornton Estate in 1994 and now runs a wide range of services employing 300 staff;
- Greenwich Leisure, which is a social enterprise that runs over 70 leisure centres within the M25 in partnership with 13 councils;
- Meden Valley Making Places, which focuses on regeneration in the former North Nottinghamshire and Derbyshire Coalfield;
- the TREES Group in Leicester (training, regeneration, education, employment, sustainability), which is one of the largest social enterprises in the East Midlands.

From a choice, empowerment and personalisation perspective, co-production and mutuality provide an interesting proactive dimension. Customers working with providers design service options and choices. Empowerment is also achieved through participation by users and communities that helps to facilitate the provision of relevant advice and information. Personalisation through individual decision making is, thus, enhanced. Co-production represents a customer-centric view of responding to the public expenditure crisis, as well as implicitly addressing costs by designing services that consumers want.

Conclusion

We wish to highlight two issues in the relationship between the public expenditure crisis and choice, empowerment and personalisation. Firstly, there are the links between the five models discussed in the previous section, and secondly, the tension between cost-driven and customer-centric approaches. We conclude with some thoughts on the future development of public services, now discussed in turn.

The five models are not mutually exclusive. For instance, Halpern (2010) points out that the concepts of a libertarian paternalistic state and co-production are not alternatives. He argues that the former will be effective only if it embraces the latter so that nudges are received from other citizens and neighbourhood groups as well as from government. However, John et al (2009), while acknowledging that traditional mechanisms of regulatory and financial incentives to change behaviour are ineffective, contrast the differences between choice architecture and 'deliberative participation', that is, involvement of local people and organisations in deciding on priorities and actions through initiatives such as participatory budgeting. They agree, nevertheless, with Halpern that the two approaches benefit from an engagement with each other, as both concentrate on improving outcomes through an engagement with the customer, citizen and community.

From a practical viewpoint, the overlaps can be illustrated through the example of Hull and the focus on improving public health. The city is faced with a crisis. The health of the people in Hull is worse than the national average, especially in relation to life expectancy, deaths from smoking, and early deaths from cancer, heart disease and stroke. Over 50% of the population live in the most deprived 20% of neighbourhoods in England. Potential cut-backs in public expenditure present an unwelcome possibility of targeting eligibility on specific groups and neighbourhoods. There is also the potential case for a greater role for staff in determining access to services. The emphasis has, however, been on 'nudge'. NHS Hull has focused attention on social marketing (see above). But there have been differences of opinion as to whether social marketing will achieve reductions in smoking, alcohol abuse and obesity. One school of thought is that a return to a traditional professional-led welfare-state regulatory approach, such as banning smoking in public places, would be more effective. However, the Liberal Democrat leader of the city council is quoted in the local paper as saying:

> I do not believe in an extension of the existing smoking ban, either locally or nationally ... In my view it would fundamentally undermine civil liberties and freedom of choice. (*Hull Daily Mail*, 2009)

From a choice, empowerment and personalisation viewpoint, the overlap between and the mix of models presents a challenging picture. Retrenchment, traditional welfare and the 'easyBorough' models centre on a cost-driven approach for responding to the public expenditure crisis. Co-production, libertarian paternalism and gold service standards potentially shift the agenda to a customer orientation. Users would have greater choice, through empowerment by information and advice, to enable realistic individual decisions to made. Bringing together the two families of models requires a balance between customer-centric and cost-driven approaches. As Cole and Parston (2006) pointed out, customers and communities want both, that is, better public services, including choice, at less cost.

Finally, the impact of the financial crisis and planning for an upturn will result in a different pattern of delivery of public services by 2020. Choice, personalisation and empowerment will remain as an important part of the political landscape. But the detailed policies and practices will vary significantly by area. The localism agenda highlighted in Chapter Six by Leach and Roberts, together with the Conservative–Liberal Democrat Coalition and its appointment of a Minister for Devolution, is likely to come to the fore. In some areas, there will be a retrenchment of public services as eligibility is curtailed, while in other towns and cities there may be a return towards a more traditional welfare state with an increased role for managers and professionals as gatekeepers. There will also, however, be examples of local innovation. In these circumstances, choice, personalisation and empowerment could be enhanced. Two-tier service models, libertarian paternalism and mutualism provide an opportunity for bringing together contrasting frameworks to develop new ideas.

References

Audit Commission (2009) *When it Comes to the Crunch ... How Councils are Responding to the Recession*, London: The Audit Commission.

Be Birmingham (2010) *Birmingham Total Place Pilot*, Birmingham: Be Birmingham.

Boyle, D. and Harris, M. (2009) *The Challenge of Co-production*, London: NESTA.

Boyle, D., Slay, J. and Stephens, L. (2010) 'Public services inside out: Putting co-production into practice', London: NEF, NESTA and The Lab.

Brown, T. (2008) 'Mortgage Rescue Schemes', unpublished paper for Hull City Council Leicester: De Montfort University,.

Brown, T. (ed) (1999) *Stakeholder Housing: A Third Way*, London: Pluto Press.

Brown, T. and King, P. (2005) 'The Power to Choose: Effective Choice and Housing Policy', *European Journal of Housing Policy*, vol 5, no 1, pp 59–75.

Brown, T. and Murphy, W. (2009) *Managing Housing Registers in England*, York: Housing Quality Network.

Brown, T. and Yates, N. (2005) 'Allocations and Lettings – Taking Customer Choice Forward in England', *European Journal of Housing Policy*, vol 5, no 3, pp 343–57.

Brown, T., Hunt, R. and Yates, N. (2000) *Lettings: A Question of Choice*, Coventry: Chartered Institute of Housing.

Cabinet Office (2010) *Mutual Benefit: Giving People Power over Public Services*, London: HM Government.

CIPFA and SOLACE (2009) *After the Downturn: Managing a Significant and Sustained Adjustment in Public Sector Funding*, London: CIPFA and SOLACE.

Clarke, M. (2010) *Challenging Choices*, Bristol: The Policy Press.

Cole, M. and Parston, G. (2006) *Unlocking Public Value*, New Jersey: John Wiley and Sons.

Commission for Rural Communities (2009) *Rural Economies Recession Intelligence – Rural Financial Inclusion*, Cheltenham: CRC.

Communities and Local Government (2009) *Fair and Flexible: Statutory Guidance on Social Housing Allocations for Local Authorities in England*, London: Department for Communities and Local Government.

Conservative Liberal Democrat Coalition (2010) *Conservative Liberal Democrat Coalition Negotiations: Agreement reached, 11 May 2010*, accessible at www.libdems.org.uk/latest_news_detail.aspx?title=Conservative_Liberal_Democrat_coalition_agreementsandpPK=2697bcdc-7483–47a7-a517–7778979458ff.

Conservative Party (2009) *Advancing Opportunity*, London: Conservative Party, accessible at www.conservatives.com/Policy/Opportunity_Agenda.aspx.

Conservative Party (2010) *Invitation to Join the Government of Britain*, London: Conservative Party.

Department of Health (2009a) *Transforming Adult Social Care*, London: Department of Health.

Department of Health (2009b) *Shaping the Future of Social Care Together*, London: The Stationery Office.

Drillsma-Milgrom, D. (2009) 'Barnet Unveils its Easy borough Model', *Local Government Chronicle*, 21 October.

Dunton, J. (2009) 'Care Funding Battle Looms', *Local Government Chronicle*, 16 July.

Equalities and Human Rights Commission (2009) *Monitoring Update on the Impact of the Recession on Various Demographic Groups*, London: EHRC.

Glasby, J. and Littlechild, R. (2002) *Social Work and Direct Payments*, Bristol: The Policy Press.

Glasby, J. and Littlechild, R. (2009) *Direct Payments and Personal Budgets*, Bristol: The Policy Press.

Gregg, P. and Cooke, G. (eds) (2010) *Liberation Welfare*, London: Demos.

Halpern, D. (2010) *The Hidden Wealth of Nations*, Cambridge: Polity Press.

HM Government (2009) *Putting the Frontline First: Smarter Government*, London: The Stationery Office.

Hull Daily Mail (2009) 'Opposition to Outdoor Smoking Ban', 29 December.

Hunt, L. (2009) 'Remote Control', *Guardian*, 29 September

Hutton, J. (2005) 'National School of Government', Speaking notes, National School of Government, London, 24 June, accessible at www.nationalschool.gov.uk/news_events/stories/john_hutton_speech.asp.

John, P., Smith, G. and Stoker, G. (2009) 'Nudge, Nudge, Think, Think', *Political Quarterly*, vol 80, no 3, pp 361–70.

Jones, A., Lee, N. and Morris, K. (2009) *Recession and Recovery: How UK Cities can Respond and Drive the Recovery*, London: The Work Foundation.

Jowell, T. (2009) 'The Mutual Movement: How Progressives can capture the ownership agenda', Speech to Autumn Lecture Series, Progress and the Co-operative Party, 15 December.

Kotler, P. and Lee, N. (2008) *Social Marketing: Influencing Behaviors for Good*, London: Sage.

Labour Party (2010) *A Future Fair For All*, London: Labour Party.

Le Grand, J. (2007) *The Other Invisible Hand*, Princeton, NJ: Princeton University Press.

Liberal Democrats (2010) *Liberal Democrat Manifesto 2010*, London: Liberal Democrats.

Moore, M. (1995) *Creating Public Value: Strategic Management in Government*, Cambridge, MA: Harvard University Press.

New Economics Foundation (2009) *Localism: Unravelling the Supplicant State*, London: NEF.

Policy Projects Team (2009) *Are We Being Served? Policies on Accessing Goods and Services*, London: Liberal Democrats.

Richardson, J. (ed) (2010) *Housing and the Customer: Understanding Needs and Delivering Services*, Coventry: Chartered Institute of Housing.

Richardson, W. (2009), as quoted in NHS Hull (2009) 'Hull set to be Altogether Healthier with new campaigns', Press release, 18 May, Hull: NHS Hull, accessible at www.hullpct.nhs.uk/templates/page. aspx?id=5272.

Rosewell, B., Cooper, E. and Alldritt, C. (2009) *The Fiscal Landscape: Understanding Contributions and Benefits*, London: 2020 Public Services Trust.

Schwartz, B. (2004) *The Paradox of Choice: Why More is Less*, New York: Harper Collins.

Simmons, R., Powell, M. and Greener, I. (eds) (2009) *The Consumer in Public Services*, Bristol: The Policy Press.

Stratton, A. (2010) 'Labour's Plan for First "John Lewis" Council', *Guardian*, 18 February, p 1.

Thaler, R. and Sunstein, C. (2009) *Nudge: Improving Decisions about Health, Wealth and Happiness*, London: Penguin.

NINE

Governing the mix: how local government still matters

Helen Sullivan

Introduction

The recession and subsequent public spending squeeze have focused attention on how local government will respond to predicted increases in levels of need among local communities while at the same time working within reduced budgets. The Conservative–Liberal Democrat Coalition government's determination to implement £6 billion of efficiency savings in its first year in office indicates an intensification of the pursuit of 'efficiency gains' within local government and across local public services that was begun under the previous Labour administration. In this context the coalition's initial agreement published on 11 May 2010 to 'promote the radical devolution of power and greater financial autonomy to local government and community groups … [including] a full review of local government finance' (Conservatives and Liberal Democrats, 2010) could prove to be a double-edged sword – long-sought-after autonomy accompanied by very limited room for local manoeuvre, given the financial constraints. Even prior to the 2010 general election, local councils were reporting the likelihood of redundancies among staff. The post-election announcements about public spending suggest that these initial redundancies will not be the last. While local government policy has been devolved to the different governments of the UK and so is outwith the direction of the coalition, the pressure on public spending will have a significant impact on how those administrations review the possibilities for local government.

Amid the speculation about how bad the immediate future will be for local government and local services, two arguments have come to define the terms of the debate. Both are underpinned by an emphasis on efficiency, though they are often articulated slightly differently. The first argument focuses on extending the role of the market in local service provision. At a minimum this involves local councils applying market disciplines to determine where they can benefit from 'sharing services'. While this may sound appealing in principle, the reported 'collapse' of shared services plans among local councils, such as in South East Wales, illustrates how tricky these relationships can be (*Western Mail*, 9 March 2010). Beyond that, local councils are encouraged to make greater use of a range of existing instruments, including 'outsourcing' or 'partnership working' with commercial or third sector providers to deliver services to localities more efficiently. Where markets do not exist, councils are exhorted to 'make them', to invest in initiatives that will generate potential suppliers particularly from within the third sector. Social enterprises and other forms of 'mutual' organisations received considerable attention from the last Labour administration as important suppliers of local services, and this attention is likely to continue, given the enthusiasm of both the partners in the coalition government for new kinds of service delivery – for example, both the Tory and Liberal Democrat manifestos extolled the potential of employee-led cooperatives.

The second argument focuses on extending the role of the citizen in local service provision. Again, both coalition government partners are enthusiasts for an increased role for the citizen, whether in determining local priorities or in delivering local services themselves. Local councils are ahead of national government here, though examples illustrate that citizen involvement can occur in very different ways. For example, Barnet Council has been praised and vilified in equal measure for its efficiency programme, which includes local citizens opting to pay for a level of service over and above that which the council offers within the council tax (see Brown and Yates in Chapter Eight). Other councils have embraced the idea of 'co-production', in which service users become much more closely involved in the delivery of services, for example, through the operation of personalised budgets in health and social care. Finally, some councils have explored the possibility of citizens taking over services entirely, for example, some local libraries are now operated by local volunteers.

These arguments have come to be seen as 'inevitable' or 'common-sense' in describing the future of local service provision. How this has happened is of interest in itself. However, of concern in this chapter is what they mean for the institution of local government, what it does and how it is understood. In relation to policy, the implications for local government are quite clearly expressed. Local government is recast as a 'leader', 'enabler' or 'commissioner' of services. In this role it is charged with putting in place the mechanisms to enable citizens to articulate their priorities, working with other public services to identify areas of common concern, seeking out potential providers (from the private, third and possibly public sectors) to supply the necessary services, and establishing a 'performance framework' for ensuring that suppliers deliver and taking them to task should they fail. These ideas are not new, indeed they have been part of the policy discourse since the 1980s, but the recession appears to have acted as the 'tipping point' providing the confluence of circumstances which renders the idea of 'enabling' as 'common sense'.

This chapter explores the background to the apparent dominance of the idea of the enabling role for local government, reviewing key contributions from politicians and academics, highlighting the different interpretations of 'enabling' that are offered and their treatment of local government as a service provider and political actor. It argues that New Labour's use of the idea of enabling drew from these interpretations, but in such a way as to offer a diminished rather than enhanced role for local government. This is partly because New Labour's policies on enabling were underpinned by two powerful ideas: first, that who delivers public services is irrelevant, provided that services are delivered to an appropriate standard and at an acceptable cost; and second, that popular representation (in the sense of elected local politicians) is less legitimate than representation by 'experts', whether 'elites' or citizens with particular life experience. The representation of these ideas in policy and practice undercut the relationship between service provision and politics integral to UK local government and marginalised the role of politics in local decision making. Notwithstanding the Conservative–Liberal Democrat Coalition government's commitment to a 'new politics', these two ideas continue to be powerful drivers for local government policy, illustrated in part by David Cameron's narrative of the 'Big Society', in which citizens are valorised as sources of expertise and energy in localities.

The chapter begins by exploring the genesis of the idea of 'enabling', discussing three interpretations offered by politicians and academics in the 1980s and 1990s. Focusing on New Labour's time in office it argues that during this period a specific interpretation of enabling became dominant, one which separated service provision from politics and which consequently raised questions about the democratic dimension of enabling. The chapter then considers what is meant by 'the political' in a 'local democratic politics' and offers a re-articulation of enabling to address the democratic dimension. It does so by re-establishing the interconnectedness of service provision and politics in the governing of localities and rehabilitating politics as practice for both politicians and citizens. In conclusion, the chapter reasserts the continued significance of local government to local governance because of its specific role in 'governing the mix': of modes of coordination, of knowledge in decision making and because of its symbolic role in articulating and representing a local government and local democracy 'to come'.

The emergence of enabling as the new 'common sense'

Service provision has been an integral element of UK local government ever since the ideas and practice of local government became institutionalised into a political system in the late 19th century (Wilson and Game, 2006). This is partly because of the influence of J.S. Mill (1962) on the idea and practice of UK local government. His three core values of local government – liberty, participation and efficiency – have shaped discussion across the political spectrum. For Mill, local government ensures liberty by acting as a source of resistance to the overweening power of the central state. It supports participation by enabling citizens to get involved in decision making on matters of local concern and to aid their self-development as citizens in the process. Finally, it can secure the allocation of public goods and services in the most efficient way while respecting the specific needs of the area. Drawing on these values, local government has been conceived as an institution where local deliberation and decision making by elected representatives on behalf of or with local citizens in geographical areas of governable size results in the satisfaction of local interests and needs in ways that are appropriate to the peculiarities of that locality (Stewart, 1983).

While these values have proved enduring, they are not unproblematic. For example, in what remains a unitary (if now fragmented) UK system, to what extent can local government promote liberty by resisting the power of the central administration, and how far should that liberty be permitted if it generates inequitable outcomes for some communities, particularly as a consequence of the application of the efficiency value? Social democrats' concern with this led them to add a further value to local government, that of redistribution, which they argued would counter the negative tendencies of the value of efficiency (King, 1995). However, it also further diluted liberty, as the act of redistribution through progressive taxation needed to be undertaken nationally, not locally.

Different political perspectives have theorised and represented these values in different ways. In the postwar period the establishment of the welfare state and the Labour government's commitment to universal provision and the promotion of opportunity through redistribution negated the other values of local government and redefined its role as principally an agent of the central state, attaching to it a wide range of new service responsibilities in education and social care. In the 1970s the Conservative 'New Right' privileged allocative efficiency above all other values. Local government's role was to provide good services as efficiently as possible, albeit within a governance framework designed and closely controlled by central government. By contrast, the socialist 'Urban Left' movement in the 1970s and 1980s rooted its programme in the locality, trying to combine a commitment to local redistributive policies fuelled through local economic development activity with much greater participation by local citizens, for example, through representation on new local institutions for race and gender equality. Where these different political programmes held sway nationally, they were able to influence the shape and nature of local government and the relationship between politics and service provision in profound ways. The reason for this is the constitutional insecurity of UK local government, which allows central administration to meddle with the size, structure, functioning and financing of local councils in ways not possible in other developed democracies.

In one of the most influential articles about local government published in the 1970s, Sharpe made the case for a reappraisal of values to assess 'the validity of past theories for modern conditions in a democracy rather than their history' (Sharpe, 1970, 11). His review concluded that efficiency rather than liberty or participation was of most relevance in the prevailing context, but he also suggested that local government had to express this value in new ways: via its role as a horizontal coordinator of services, as an institution for reconciling competing community interests, as a pressure group on behalf of those without resource power, as an agent for responding to rising service demand in key areas, and as a counterweight to the interests of professionals.

Prescient though Sharpe's analysis of future economic and political conditions may have been, by legitimising the idea of local government values as not merely elastic but also possibly contingent, Sharpe allowed for the subsequent and regular redefinition of these values in relation to the prevailing contextual drivers. More prosaically, these theoretical developments offered additional comfort to central government that it could refashion local government regularly to meet the needs of the time and the prevailing modes of governance without there being any risk to services or democracy. It was in this context that the idea of enabling emerged and evolved in subsequent programmes of local government reform. Three particularly influential interpretations of enabling are considered here.

The first comes from the Conservative 'New Right' and its refashioning of local government in the 1970s and 1980s. New Right policies created a significant cleavage within the relationship between political decision making and service provision as its supporters argued that politics was discredited as a means of allocating resources. It had proved too amenable to 'producer interests' and it lacked the discipline necessary to secure 'allocative' efficiency. Politics had failed citizens as taxpayers and as beneficiaries of services. The market was offered as an appropriate disciplining instrument, able to challenge the producer interests protected by the hierarchical bureaucracy of local government and to better meet the aspirations of taxpayers and customers. In practice this meant keeping local politics 'at bay' from service decisions in order to promote their efficient delivery.

The means of keeping politics 'at bay' was via the promotion of a new role for local government – one characterised as 'enabling' by its chief architect, Nicholas Ridley (1988). The enabling authority was the ultimate expression of his desire for the 'small state' at the local level (framed by strong central direction, it is important to note). It was associated with the adoption of the mixed economy, compulsory competitive tendering, public–private partnerships, increasing engagement of the third sector as providers, and the identification of the citizen through its role as either consumer or taxpayer. More and more local government 'business' could be 'outsourced' to others, increasing the efficiency of service delivery that taxpayers were happy to fund and at the same time offering reductions both in the number of local government staff and, crucially, in the number of local elected councillors. The role of the council would, in an oft-repeated phrase, be 'to meet once a year to agree contracts'. This interpretation of enabling was built on a belief in the primacy of the market, on the desire of individual citizens to be as unencumbered by the state as possible and on the ability of all council activities to be subject to calculation in order to render them marketable or obsolete. The political/democratic dimension of local government was articulated in the expression of the people's will at elections and in representing that will in the allocation of contracts – it was never assumed that the people would want any alternative, given a choice. These development presaged the era of what Hirst (2000) described as the 'post political', in which, in his view, democracy came to be in service to rather than being served by the market.

The second interpretation of enabling was developed in the 1990s in response to recognition by some politicians and academics that governing was becoming more complex and challenging, and that single approaches to governing rooted either in markets or in traditional bureaucracies were unlikely to be sufficient. Rather, what was needed was a means of governing that could accommodate the diversity of local interests and the complexity of what were regarded as 'wicked' problems. John Stewart (1995) was a key contributor to this debate. For him, enabling was synonymous with community leadership and empowerment – local government leading by listening to and acting on local views and manifesting itself as an expression of community will. In this version of enabling, citizens are stakeholders, as are other local providers, whose actions need to be 'orchestrated' or 'influenced' by local government to meet community goals. In these expressions of enabling, service provision was the consequence of the expression of 'community will' in a local democratic context.

The final interpretation of enabling to be considered here is Gerry Stoker's appeal for the reinvention of local democracy in the 1990s. Stoker was explicitly not concerned with service provision, arguing instead that local government in the UK ought to learn from its US and European counterparts. Stoker (1996) wanted to 'redefine local government' to go 'beyond service delivery'. Local government should be the arena for political conflict, for deliberation and debate about 'who gets what, when and how'. Local government's focus on provision and its role as a direct deliverer of services was identified as a distraction from the practice of democratic decision making to determine and realise the kind of community well-being that John Stewart referred to. In Stoker's view, local government should be concerned with the big issues of the day and 'the search for consent' in ambiguous circumstances. Local government sat at the hub of a range of networks of actors and its role was to coordinate the 'capacity to act' via much closer and deeper engagement with citizens, and also with other public, private and voluntary sector actors to shape their contributions.

Post 1997, 'New Labour's' determination to 'modernise' local government appeared to draw on each of the above interpretations of enabling. An early policy, 'Best Value', focused attention on service delivery and the need for local councils to enable delivery by the most appropriate provider. By 2006, the White Paper *Strong and Prosperous Communities* offered a much clearer link to Ridley's vision, arguing that local councils should be 'strategic commissioners' of services, facilitated through but not provided by local government (DCLG, 2006). From 1997 a broad suite of area-based or thematic policies, including neighbourhood renewal, health action zones, and crime and disorder reduction partnerships, drew on Stewart's idea of enabling as community leadership, with the local authority working in tandem with other providers and local citizens to determine and meet local needs. Similarly, proposals for extending and enhancing democracy in a 'network context' drew on Stoker's vision of the enabling authority and a range of innovations were supported, including elected mayors, local strategic partnerships (partnerships of partnerships) and new forms of citizen empowerment and democratic participation. Traces of Stewart's and Stoker's visions can also be found in the 2006 White Paper, as the 'strategic commissioner' role for local government was linked to a 'community leadership' responsibility that charged the local authority with ensuring that the interests and wishes of its citizens were sought and secured with their active participation.

However, closer examination of what happened in localities between 1997 and 2010 reveals that it was a version of Ridley's vision of enabling that came to dominate, notwithstanding the institutions and initiatives that appeared to reflect Stewart's and Stoker's perspectives. So, while it is possible to identify ways in which local government was represented as 'the community leader' at the centre of a range of networks focused on the achievement of community well-being, for example in England this was expressed through the agreement of key local priorities in the sustainable community strategy, overseen by the multi-sectoral local strategic partnership and delivered through the local area agreement, in practice any room for the expression of community leadership was heavily constrained by the persistence of strong central performance targets that continued to drive local action. As well as being relatively powerless in the face of the centre, local government was also subject to the judgements of the national regulator – the Audit Commission – part of whose job under the new inspection regime was to assess its performance as an enabler, particularly in political leadership and partnership.

In addition, the local strategic partnership (LSP) was not the place where 'strategic commissioning' was undertaken; rather, the practice of service commissioning remained within service areas, managed and operated by local government and other officers in consultation with service users and within predetermined limits. Political engagement in these arenas, in the sense of democratic debate among politicians, users and citizens about service decisions, was absent or limited. This example is indicative of the failure of enabling to fulfil Stoker's vision of it as a means of reinventing local democracy. As the search for consent in ambiguous circumstances, it is possible to claim that LSP performed that function by bringing together institutions and interests to consider how to balance key local priorities. However, evidence from the national evaluation of LSPs suggests that these institutions did not tackle 'the big issues of the day', but instead engaged primarily in 'games' about acquiring and retaining resources (ODPM/DoT, 2006). Critically for Stoker's vision of a reinvented demos, citizen stakeholders remained on the periphery of LSPs, as did elected politicians. Some academics have characterised engagement with LSPs as 'metagoverning' or 'steering', but in practice it often looked suspiciously like redundancy (Sørenson, 2006). More and more 'partnership' institutions were established at 'arm's length' from local government with no direct political oversight, and populated by local government and officials from other organisations whose engagement was valued because they were not political – politics was seen to interfere with good governance, again echoing Ridley's vision.

The example of neighbourhood governance provides a good illustration of how Ridley's vision of enabling dominated local practice. Promoted by New Labour as a means of empowering citizens to get involved in making decisions about their areas alongside local politicians, and working with providers to ensure that services were responsive and appropriate to local needs, neighbourhood governance struggled to hold the imagination of local communities. One reason for this may be that the dominant model of neighbourhood governance was that of neighbourhood management, which offered a much narrower agenda of possibility than that initially envisaged in bold speeches about devolving power and empowering citizens. In practice, neighbourhood management not only limited citizen involvement to the management of services and also limited their involvement *in* the management of those services. Citizens were not encouraged to make big choices about what services are provided and how, but rather were offered opportunities to get involved in 'setting priorities' or 'performance managing' services against existing specifications. In addition, they were often engaged in setting up governance structures, spending time discussing matters of representation and accountability when there was little to represent or to be held accountable for (Griggs and Roberts, forthcoming).

At the point at which New Labour left office, enabling was practised in ways which marginalised politicians and politics, engaged citizens only as consumers and focused managers' attention upwards towards central government, not outwards to localities or communities. For any future administration wishing to realise enabling as a democratic political practice, restoring the connection between service provision and 'the political' in local government and local governance would be key. These issues are addressed in the following section.

Restoring 'the political'

Debates about 'the political' in local democratic governance generally address two linked features. The first concerns the democratic principles that underpin local governance institutions, specifically the relationship between representative and participative principles. The second concerns the democratic practices that are engaged in within those institutions, particularly the role of deliberation as a means of arriving at democratic decisions. Barber's (2003) study of democracy addresses both of these features and starts from a theoretical analysis that locates 'the liberal tradition' as the fundamental obstacle to a healthy democracy. He considers that most democratic institutions in the West practice what he terms 'thin democracy', representative democratic systems rooted in liberal values which, he argues, serve to promote individual liberty and private interests rather than justice and public goods. For Barber, the development of a 'strong democracy' requires a transformation of the prevailing representative models, a departure from the reliance on liberal values and their replacement by democratic institutions and practices that are participative and view active self-governing by citizens as the ideal. Although he acknowledges that citizens may not be able to govern themselves at all times and over all issues, he is adamant that they should do so sufficiently often and over sufficiently important issues, such as key policy questions and decisions about power and resources, as to feel themselves authentic self-governors. Rather than displacing the conflict that arises in processes of democratic decision making to inadequate representatives, Barber's prescription is that conflict is resolved through participative processes that enable citizens to transform private interests to public goods and, through the processes of deliberation, create a political self-governing community. Communication is vital in developing and maintaining political relations, and governing requires engagement with strangers.

Local government plays a key role in Barber's prescription for 'strong democracy', though it is a radically different local government from the representative model that currently dominates. Likewise in the UK, Phillips' (1996) reappraisal of the value of local government identified political participation as the primary value because of its potential to enhance the quality of democracy. Phillips identified several features that position local democracy as one of the 'cornerstones' of a strong democracy: most political participation is local, a wider variety of interests (including parties) get represented locally, and local governments tend to distribute power and resources more in accordance with this variation. However, it is important to note that Phillips, like Barber, is critical of local government's performance in relation to protecting and promoting local democracy. Her prescription for local government in the UK involves enhancing the institutions of representative democracy and developing participative and direct democratic innovations to engage citizens more often and more deeply.

The concepts of 'strong' and 'thin' are also useful for thinking about how to understand politics and the political at the local level, particularly in relation to the operation of democratic decision making. Drawing on Mouffe's (1993; 2005) analyses, it is possible to conceptualise 'strong' politics as based on the expectation that there will be ideological differences between parties to governance (with both small and big 'p'), that individual preferences and identities are neither given nor fixed but are constituted through processes of continual discussion, debate and disagreement to define what 'the problem' is and how it might be addressed, and that conflict is essential in the formation of identities and the practice of politics. 'Thin' politics, by contrast, is politics in which preferences are given, identities are more or less fixed, and the terms of the debate are set so as to promote consensus and dialogue. As a result, 'difference' is either excluded or suppressed, and the role of the political becomes to legitimise managing 'the middle ground' and applying better techniques to the processes of problem solving. This distinction between 'strong' and 'thin' politics cuts across representative/participative/deliberative models and is not necessarily aligned to one or another. So, for example, a 'strong' democracy that privileges consensus, rationality and dialogue over conflict, intuition and affect is characterised by 'thin', not 'thick' politics.

For Mouffe (1993), conflict is inherent in and constitutive of political relations, with actors identified as 'friends or enemies' in processes of decision making. Therefore even in a 'strong' agonistic politics the presence of conflict will generate attempts to exclude those identified as 'enemies' from contributing to determining political goals. This in turn generates a democratic challenge – how to find ways of involving those identified as 'enemies', and legitimising conflict as a necessary condition for meeting the challenges in and to democracy. Norval's (2007) concept of 'adversarial legitimacy' is helpful here. It offers actors 'temporary identities' that can serve to express dissent or disagreement, so reducing the risk of damaging encounters between actors whose identities are constituted as 'friends' or 'enemies' in a particular decision-making context.

Mouffe's challenge to democrats to acknowledge and embrace conflict is particularly apt, given the valorisation of 'consensus' in the partnership discourse evident in the UK under New Labour, and the consequent marginalisation of those who attempted to challenge or subvert institutional arrangements designed to 'deliver consensus'. In Mouffe's terms, this focus on consensus was an expression of a 'thin' politics, in which partnerships were merely managerial instruments offering limited options about the means and ends of local governance. In similar vein, New Labour policies in support of 'democratic renewal' also reflected a 'thin' conception of politics in the way they sought to sideline formal politics and local politicians by devising and implementing 'empowerment' initiatives in and through institutions of central government. This approach was argued to be justified, on the basis that local government and local politicians had lost their legitimacy with local people and that citizens with 'lay knowledge' had greater legitimacy and could be activated by direct appeals. However, in practice what it was to be 'active' or 'empowered' was defined for citizens by policy makers, and the expectation was that 'responsible' citizens would work within parameters set for them by central government (Barnes et al, 2007).

The growth in 'arm's length' governing institutions and the separation of local citizens from formal local politics were considered a plus by many who sought to govern 'beyond the politics'. However, these developments reflected a 'thin' politics unable to respond to what Barber calls 'the tension and paradox' of the 'delicately dialectical relationships between equality and liberty, community and individualism and participatory and representative democracy' (Barber, 2003, ix). As indicated above, this found clear expression in the dominant model of enabling which reduced the practices of citizenship to consumption, of representation to meta-governance and of civic activism to an alternative expression of service provision.

While recession puts pressure on existing services and makes new demands as people, businesses and voluntary organisations experience the consequences of the downturn, it also draws attention to the importance of politics in making choices about how shrinking resources are allocated. 'Strong' politics and 'thin' politics offer very different approaches to making these choices, though in neither case will single solutions arise, as local political contexts will generate variation. Rather, the principles underpinning 'strong' or 'thin' politics will frame how local priorities are arrived at in ways that fit with local circumstances.

One likely option for local government is to refocus on what is termed the 'core business' and to strip out of its activities anything that doesn't fit. There are a couple of points to make here. A focus on 'core business' does not necessarily equate to 'thin' politics – it depends on how decisions are made and what is agreed to constitute 'core business' for that locality. The risk of a 'core business' approach in a context of 'thin' politics is that it depoliticises discussions about what possible choices might be, for example, limiting the discussion of inequality, need and resources in favour of rendering all decisions somehow technical matters that can be assessed by using ever more sophisticated versions of 'value for money' calculations. It also risks limiting local government's engagement in new/existing areas of activity that are not necessarily about providing services but are about contributing to community well-being, such as preventive interventions, economic innovations and support, including the development of local banks, as in Essex.

Annmarie Mol (2008) offers another way of thinking about public service provision that can complement the idea of a 'strong' or 'thin' politics. Drawing on research in healthcare, she contrasts what she terms has become a dominant logic in healthcare – the 'logic of choice' – with an alternative logic – 'the logic of care'. The 'logic of choice' is popular with many across the political spectrum, as it is suggestive of autonomous consumers exercising individual judgements over possible service options, with professionals providing the relevant information and the market making different options available. It fits well with the preferences of the main UK political parties for consumer rights, personalisation and marketisation. However, Mol argues that in the context of health services (and, I would argue, many other public services) this analysis is flawed and that the 'logic of care' offers a more apposite mode of understanding health service practices. The 'logic of care' begins from a position that we do not act as autonomous rational individuals, but are always situated in collectives (or communities) of one form or another that influence how we perceive ourselves and our options. In healthcare, patients are not necessarily passive but exist in an interdependent and collaborative relationship with professionals. Between them, they are engaged in an ongoing relationship in which judgements are regularly made and remade to attune knowledge and technologies to their complex lives. Adaptation and tinkering are expected and encouraged in order to ensure that the patient receives the best care. The 'logic of care' offers a more meaningful way of expressing what is being sought and offered on the part of patients and providers, including those interactions that are not calculable but are central to the experience of giving and receiving care. Applying the 'logic of care' to public services more widely offers a different way of appraising service provision in local government and deciding what should be provided, in what way and by whom. Wainwright and Little's (2009) reporting of Newcastle City Council's experience may be considered a case study of the application of the 'logic of care' to local government services. According to Wainwright and Little, the city's unhappy experience of 'modernisation' in the 1990s (partnerships with the private sector) led to a re-emphasis on the role of the local authority as a direct service provider in accordance with a set of values and democratic practices that were considered essential in shaping how the council responded to changing circumstances. Unions and politicians were identified as key drivers of this process, working closely together and with senior managers (Wainwright and Little, 2009).

Combining the ideas of 'strong' and 'thin' politics with the 'logics of care and choice' generates a range of ways of representing 'enabling' and offers local government and local citizens a number of possible options which are not necessarily mutually exclusive but may coexist in different policy/service areas. These are illustrated in Figure 9.1.

Figure 9.1: Options for 'enabling' local government

Strong politics

Local government facilitates network of delivery options reflecting decisions made through collective encounters between communities, politicians and professionals

Local government promotes and regulates a 'market' of service providers reflecting preferences of budget-holding users who commission directly through user-led consortia

Logic of care ← → **Logic of choice**

Local government determines what should be provided and how based on local priorities balancing technical assessments of need with political demands mediated by local representatives

Local government facilitates a 'market' of service providers to meet the preferences of individual users

Thin politics

Conclusion: towards a new common sense of enabling?

Understanding how local government matters in and beyond the recession requires an appreciation of the particularities of the local government tradition in the UK, combined with an ability to offer a positive vision for its future. Central to this is the need to reinterpret the service provider/politics dynamic. Attempts to reimagine local government without a service dimension have not taken hold, in part because the history and memory of UK local government is shaped by its role as a service provider. Without this it has a very limited basis upon which to promote participation or to represent local interests against the over-mighty power of the centre.

However, this is not to conclude that local government need not be reimagined, nor that service provision necessarily equates to direct service delivery. Instead, this chapter has reviewed different interpretations and practices associated with the idea of 'the enabling authority' and offered an alternative interpretation that reasserts the interconnectedness of service provision and politics in the governing of localities, and rehabilitates politics as practice for both politicians and citizens. In this conception of enabling it does matter who delivers local services, and so decisions about this need to be made within a framework of values generated and endorsed by local citizens. In an environment in which local needs, communities and aspirations are increasingly diverse, popular representation becomes more important as a means of finding a path to resolution that can link 'lay' and 'expert' knowledge in any given situation.

Local government's enabling role becomes one of 'governing the mix'; of modes of coordination and of knowledge in decision making. This means that local government needs to ensure not just that the process of making decisions about service provision is democratic but also that it has the necessary capacity to govern whatever mix of hierarchies, markets and networks emerges. This requires attention both to formal political systems and processes and also management systems of monitoring and support. It is also necessary for local government to be able to situate lay, expert and political knowledge within the context of the logics of care/choice and to redefine the roles of politicians and of professionals and citizens in line with these logics.

What local government does and what it looks like will vary, depending upon local circumstances (as indicated in Figure 9.1), but a typical enabling authority is likely to perform a number of roles. Acting as a 'safety net', it would offer protection to all in some service areas and to vulnerable groups in others, built on an acknowledgement of basic citizen rights. In support of a 'securing role' it would offer a 'selection box' of services to ensure the supply of an agreed (with communities) range of services and activities through different modes of provision. Finally, it would also act as a 'springboard', performing as an innovator both to improve efficiency, for example, using social media to improve service reach, and in meeting new community needs, for example, establishing community banks.

This reimagining of enabling also has implications for central government, as in order to be sustainable, the practice of 'strong politics' and making choices about which logics to pursue requires limited central government interference and increased local autonomy.

References

Barber, B.R. (2003) *Strong Democracy: Participatory Politics for a New Age*, 20th anniversary edition, California: University of California Press.

Barnes, M., Newman, J. and Sullivan, H. (2007) *Power, Participation and Political Renewal: Case Studies in Public Participation*, Bristol: The Policy Press.

Conservatives and Liberal Democrats (2010) *Conservative Liberal Democrat Coalition Negotiations, Agreements Reached, 11 May 2010*, www.conservatives.com/News/News_stories/2010/05/Coalition_Agreement_published.aspx, accessed 16 May 2010.

DCLG (Department for Communities and Local Government) (2006) *Strong and Prosperous Communities*, Local Government White Paper, London: DCLG.

Griggs, S. and Roberts, M. (2011, forthcoming) *From Neighbourhood Governance to Neighbourhood Management: a Neo-liberal Pattern to Devolved Governance?* Local Government Studies.

Hirst, P. (2000) 'Democracy and Governance', in J. Pierre (ed) *Debating Governance: Authority, Steering and Democracy*, Oxford: Oxford University Press.

King, D. (1995) 'From the Urban Left to the New Right: Normative Theory and Local Government', in J. Stewart and G. Stoker (eds) *Local Government in the 1990s*, Basingstoke: Macmillan, pp 228–48.

Mill, J.S. (1962) *Utilitarianism, On Liberty and Representative Government*, London: Everyman.

Mol, A. (2008) *The Logic of Care*, London: Routledge.

Mouffe, C. (1993) *The Return of the Political*, London: Verso.

Mouffe, C. (2005) *On the Political*, London: Routledge.

Norval, A. (2007) *Aversive Democracy*, Cambridge: Cambridge University Press.

ODPM/DoT (Office of the Deputy Prime Minister/Department of Transport) (2006) *Evaluation of LSPs: A Final Report from the Universities of Warwick, Liverpool John Moores, West of England and the Office for Public Management*, London: ODPM.

Phillips, A. (1996) 'Why does local democracy matter?' in L. Pratchett and D. Wilson (eds) *Local Democracy and Local Government*, London: Macmillan, pp 20–37.

Ridley, N. (1988) *The Local Right*, London: Centre for Policy Studies.

Sharpe, J. (1970) 'Theories and values of local government', *Political Studies*, vol 18, no 2, pp 153–74.

Sørensen, E. (2006) 'Metagovernance: The changing role of politicians in processes of democratic governance', *American Review of Public Administration*, vol 36, no 1, pp 98–114.

Stewart, J. (1983) *The Conditions of Local Choice*, London: George Allen and Unwin.

Stewart, J. (1995) 'A future for local authorities as community government', in J. Stewart and G. Stoker (eds) *Local Government in the 1990s*, Basingstoke: Macmillan pp 249–68.

Stoker, G. (1996) 'Redefining local democracy', in L. Pratchett and D. Wilson (eds) *Local Democracy and Local Government*, London: Macmillan, pp 188–209.

Wainwright, H. with Little, M. (2009) *Public Service Reform ... but not as we know it*, Hove: Compass with Unison.

Wilson, D. and Game, C. (2006) *Local Government in the United Kingdom*, Basingstoke: Palgrave.

Part Three
Conclusion

TEN

Conclusion: from recession to renewal?

Joanna Richardson

> Will we seize the opportunity to restore our sense of balance between the market and the state, between individualism and the community, between man and nature, between means and ends? (Joseph Stiglitz, 2010, 296)

It's a matter of trust

The essential ingredient in the understanding of money and exchange of goods and services is trust (Ferguson, 2008; Lonergan, 2009). It is also vital for social order and good governance. Stiglitz (2010, 289) says that 'trust is the grease that makes society function'. Society, however, feels let down by the systems of the market that resulted in the credit crunch, leading to closure of businesses, increasing unemployment and house repossessions; and yet bankers' bonuses were still eye-wateringly large in 2010, as a result of profits made following quick recovery on the markets. British people also felt that their trust in government was eroded after the scandals in 2009 over the behaviour of some politicians in relation to their expenses.

There was public scepticism over the opacity of the banking system, and what appeared to be a self-serving system of expenses for politicians. Trust was in low supply. In order to rebuild trust, it is important to have a proper understanding of what happened in the financial crisis.

This book has sought to identify some of the social outcomes of the financial crisis and examined their impact on public services, government and citizens. Rather than providing analysis, or simple predictions, it has aimed to stimulate thought about the wider themes to be addressed, such as governance and empowerment. In the early part of the book both Lambie and Holland provoked us to think about the radical changes needed to prevent such a crisis happening again. Such changes are not about tweaking the regulation of banks, or debating public spending cuts, but a fundamental rethink about how we see society, government – the world. Hutton (2010) galvanises us to think this through: 'We have, in short, lived through an epic economic mistake culminating in a first order financial crisis. There cannot be a return to business as usual'. Other commentators exhort us to look beyond the economic causes and implications of the recent crisis. O'Toole (2009, 219) says about the crisis in Ireland that: 'Unless there is an attitudinal revolution in which honesty, responsibility and a concern for the future become basic social values, nothing else is going to change'. He describes three cornerstones of an Irish recovery: (1) recognition that the crisis was moral as well as economic; (2) need to renew and reform institutions of government; and (3) articulation of a social vision. One could add that in Britain financial institutions, as well as government, need reform to increase trust; but by any measure against O'Toole's cornerstones, there has been a failure: there has been very little introspection by either government or the financial sector on the moral causes and impacts of the crisis. There was also a failure by the previous Labour government to articulate a social vision, and while the Conservative pre-election rhetoric of 'big society' purported to fill that gap, the reality was a vision with a more individual focus through an ideologically driven retraction of state support for the less well-off.

Debt, risk and cuts

As discussed in the first chapter of this book, the narrative of the financial crisis started off with private debt – that of both individuals and banks being too highly leveraged against falsely inflated house values. This moved quite swiftly on to sovereign debt, and without too much introspection there was a call to cut public debt. In early 2010 the main political parties may have had differing time frames for the cuts, but there was a consensus that public debt must be reduced. Roxburgh et al (2010) produced a report for McKinsey and Co. analysing previous crises, in which they explained the differences around the globe and over 45 episodes, but found that deleveraging nearly always follows a crisis. They found four main responses to crises; the most common route was deleveraging through periods of austerity or 'belt-tightening', while other responses included 'high inflation', 'massive default' or 'growing out of debt' (p 39). The McKinsey report also suggested that the crisis could have been predicted by use of the right tools. Its first recommendation is that 'Policy makers should work toward developing an international system for tracking leverage at a granular sector level across countries and over time' (p 46). The OECD reflected this: 'Unwarranted build-ups of leverage, risk-taking and asset prices, as occurred before the crisis, must not be repeated' (Elmeskov, 2009, 5). The International Monetary Fund (IMF) has joined the debate on revising current assumptions in models with its question on whether inflation targets should be raised in 'normal' times to allow more of a cushion during times of shock or crisis (Blanchard et al, 2010) and in its report for the G20 in April 2010, the IMF suggested two taxes on banks – a Financial Stability Contribution, charged initially at a flat rate per bank as a contribution towards a bail-out in the next financial crisis, and a Financial Activities Tax, to be levied on profits and bankers' pay (IMF, 2010a).

The responses to private and public debt and the subsequent deleveraging processes, through austerity measures, seem to be offered as a way of patching up existing market models. For all the talk of a new direction, the emphasis appears to be on reducing public debt while introducing some measures to try to protect against mass unemployment and other effects that would impact on society and communities. Alongside this runs an argument of better regulation and restructuring to avoid the problem of 'too big to fail' banks (for example, the manifesto from the New Economics Foundation, 2010) and so-called innovative products which allow investors to bet against the productivity of the market; however, there seems to be little political appetite for dealing with the moral causes of the crisis (the greed of bankers and those with investments in the bond and stock markets). Both Lambie and Holland (Chapters Two and Three in this book) have demonstrated the complexity in the build-up to the financial crisis both globally and on a European level, and they equally point to the challenges in the responses needed: they suggest that more needs to be done than tweaking the current global system of markets. Stiglitz (2010) also urges us not to lose the opportunity for a more radical look at future directions. A new economic and social model could emerge from the crisis, rather than patching up the old predominant free-market order that has dominated the economic landscape since the 1980s.

Alternative macro-economic models

For a time, at the beginning of the crisis, Keynes was back in vogue (Skidelsky, 2009) after a period of laissez-faire economic models, which gained particular strength in the 1980s (see further Skousen, 2005; de Soto, 2008). There is much argument and debate between proponents of different schools, and particularly between the broad approaches of laissez-faire and government intervention approaches. At the beginning of the crisis the interventionists put great store in the death of unfettered capitalism, but as the private sector recovered and the banks started returning large profits again, this death knell weakened and libertarians argued that time had shown that the markets could work. The alarmist discourse on the size of the government debt in Britain, the United States and countries in Europe also gave cause to the argument of less government intervention and lower public debt. Nevertheless, caution is still advised in cutting public debt too quickly. The IMF said in February 2010 that 'the potential risks associated with an early withdrawal of policy stimulus seem to outweigh the risks of maintaining it for longer than possibly needed' (IMF, 2010a, 5), albeit this caution was not heeded by the new Conservative–Liberal Democrat Coalition government when it confirmed plans to cut public spending by £6 billion in 2010–11.

Buchanan et al (2009) examine what they call the 'UK national business model' to talk about welfare distribution through employment. They suggest that the public and the 'para-state' (private organisations supported by state spending) have made up more than half of all job creation since 1998 and say that 'the UK has an undisclosed business model of using publicly supported employment to cover the continuing failure of the private sector to generate and distribute welfare through job creation' (p 2). If the private sector has been failing to create sufficient jobs and the public sector has been covering that gap, the prospect of immediate public sector budget cuts, along with job cuts in local government and quasi-public organisations, could have an extremely damaging effect on the recovery of Britain from the financial crisis.

Alternative economic models need to be found, not just in order to regain a more equitable society, but also to take account of risk in a globalised economy. The interconnectivity of exposure to risk was shown in the banking crisis and was part of the reason why the government stepped in to bail out. With banks having merged, there was a risk that, if one bank had been allowed to fail, this it would have affected the remaining banks because of their holdings of 'toxic loans'. The extent of this interconnectivity had not been thoroughly examined for its potential systemic risk to the global market order; instead, banks and government regulators had taken more of a silo approach to examining risk. A similar issue of interconnectivity in the risk of sovereign debt 'contagion' was also seen in the problems with the Greek public debt, its links with the debts of other eurozone members, the future validity of the euro, and the exposure to 'junk' bonds held by the very banks who were seeing a return to massive profits. The cyclical and networked problems of globalised banks and global governance became all too apparent.

Scientists suggest that a larger system perspective is necessary in ecology, so that issues are looked at not on a species-by-species basis, but instead in a wider eco-system/environmental context, and researchers such as May et al (2008) state that these lessons might also apply to the global economy. Global networks in the economy might hide potential tipping points (Gladwell, 2001) that have the potential for a financial crisis. Mathematical and network theories might offer some ideas for new economic models more realistically rooted in the globalised market; for example, Reed (1999) referred to a huge underestimation of the growth in number of users of the internet, based on previous mathematical models suggesting that a network grows in proportion to the square of the number of users (n^2), and stated that in fact group formation was the key – so not one user talking to one user, but groups of two, three and so on. Not only has the exponential growth in connections due to the advance of technology to be taken into account in assessing the risk of systemic failure, but also network theory can be used to examine business cycles on a macroeconomic level (Gatti et al, 2008). These emerging formulae and models should be considered in the revision of economic models, especially if the status quo of free markets holds in a rapidly expanding global order.

Arguments between economists will continue through this crisis and through recessions in the future. Models may work well in theory, but are based on sets of assumptions that may not present themselves in reality; free market proponents, for example, assume that perfect information is available to actors in the market. Stiglitz (2010) refers to the problem with the assumptions of the laissez-faire economic models, and Levitt and Dubner (2009) also show that what many of us presume to be true can be turned on its head, because actual behaviour is different to assumed behaviour. Information available to investors and, indeed, to governments, is less than perfect, and decision making by individuals and their political representatives can be less than rational. A number of behavioural science researchers have investigated the influence of others in society on the way we act (Earls, 2009), the influence that individual bias has in decision making (Thaler and Sunstein, 2009) and the role of emotion in the choices we make in the market-place (Hill, 2008). Turner (2010a) also warns against oversimplification and an overconfident view of markets as rational and self-equilibrating, and suggests (2010b) that some 'radical' solutions are not radical enough and that a simple structural solution to resolving the problems in the financial sector is insufficient. Turner says that: 'Instead we need to deploy a wide range of regulatory and macro-prudential tools, informed by a philosophy deeply sceptical of past arguments that financial liberalisation, innovation, and deepening is axiomatically beneficial' (2010b, p 31).

Sen (1999) offers a critique of the narrow approach of traditional economic models of understanding human behaviour, preferring instead to look at a person's 'interests' as defined by 'well-being' and 'advantage'. Well-being is broadly concerned with individual achievement, and advantage is related to the opportunity to fulfil wishes, particularly when compared with others' opportunities. Toynbee and Walker (2009) examine this entrenchment of the disparity in ownership of assets with the opportunity and advantage afforded to successive generations. The financial crisis has made it harder for all first-time buyers to secure a mortgage, but the children of existing home owners have an advantage over those whose families have no capital assets. Rather than the gap between the haves and have nots narrowing with progressive social policies, the boom in house prices under New Labour further widened this gap. In their research Wilkinson and Pickett (2009) look at well-being in rich countries, and they find that it does not grow exponentially in line with economic growth and individual income. They suggest that economic growth has largely done its work in rich countries, and instead they find that lack of well-being – whether social, health or some other measure – is dependent more on inequality than on overall levels of poverty. This also echoes Sen's (1999) notion that the freedom of opportunity to achieve well-being, rather than well-being itself, is a more appropriate measure in the study of inequality.

Economic and environmental resources are finite, and so it is surely the responsibility of government now to examine ways of securing equality of access to well-being, rather than to chase an impossible infinite economic growth. Simms et al (2010) call for a new economic direction. This need has been highlighted by Mear (in Chapter Four) as being due to the failure of existing economic models based on the premise of an always fully functioning banking system. However, the need for new models is also the result of issues of inequality in opportunities for individual and societal well-being. These need to go further than practical initiatives at service-delivery level, and instead take a more holistic economic and environmental view which re-examines consumption of scarce resources, from fossil fuels to land, through the use of mutuality, cooperation and shared ownership (Ostrom, 1990; Simms et al, 2010).

There has been ongoing work by prominent experts in Europe, such as Holland (who writes Chapter Three in this book), on alternative economic models. Holland's ideas offer an alternative approach for European governments to add economic, social and political value. Stiglitz (2010) also challenges those in power to find a new moral economic model, one that will counter the current social inequalities and reduce the risks of banks that are 'too big to fail'. He argues for more than just a tweaking of the old order, and for a more rigorous rethink.

Public service delivery models

Place-based budgets (formerly known as 'Total Place'/'total capital') have been recommended by Hutton and Jones (2010) as part of a basis for a new 'partnership' with government. HM Treasury (2010) analysed the results of the 'Total Place' pilots and reported on savings that could be made in a number of ways – predictable among these were areas such as 'back office' and 'support' functions through reduction in duplication, and also service redesign and reduced costs from better outcomes (for example, in Birmingham it was estimated that every £1 spent now on funding for drug misuse will save £2.50 in the future social costs that might be incurred if drug initiatives were not in place: HM Treasury, 2010, 29). Coming out of the 13 pilot schemes is an emerging concept which aims to take a holistic view to capital investment. The Coalition government also announced a 'transformation' of public service delivery – a local, devolved approach – through four 'vanguard' community pilots (Cameron, 2010). Whatever the label applied, the concept of local government organisations taking a holistic view of their communities and the public budgets available for those communities seems to be a useful framework for the delivery of local public services. Counties and sub-regions across the country are already examining a number of service areas across council boundaries to analyse where duplication can be avoided and savings made.

There have also been innovative suggestions from registered social landlords for the future financing of housing organisations. Hyde Group announced plans to enter the bond market after being given an Aa2 rating; its hope was to raise £200 million in this way. Another housing association – London and Quadrant – had already made £300 million in a bond deal (*Inside Housing*, 2010). Places for People raised £76 million funding on the Japanese bond market (Brown, 2010a) and Notting Hill Housing Trust raised a £180 million bond with highly competitively prices interest rates (Brown, 2010b).

The use of innovative finance for housing and urban development was also discussed by the All Party Urban Development Group in its (2009) report which asked for Tax Increment Funding (TIF)/Accelerated

Development Zone (ADZ) pilots in a number of cities straight away, with a roll-out to a national scheme from 2011; TIF/ADZ allows future increases in tax revenue from a development to be used to fund infrastructure on that development. A number of solutions have been suggested across the housing sector to examine a range of changes to planning, land acquisition and mortgage finance, as well as an analysis of the roles of the state and the private sector in facilitating new housing development (Shelter, 2009). The range of suggested levers to unlock development of social house building is varied, but also confused in direction. The rationale behind some changes, such as not including private sale profits in Private Finance Initiative business plans, suggests an unwinding of the bind between private profit and social build; yet others, such as TIF/ADZ schemes, seem to tighten that bind.

'Big markets'/'big government' – moving towards a 'big society'?

At the beginning of the financial crisis, there was a growing discourse of 'anti-capitalist' market sceptics, who felt that there needed to be a new world order and that the power of the market had to be reduced. Some said that it was the power of the 'big' market that had caused the crisis, and that only 'big' government could lead the way to recovery.

Cohen (2009) suggests that market socialism is an option to taper the effects of the 'big' market. He offers a scenario which empowers individuals to make the best decisions for themselves, while not disadvantaging the wider group. Sandel (2009a) also voices concerns over freedom of choice; he asks, 'How free are the choices we make in the free market? And are there certain values and higher goods that markets do not honor and money cannot buy?' (p 102). Schweickart (1998) shares the view that market socialism is a beneficial system. He refutes pure socialism as 'either economically non-viable or normatively undesirable, often both at once' (p 10). The retention of a market system would coordinate the economy, but ownership of the means of production would not be solely by private organisations.

However, as the financial crisis progressed, the discourse turned increasingly to the problems of 'big' government and how public debt and high public spending had in fact been at fault. Both the Labour government and opposition parties competed in discourses of gloom over cuts in public spending. Not a usual state of affairs in the pre-election conference season, but politicians seemed sure that strong cuts in spending were necessary, and spelt out the coming situation to the public. Cameron put government in its place in his conference speech

(2009a) when he said 'the state is your servant, never your master'. He went on to say: 'Labour say that to solve the country's problems, we need more government. Don't they see? It is more government that got us into this mess.' Where government equals arbitrary performance indicators and targets, O'Donovan and Seddon (Chapter Seven) argue for a rethink along the lines of systems thinking in public sector services. In a later speech on the role of government, Cameron (2009b) seemed to qualify his earlier suggestion that the state should be rolled back and referred instead to the need for a 'big society'. He also suggested a 'big society bank' where funds from dormant accounts would be collected to pay for social entrepreneurial projects (Watt, 2010). During the election campaign period in April and early May 2010, commentators and politicians from Labour and other parties suggested that 'big society' was no more than the withdrawal of government responsibility and that it equated to 'do it yourself'; political sketch writers made fun of the notion of DIY health services and policing, but some writers made more sense of the concept by suggesting that a 'National Trust' model might work for the management of parks and libraries if councils needed to cut their spending (Hetherington, 2010). One of the first speeches of the Conservative–Liberal Democrat government in May (Cameron and Clegg, 2010) was on 'big society', promising to give communities more power, devolve power from the centre to local government, encourage people to be an active part of their communities, support co-ops and enterprises, and publish government data to inform the public.

Reeves and Collins (2009) caution that: 'There is a grave danger that recent economic events will blind us to the overwhelmingly positive contribution of free markets to prosperity and liberty' (p 10). They argue instead for the power of markets to be divested to communities. Financial markets and governments are there to support, not dictate, the choices that individuals can make. Le Grand (2007) argues that choice and competition should be used to deliver efficient public services and states that this approach should not be anathema to either the conservative right or the social democratic left. This issue of choice and empowerment in the public sector was examined in more depth by Brown and Yates (Chapter Eight) and they suggested that although there are challenges in service delivery, there is an opportunity through innovation to enhance choice, personalisation and empowerment.

The political and discursive shift away from criticism of the market, to a discourse of cutting spending was not driven by the mood of the electorate, however, with many public voices suggesting that cuts were not necessarily the best way forward.[1] The size of the public deficit seems to be the driver. Budget 2010 forecast a slow return to growth in the economy. The reliance on growth, particularly as measured by GDP, has been highlighted in a report by Stiglitz et al (2009) for the French government. They question the validity of such economic indicators for the measurement of overall social well-being. Indeed, social well-being, however difficult to measure, should not be forgotten in the drive to reduce deficits. In their analysis of the economics of social problems, Le Grand et al (2008) refer to the need of governments to balance efficiency and effectiveness in meeting social objectives and to keep in mind not just social costs but also social benefits. Leach and Roberts (Chapter Six) have also called for a more subtle approach to the public sector debt than the 'slash and burn' discourse of the early part of 2010. They have provided a conceptual framework based on institutional theory to show how the pattern of responses to the crisis by councils shows more variation than at first suggested.

Markets and morals – in pursuit of social justice

> 'Greed is good' is no prescription for the good society, but neither is it the mark of a good economy. It is the progressive values – rewarding hard work, co-operation, responsibility while penalising excess and reckless risk-taking – which will ensure our market economy works efficiently and fairly. (Brown, 2008, 29)

There have been suggestions for a mix of approaches and strategies in the banking sector to bring about equilibrium – such as understanding bankers' behaviour, or narrowing the scope of their impact through consideration of reform to limited-purpose banking (Kotlikoff, 2010). The behaviour of bankers, prior to the crisis in 2007, was perceived to be singularly motivated by profit making in the short term in order to be rewarded by large bonuses. The field of economics has used game theory modelling for some time to understand and predict how behaviours will impact on outcomes (for example, Allen and Morris, 1998). For example, the application of game theory, particularly the Hawk-Dove game, has attempted to understand the decisions made by individual bankers investing money for people. Hanauske et al (2009) developed applied Quantum Game Theory to reformulate the classic Hawk-Dove scenario modelling. They suggest that by creating a high-enough level of interconnectedness between hawk and dove banker strategies, there will be a more consensual, less aggressive, lower-risk approach to investment: morals injected into markets.

Just as there is a suggestion for a mix of approaches in the future of the banking sector, one can also see options for mixing private and public strategies for the future of government and public service delivery. The answer is not simply to roll back the power of markets entirely, or to roll back the state entirely, but instead to inject morals into markets and empower individuals in society.

There is a question of whether British society is 'big' enough and cohesive enough to share the burden of recovery and to prevent breakdown in social order in the event of an acute shortage of resources. There is a need for some sort of equitable approach to sharing the pain of the financial crisis. In the Japanese recession of the 1990s there appeared to be a consensus to continue to buy Japanese government bonds by way of propping up government debt and supporting recovery of the economy. However, different countries have starkly different cultural contexts and there seems to be no such consensus in Britain (Lea, 2009, suggests that any downgrade of Britain's AAA rating would lead to an investors' strike in the gilt market – there would be no automatic, consensual propping up of government bonds). Indeed, the outcry over bankers' bonuses continued to be ignored, with large financial rewards persisting in 2010. This perceived unfairness, this lack of sharing the pain by those in the financial services sector, suggests a society that is not cohesive, a society with an unfair system of rewarding 'success', and a society that needs building up before it is big enough to recover and renew.

Consideration should also be given to the impact of the last three decades' embrace of an individualised, marketised approach to governance of the economy and society in its broadest sense. For some time, there has been an assumption that individuals have positive control over their own destinies, and that as long as harm is not being done to others, then individuals should be encouraged to make money and to provide for themselves. While the safety net of the welfare state still functions for those who cannot or will not do this for themselves, a wider cultural discourse on 'deserving and undeserving poor' persists. Referencing the times of Octavia Hill in her management of social housing through the Murray (1994) debate on the 'deepening Underclass' in Britain, the issue of individual responsibility for one's destiny has an impact on the distribution of resources. Ehrenreich (2010) discusses this individual responsibility to be positive in order to secure a successful outcome in the context of illness, specifically, cancer. She suggests that there is a 'tyranny' of positive thought which suggests that individuals can secure health, wealth and happiness if only they themselves are positive. She goes so far as to suggest, in a different context, that this unfettered positivity could have, in part, led to financial institutions and governments ignoring the warnings of individuals that the financial system could not be sustained, because their views were not 'positive'. Equally, she suggests that if individuals are held responsible for their own destiny (if you're positive, then redundancy is an 'opportunity' rather than a threat), this negates the need for the state or private employers to support those who find themselves out of a job due to the crisis. This issue was examined in part in Chapter Five, looking at the impact of the financial crisis on vulnerable groups and individuals.

A wide debate has been had on recognising different elements of society more equally, rather than assuming that money making is king. Stiglitz (2009) referred to the injustice of the value placed on contribution to society by comparing the efforts of the late Nobel peace prize-winner Borlaug with the money incentive-driven behaviour of the bankers. The New Economics Foundation (2009) also looked at this issue in calculating the 'real' value to society of different professions. It found, for example, that although bankers are paid considerably more, childcare workers are worth more to society. In his fourth lecture for the 2009 BBC Reith Lectures, Sandel (2009b) called for a new public debate about the moral limits of markets and a more robust public discourse engaging with moral issues. Examining the shortcomings of using markets to organise public services – or 'market mimicking governance' – he said that there was great difficulty in placing a monetary value on human life. He also suggested that market mimicking creates a non-scientific, technocratic decision-making process, when instead there should be a democratic debate. In making a case for a 'politics of the common good', Sandel suggests that this would help to rebuild institutions and the structure of civic and public life. Where Stiglitz suggested that there needed to be more Borlaugs, and fewer bankers, but that the former were in short supply, Sandel suggests that altruism is not a scarce resource, but that this and moral guidance are characteristics that, like muscles in the body, can grow stronger with exercise.

Social justice is a strongly emerging rationale for not allowing unfettered markets to operate at any cost. Intervention to secure equality of opportunity and access to resources is an abiding drive for those proposing stronger governance and regulation of markets. Cramme and Diamond (2009), Wilkinson and Pickett (2009) and Dorling (2010) analyse social justice and social inequalities in more depth, but some of the issues of the impact of the financial crisis for communities and vulnerable groups have been examined in this volume in Chapter Five.

The wider theoretical debate on the rationale for government and governance was also analysed in Chapter Nine by Sullivan.

New opportunities and new models

The financial crisis, along with a changing global order of political and cultural influence (Cohen and DeLong, 2010), requires us to stop and think fundamentally about what economic and social models will work in this changing world. Therefore, it is perhaps not the most appropriate way forward to focus on defining and refining economic models as though they were dependable structural frameworks where information is perfect and actors are rational. Instead, new models are required where structures, agents, actors, emotions and behaviours are all recognised as having an impact. New economic frameworks are desirable not just for the purposes of renewing the economy and the well-being of individuals and communities, but also for environmental reasons, so that production and consumption at all costs does not deplete natural resources any further. The New Economics Foundation (Simms et al, 2010) talked about the need for a new direction that will unlock us from high-consuming life-styles which are driven by the economic, technological and cultural context. They again refer to Wilkinson and Pickett's (2009) argument that it is not overall national wealth that improves well-being, and that relative social inequality within countries can have a big drag on well-being.

Ostrom (1990) suggests a more fluid 'ownership' of resources. She analyses a range of economic models in delivering collective benefits (the tragedy of the commons, the prisoner's dilemma and the logic of collective action), and critiques the policy responses seen so far – 'Leviathan' as the only way and privatisation as the only way, and also the notion that there is an 'only way' – and says that instead a range of responses are needed in the ownership and sharing of resources, particularly common-pool resources. Amin (2009) also looks at alternative responses and attempts to locate the social economy to see whether this can offer a different kind of system. In the market-place, there are suggestions for a national 'e-market' to allow people to trade labour, short-term loans or indeed any small assets, particularly focusing on four areas of formal work, local services, hire of goods and borrowing cash. Rowan (2010) suggests that this is a model not for government to provide, but that instead it should act as a catalyst and regulator. He suggests that such a model could help to tackle worklessness, target public services more precisely and develop a new model for skills sharing. It could be that elements such as short-term, small cash loans at a reasonable rate of interest might go some way to reducing the impact of loan-shark practices on individuals and neighbourhoods.

While thought and debate are being undertaken in relation to the big picture, there are already ideas on adapting the existing system of public service delivery. The Commission on 2020 Public Services was talking in the early part of 2010 about a new strategic direction for public services in a 'post-Beveridge' welfare state. In a round of debates as part of the *Guardian's* Public Services Summit 2010, there was concern over the scale of cuts, but optimism that, undertaken sensitively, more efficient methods of delivery could provide better services in some areas. Individual budgets were one example cited as a way of making savings, allowing recipients to spend their budget on a service specific to their own needs, rather than on one the state presumed they needed. In January 2010 the Department of Health announced that personal budgets were cost-effective and that individuals were spending a little less on their own care than local authorities would have done on their behalf (Brindle, 2010).

Innovation and experimentation in public service delivery and local governance should be encouraged and supported. While it is tempting to make short-term cuts, there are longer-term consequences. Instead, funding and support should be given to experimenting, such as the approach in the Netherlands by the Housing Experiments Steering Group (SEU) which aims to find innovative and effective solutions. Fundamentally, policy should be based on evidence, not just on ideology.

There are opportunities for co-production of services in both the public sector and the wider market-place and there have been proposals from all parties on creating new such models of provision, with Labour in the early part of 2010 working explicitly with the Co-operative party to integrate cooperative and mutual values into its proposals. One example of how this might work is in the London Borough of Lambeth, where the so-called 'John Lewis' council has community-led public service provision. This contrasts with another new model in Barnet (nicknamed the 'easyBorough' council), which offers consumers choice over which services they want to prioritise on an individual level by charging more for 'extras'. Both examples were discussed by Brown and Yates in this book (Chapter Eight). More time is needed before a proper analysis of the two approaches can be taken, but initially there is concern that the latter model could exacerbate the very social inequality that the public sector should be looking to ameliorate, and that while consumers may have a 'choice', this is dependent on their ability to pay.

A report by the Institute for Public Policy Research and PricewaterhouseCooper (IPPR and PWC, 2010) notes that citizens are now more assertive and better informed, and that public sector services should change in order to keep up – they call for a new partnership between citizens and public services. The action plan published by Labour at the end of 2009, *Putting the Frontline First: Smarter Government* (HM Government, 2009), called for a greater role for the citizen, and the Conservatives' (2010) suggested new economic model also sought to give more power to the consumer. Whichever models are used on a national and local level in the future, there seems to be a political consensus that citizens/consumers will have a stronger role in the delivery of public services.

However, a note of caution is required. As discussed in Chapter Five, a wide range of groups and areas have been and will continue to be affected by the financial crisis. Some of the emerging 'innovative' models being tried in councils like Barnet could signal withdrawal of support services from people at the very time they need them the most. If the government takes away the safety net of robust, government-led services in favour of letting individuals and communities provide for themselves through private or quasi-private agencies, then this might be privatisation by another name. Evidence from reports like that of Buchanan et al (2009) suggests that the state is propping up the private market, not vice versa, so withdrawal of the state from the delivery of services to neighbourhoods could be disastrous on a number of levels: the impact on employment, the needs of vulnerable groups, and the longer-term recovery of the wider economy.

There is also a need to remember the devastation wrought by the over-reliance of government on the 'innovation' of the financial services sector. Government has been in thrall to financial services organisations for too long and, despite strong words at the beginning of the recession, memories seem to be short while bonuses and regulation concessions continue apace in 2010. Cox (2010) reminds us of the comparable GDP contribution of the physics-based industry, which had £3.3 billion investment for the whole science budget in 2009, compared to the £1.3 trillion bail-out of the financial services sector. Physics-based industry and research is inspiring a new generation and has the power to transform our understanding of the universe, as well as to frame future transformative technology. It is areas such as this which need to be nurtured and led. Gardner (2008) explained the need to understand the changing knowledge economy in his *5 Minds of the Future*, and it is the opportunity to look forward to changing technologies, breakthroughs in science and transformative future products that the government should enable through public spending and inspirational leadership.

The issue of the need for historical context before examining public debt has already been referred to, but it is readily forgotten in the hysterical debate on how to cut the public debt. Upon reflection, and in the context of historical figures, global comparisons, and comparisons with private debt, there is an opportunity to calm the debate and see the rationale for retaining current public debt levels if this helps to support social cohesion, to grow modern technological and intellectual industry through education and training, and investment in technological infrastructure. Britain needs leading out of the crisis, not rushing towards future pain with poorly devised hard and fast cuts in spending. The Audit Commission report (2010) demonstrated this in its assessment that more can be done for less in a thoughtful redesign, but this takes time and effort.

Conclusion

This book has attempted to provide an overview of the financial crisis that started in Britain in 2008 (Chapter One) and has given a brief, recent historical context and a detailed account of the global and European implications for the economy (Chapters Two and Three). The flaws in current economic models and implications for the financial mechanisms open to councils were examined (Chapter Four), as were concerns that although efficiencies can be made, deep cuts in public spending and service delivery could have a profound effect on communities and vulnerable groups (Chapter Five). A theoretical framework for analysing the responses from local authorities through a neighbourhood management locus in Britain was reviewed (Chapter Six). As the debate has moved from private to sovereign debt and the clamour for cuts and 'efficiency' savings grows louder, there are suggestions for understanding public service systems from the customer's point of view, rather than through the historical focus on targets and performance indicators (Chapters Seven and Eight). There has also been an attempt to uncover the role of local government, not just as a public service provider, but as a provider of leadership and governance (Chapter Nine). It is this leadership which is key. Roosevelt (1938) said in one of his presidential fireside chats during the 1930s recession in the United States: 'For to reach a port, we must sail – sail, not lie at anchor, sail, not drift'. There are a number of structural and economic models that could be taken to develop a new framework, but without a moral direction and leadership, the opportunity for renewal to come out of the financial crisis will be lost.

Note

[1] An Ipsos Mori poll in September 2009 showed that just a quarter of respondents in Britain saw the necessity of spending cuts.

References

All Party Urban Development Group (2009) *Regeneration and the Recession, Unlocking the Money*, London: All Party Urban Development Group.

Allen, F. and Morris, S. (1998) *Finance Applications of Game Theory*, Working Paper Series, Financial Institutions Center, The Wharton School, University of Pennsylvania.

Amin, A. (2009) *The Social Economy: International Perspectives on Economic Solidarity*, London: Zed Books.

Audit Commission (2010) *Surviving the Crunch: Local Finances in the Recession and Beyond*, London: Audit Commission.

Blanchard, O., Dell'Ariccia, G. and Mauro, P. (2010) 'Rethinking Macroeconomic Policy', IMF Staff Position Note, 12 February, www.imf.org.

Brindle, D. (2010) 'Boost for "cost-effective" individual budgets', *Guardian*, 28 January, www.guardian.co.uk.

Brown, G. (2008) 'America has embraced the values of progress. The election of Obama has inspired millions around the world. It shows how voters need government to provide security in troubled times', *The Observer*, 9 November, p 29.

Brown, C. (2010a) 'Landlord raises £76m in Japan', *Inside Housing*, 2 July, p 2.

Brown, C. (2010b) 'Notting Hill issues £180 million bond', *Inside Housing*, 9 July, p 9.

Buchanan, J., Froud, J., Johal, S., Leaver, A. and Williams, K. (2009) *Undisclosed and Unsustainable: Problems of the UK National Business Model*, Manchester: CRESC.

Cameron, D. (2009a) Speech to the Conservative Party Conference, 8 October, Manchester.

Cameron, D. (2009b) 'The Big Society', Speech, 10 November, www.conservatives.com.

Cameron, D. (2010) Big Society Speech, 19 July, www.number10.gov.uk.

Cameron, D. and Clegg, N. (2010) 'Big Society' launch speech, 18 May www.number10.gov.uk.

Cohen, G.A. (2009) *Why Not Socialism?,* Princeton, NJ: Princeton University Press.

Cohen, S. and DeLong, J. (2010) *The End of Influence: What Happens When Other Countries Have the Money,* New York: Basic Books.

Conservatives (2010) *A New Economic Model: Eight Benchmarks for Britain,* London: Conservatives.

Cox, B. (2010) 'How the geeks inherited the earth', *Guardian* G2, p 2, 13 April.

Cramme, O. and Diamond, P. (2009) *Social Justice in the Global Age,* Cambridge: Polity Press.

de Soto, J. (2008) *The Austrian School, Market Order and Entrepreneurial Creativity,* Cheltenham: Edward Elgar Publishing Ltd.

Dorling, D. (2010) *Injustice: Why Social Inequality Persists,* Bristol: The Policy Press.

Earls, M. (2009) *Herd: How to Change Mass Behaviour by Harnessing our True Nature,* London: John Wiley and Sons.

Ehrenreich, B. (2010) *Smile or Die: How Positive Thinking Fooled America and the World,* London: Granta Books.

Elmeskov, J. (2009) Economic Outlook No 86, Press Conference, 19 November, Paris: OECD, www.oecd.org.

Ferguson, N. (2008) *The Ascent of Money: A Financial History of the World,* London: Allen Lane.

Gardner, H. (2008) *5 Minds for the Future,* Massachusetts: Harvard Business Press.

Gatti, D., Gallegati, M., Greenwald, B., Russo, A. and Stiglitz, J. (2008) 'Financially Constrained Fluctuations in an Evolving Network Economy', NBER Working Paper, No W14112, June, Social Science Research Network, http://ssm.com.

Gladwell, M. (2001) *The Tipping Point: How Little Things Can Make a Big Difference,* London: Abacus.

Hanauske, M., Kunz, J., Bernius, S. and Konig, W. (2009) 'Doves and hawks in economics revisited; an evolutionary quantum game theory-based analysis of financial crises', submitted 14 April to arXiv:0904.2113v1 [q-fin.GN], available at http://arXiv.org/abs/0904.2113.

Hetherington, P. (2010) 'In our hands', *Society Guardian,* 12 May, p 1.

Hill, D. (2008) *Emotionomics,* London: Kogan Page.

HM Government (2009) *Putting the Frontline First: Smarter Government,* London: HM Government.

HM Treasury (2009) *Pre-Budget Report*, December, London: HM Treasury.

HM Treasury (2010) *Total Place: A Whole Area Approach to Public Services*, London: HM Treasury.

Hutton, W. (2010) 'This country's renewal is being betrayed by cheap, paltry politics', *Guardian*, 11 April, p 29.

Hutton, W. and Jones, A. (2010) *Driving Economic Recovery: Core Cities – a new partnership with government*, Manchester: Core Cities/Tenant Services Authority.

IMF (International Monetary Fund) (2010a) *Exiting from Crisis Intervention Policies*, Washington, DC: IMF, www.imf.org.

IMF (2010b) *A Fair and Substantial Contribution by the Financial Sector*, Interim report for the G20, 2010, Washington, DC: IMF.

Inside Housing (2010) 'Hyde sets its sights on £200m bond deal', 5 February, p 2.

IPPR (Institute for Public Policy Research) and PWC (PricewaterhouseCoopers) (2010) *Capable Communities: Public Service Reform: The Next Chapter*, London: IPPR and PWC.

Kotlikoff, L. (2010) *Jimmy Stewart is Dead: Ending the World's Ongoing Financial Plague with Limited Purpose Banking*, New Jersey: John Wiley and Sons.

Le Grand, J. (2007) *The Other Invisible Hand: Delivering Public Services Through Choice and Competition*, Princeton, NJ: Princeton University Press.

Le Grand, J., Propper, C. and Smith, S. (2008) *The Economics of Social Problems* (4th edn), Basingstoke: Palgrave Macmillan.

Lea, R. (2009) 'The IMF is right: quicker action needed on the public finances', Arbuthnot Banking Group Perspective, www.arbuthnot. co.uk.

Levitt, S. and Dubner, S. (2009) *Super Freakonomics: Global Cooling, Patriotic Prostitutes and Why Suicide Bombers Should Buy Life Insurance*, London: Allen Lane.

Lonergan, E. (2009) *Money*, Durham: Acumen Publishing Ltd.

May, R., Levin, S. and Sugihara, G. (2008) 'Ecology for Bankers', *Nature*, vol 451, no 21, February, pp 893–95.

Murray, C. (1994) *Underclass: The Crisis Deepens*, London: IEA Health and Welfare Unit.

New Economics Foundation (2009) *A Bit Rich: Calculating the Real Value to Society of Different Professionals*, London: NEF.

New Economics Foundation (2010) *Better Banking: A Manifesto to Re-organise the UK Banking System to Serve and Strengthen the British Economy Through Structural Reform*, London: NEF/Compass.

O'Toole, F. (2009) *Ship of Fools: How Stupidity and Corruption Sank the Celtic Tiger*, London: Faber and Faber.

Ollman, B. (ed) (1998) *Market Socialism, The Debate Among Socialists*, London: Routledge.

Ostrom, E. (1990) *Governing the Commons: The Evolution of Institutions for Collective Action*, Cambridge: Cambridge University Press.

Reed, D. (1999) 'Weapon of Math Destruction, a simple formula explains why the Internet is wreaking havoc on business models', *Context*, Spring issue, www.contextmag.com.

Reeves, R. and Collins, P. (2009) *The Liberal Republic*, London: Demos.

Roosevelt, F.D. (1938) 'Fireside Chat', 14 April, available at www.mhric.org/fdr.

Rowan, W. (2010) *Could Online Marketplaces Tackle Poverty?*, York: Joseph Rowntree Foundation.

Roxburgh, C., Lund, S., Wimmer, T., Amar, E., Atkins, C., Kwek, J., Dobbs, R. and Manyika, J. (2010) *Debt and Deleveraging: The Global Credit Bubble and its Economic Consequences*, McKinsey and Co., www.mckinsey.com.

Sandel, M. (2009a) *Justice: What's the Right Thing to Do?*, London: Allen Lane.

Sandel, M. (2009b) *Reith Lectures 2009: A New Citizenship*, Lecture 4, BBC Radio 4, 30 June.

Schweickart, D. (1998) 'Market socialism: a defence', in B. Ollman (ed) *Market Socialism: The Debate Among Socialists*, London: Routledge.

Sen, A. (1999) *Commodities and Capabilities*, New Delhi: Oxford University Press.

Shelter (2009) *Ground Breaking: New Ideas on Housing Delivery*, London: Shelter.

Simms, A., Johnson, V. and Chowla, P. (2010) *Growth isn't Possible: Why We Need a New Economic Direction*, London: New Economics Foundation.

Skidelsky, R. (2009) *Keynes: The Return of the Master*, London: Allen Lane.

Skousen, M. (2005) *Vienna and Chicago, Friends or Foes? A Tale of Two Schools of Free-market Economics*, Washington: Regnery Publishing.

Stiglitz, J. (2009) 'Borlaug and the bankers. Perhaps one of the worst effects of financial greed was to deprive the world of more people like Norman Barlaug', *Guardian*, 11 October, www.guardian.co.uk/commentisfree

Stiglitz, J. (2010) *Freefall: Free Markets and the Sinking of the Global Economy*, London: Allen Lane.

Stiglitz, J., Sen, A. and Fitoussi, J.-P. (2009) *Report by the Commission on the Measurement of Economic Performance and Social Progress*, Report for the Government of France, available on www.stiglitz-sen-fitoussi.fr.

Thaler, R. and Sunstein, C. (2009) *Nudge: Improving Decisions about Health, Wealth and Happiness*, London: Penguin.

Toynbee, P. and Walker, D. (2009) *Unjust Rewards: Ending the Greed that is Bankrupting Britain*, London: Granta.

Turner, A. (2010a) 'Economics, conventional wisdom and public policy', Paper delivered to the Institute for New Economic Thinking Inaugural Conference, Cambridge University, April.

Turner, A. (2010b) 'What do banks do, what should they do and what public policies are needed to ensure best results for the real economy?', Paper delivered to the Cass Business School, 17 March.

Watt, N. (2010) 'Big society in, big state out, say Tories, New bank to fund public services, says Cameron', *Guardian*, 1 April, p 12.

Wilkinson, R. and Pickett, K. (2009) *The Spirit Level: Why More Equal Societies Almost Always do Better*, London: Allen Lane.

Index

A

Accelerated Development Zone (ADZ) 205-6
Adenauer, K. 63
Adult Social Care (ASC) 150-1, 159
'adversarial legitimacy' concept 189
Advice UK 147
All Party Urban Development Group 205-6
Almunia, J. 64
Alternative Economic Strategy (AES) 35-6, 37, 45
Amin, A. 211
Amis, M. 99
Appleby, J. 95
Arthur Andersen 7
AstraZeneca 15
Audit Commission (AC) 14, 15-16, 145, 149, 165, 166, 186, 214

B

'back-office' activities 84, 94, 135, 140-1, 143-7, 148, 149, 158, 205
Bank of England 8, 36, 38, 42, 51
Bank of International Settlements 31
banking sector 6, 25, 43, 45, 86, 202, 208, 210
    government intervention 3-4, 44, 76, 77, 78, 87
    international 31-2, 51-2
    taxation and regulation 12, 13, 37-8, 201
Barber, B.R. 188, 190
Barnet, London Borough of 129-30, 131, 171, 172, 180, 212, 213
Barrett, T. 58
Basel Accords (1988, 2004) 6, 7
Bear Stearns 8
Belgium 55, 65, 66
Benn, Tony 35, 36
Better Banking Campaign 91
'big markets' 206-8
'Big Society' 9, 12, 18, 19, 80, 105, 173, 181, 200, 206-8, 207
Birmingham City Council 101, 113, 170, 205
'Black Wednesday' (1992) 7
Braverman, H. 29
Bretton Woods conference (1944) 25, 26-30, 32
British National Party (BNP) 103, 104, 117-18

Brown, G. 7, 8, 92, 138, 143, 208
Brown, T. 163
Buchanan, J. 202, 213
Building Britain's Future (HM Government) 19
Building Schools for the Future programme 9, 80
Bundesbank 63-4
Burgess, J. 131
Byrne, L. 3

C

Cambridge Political Economy Group 35, 45
Cameron, D. 149, 181, 206-7
capital markets 74-5, 76-7
capitalism 26-30, 34, 42, 46, 202
Centre for Cities 90
Centre for Policy Studies 43
Centre for Research on Socio-cultural Change (CRESC) 40-1, 44
Chartered Institute of Personnel and Development (CIPD) 15
Chase, R. 141
children and young people 90, 99-102, 105
China xii, xiii, 78
choice 157-64, 167-8, 170-1, 174-5, 206, 207, 212
Chote, Robert 45
Citizens Advice Bureau 165
Clarke, M. 160
co-production 172-4, 175, 180, 212
Cohen, G.A. 206
Cole, M. 159, 175
Collins, P. 207
'command and control' 19, 140, 151, 161
communities 102-5, 125-7
Communities and Local Government, Department of 115
community leadership 19, 112, 113-16, 186
Community Reinvestment Act (CRA) (1977) 6
Comprehensive Spending Review (2010) 9
Confederation of British Industry (CBI) 35, 36
Conservative Party 6, 7, 35, 36, 38, 138, 173, 180, 184

Conservative-Liberal Democrat
  Coalition Government xiii, 12, 18,
  45, 94
  'Big Society' 19, 80, 130, 173, 181,
  200, 207
  devolution and 85, 175, 179
  public expenditure and 3, 9, 13, 14, 17,
  73, 78, 89, 90, 157, 202
Constitution for Europe 61-3
'core business' approach 190-1
'corporate raiders' 33, 38
Corus 14-15
cost-driven approach 168-9, 174, 175
Council for Mortgage Lenders (CML)
  93
Cox, B. 213
credit ratings 9, 13, 14, 44, 52
credit unions 91
Crosland, A. 36
currency markets 27-8, 30, 38-9
customer relationship management 158
customer-orientated approach 158, 174,
  175

D

Dahlgren, G. 96
Daily Mail 99
Day, K. 91
debt 4, 5, 9, 14, 43, 45, 77, 79-80, 82-3,
  95, 165, 200-1, 214
decentralisation 85, 86
'deliverology' 135, 138, 139, 140
Delors, J. 54, 55, 56, 57, 58, 59, 60
demand 144-6, 148, 158
Deming, W.E. 141-2, 148-9
democracy 40, 184, 185, 188, 193
Demos 159
Denmark 103
Derby 124, 126-7
derivatives market 6, 7, 38, 51
Desai, M. 35
Development Concepts and Doctrine
  Centre (DCDC) 45
devolution 85, 86
Dodd-Frank Wall Street and Consumer
  Protection Act (2010) 9
'double-dip' recession 4, 14, 82, 86, 111
Dubner, S. 203
Dunleavy, P. 139
Duxbury, N. 94

E

East Midlands Housing Group 93
East Sussex County Council 89, 95
'easyBorough' model 129, 130-1, 167,
  168, 171, 172, 175, 212
economic modelling 73-4, 201-5,
  211-14

Economic and Social Research Council
  (ESRC) 159
economies of scale 147-9
Economist Intelligence Unit (EIU)
  102-3
education 79-80, 84-5, 86, 100-1, 157
'efficiencies' 135, 179, 180, 182, 183,
  184
Ehrenreich, B. 209-10
'The emperor has no growth: Declining
  economic growth rates in the era of
  globalisation' (Weisbrot et al) 40
employment 41, 56-7, 59
empowerment 20, 157-8, 159-62, 164,
  167-8, 169, 173-4, 175, 187, 206,
  207
'enabling' 181-8, 192, 193-4
Engdahl, W. 32
Equalities and Human Rights
  Commission 104, 165
Essen European Council (1994) 56, 57,
  59
Eurodollar market 6, 7, 14, 31-2, 46, 52,
  54, 202
European Central Bank 51, 63, 64, 65,
  66, 73
European Economic Recovery
  Programme 67
European Exchange Rate Mechanism
  (ERM) 7, 38
European Investment Bank/Fund (EIB/
  EIF) 54, 57-61, 62, 64, 65, 67
European Network Against Racism 103
European Union (EU) 6, 30, 54-67

F

Fannie Mae/Freddie Mac 8
Federal Bank of America 8
Federal Reserve Act (1913) (US) 27
Federal Reserve (US) 8, 10, 27, 42, 51,
  63
Fenton, A. 91, 103
Financial Activities Tax 201
financial crisis (overview) 3-23, 164-7
Financial Stability Contribution 201
'fiscal illusion' 81, 83
Fiscal Responsibility Act (2010) 13
5 Minds of the Future (Gardner) 213-14
France 38, 53, 80, 103
Freitas Ferraz, José de 58-9
Friedman, M. 53

G

Galbraith, J.K. 30
Gamble, A. 5
'game theory' 208
'gaming' 138-9
Gardner, H. 213-14

General Agreement on Tariffs and Trade (GATT) 28
Germany 53, 103
Gershon, Sir Peter 111, 145
Ghoshal, S. 140
Giscard d'Estaing, V. 62
Glass–Steagall Act (US) 6, 7, 51
Global Strategic Trends Programme 2007-2036 (DCDC) 45-6
globalisation 6, 17, 18, 25, 31, 32, 33-7, 39-44, 45, 203
gold reserves 7, 9, 30
Goldsmith, J. 33, 38
Goodin, R.E. 119
Goodwin Development Trust 173
Gordon, D. 96
Gorges, M.J. 120
governance 12, 20, 67, 112, 113-14, 127, 128, 182, 183, 187, 199, 209, 210
Greater Manchester 172
Greece 6, 9, 14, 41, 46, 52, 55, 65, 66, 75, 77, 81, 100
Greenspan, A. 51
Greenwich Leisure 173
gross domestic product (GDP) xi, xii, 4-5, 6, 54, 76, 208
Growth, Competitiveness, Cohesion (Delors) 54
Guterres, A. 58, 59, 61
Gypsies and Travellers 90, 96-8, 103, 104

H

Halpern, D. 170, 174
Hammersmith and Fulham, London Borough of 171
Hanauske, M. 208
Hays, C. 120
Healey, D. 32-3
Health and Consumer Focus, Department of (DHCF) 171
health and healthcare services 89, 94-6, 157, 168, 191, 212
hedge funds 7, 38, 51, 52
Herzog, R. 63
Higher Education Funding Council 100
Hills, J. 96
Hirst, P. 184
Holland, S. 34-5, 199, 201, 204-5
Hood, A. 91
Horton, T. 90
Housing Experiments Steering Group (SEU) 212
housing markets 4, 7, 8, 89, 93, 166-7
see also social housing
Hull City Council 92, 163, 164, 166, 174

Hull Community Legal Advice Centre 167
Human Development Reports (UNDP) 41
Hunter, G. 73
Hutton, J. 160
Hutton, W. 92, 102, 200, 205
Hyde Group 205

I

Iceland 8, 9, 75, 101
Independent Living Movement 159
India xii, 78
Infrastructure UK 87
Innovation 2000 Initiative 59
Institute of Fiscal Studies (IFS) 13, 45, 117
Institute for Public Policy Research (IPPR) 213
institutional change 118-22, 129
Instituto per la Riconstruzione Industriale 35
'Integrated Children's System' 150
Integration and Cohesion, Commission on 104
International Comparison Programme 41
International Monetary Fund (IMF) 6, 9, 28, 36, 37, 40, 52, 82, 201, 202
banking sector and 12-13, 43
financial sector and 75
healthcare and 94
Ireland 41, 75, 77, 200
Irwell Valley Housing Association 172
Italy 41, 53, 54-5, 65, 66, 100

J

Japan xii, 28, 31
'John Lewis' approach 16, 130, 167, 172-3, 212
John, P. 174
Johnson, H.T. 147
Jones, A. 92, 205
Jowell, T. 130, 172-3
JP Morgan 8

K

Kaptur, M. 46
Keynes, John Maynard 26-7, 28, 29, 30, 40, 42, 53, 136, 201
King, P. 163
Kohl, H. 58, 64
Kraft 15, 17
Kroes, N. 52

L

Labour Party 11, 18, 43, 139, 182-3, 190
choice 138, 160, 162

community leadership 113, 114-15, 116
'enabling' 181, 187
globalisation 31, 33-7
local government 185
private sector 41
public spending 13, 78, 98, 99, 206
Lambeth, London Borough of 130, 131, 212
Lancashire County Council 98
Latvia 41, 46, 75
Lawson, N. 53, 105
Le Grand, J. 160, 169, 207, 208
Lea, R. 13
Leach, S. 115-16, 208
'lean management' techniques 147
Lehman Brothers 8
Leslie, C. 86, 91
Levitt, S. 203
Liberal Democrats 162, 173, 175, 180
libertarian paternalism 170-1, 174, 175, 202
Lisbon Agenda (2000) 58-60, 61, 66
Little, M. 192
loan-sharking 90-1, 212
local government
  'back-office' services 143-7
  budget cuts 9, 18, 80-1, 89-90, 101, 104, 111
  council-led approaches 123, 165
  devolution 84, 85
  'enabling' 179-95
  housing 93-4, 97, 163-4
  place shielding 91-2
  older people 98
  responses to recessions 11, 14-17, 83
  restoring 'the political' and 188-92
Local Enterprise Partnerships (LEPs) 9
Local Government Acts (2000, 2007) 115
Local Government Association (LGA) 92, 104
local strategic partnership (LSP) 91-2, 186-7
local-central relationship 117-18
'localism' 12, 18, 115, 127, 129, 130, 151, 175
'logic of care/choice' 191-2, 194
London (City of) 31, 35, 36, 38, 43
London Interbank Offered Rate (LIBOR) 6, 8
London and Quadrant Housing Association 205
Long Term Capital Management 7, 51
Lowndes, V. 116, 119

M

'market fundamentalism' 18, 26, 42
Marmot Review (2010) 90
Marsh, D. 63
May, R. 203
Meden Valley Making Places 173
Merkel, A. 66, 67
Merrick, N. 80
middle-income households 45-6, 165
Miliband, D. 139
Milken, M. 38
Mol, A. 191
Monks, J. 64
Moore, M. 173
Mouffe, C. 189-90
Multinational Corporations (MNCs) 32
Murphy, W. 163
'Mutual Manifesto' 130
mutuality 172-4, 175, 180, 204

N

National Housing Federation (NHF) 80
'National Self-Sufficiency' (Keynes) 26-7
National Social Marketing Centre 170-1
neighbourhoods 90-1, 114-16, 122-7, 187
neoliberalism 11, 26, 35, 37, 38, 39, 40, 41, 42, 45, 51, 137
Netherlands 212
New Deal (US) 27, 32, 51, 55-6, 57, 60, 65, 66
New Economics Foundation 169, 201, 210, 211
New Local Government Network (NLGN) 89, 92
'new public management' (NPM) 137-8, 139
Newcastle City Council 192
NHS Confederation 95
NHS Hull 164, 171, 174
Northern Rock 8, 76, 81
Notting Hill Housing Trust 205
Nottingham City Council 104
Nottingham City Homes 93

O

Ohno, T. 142-3
older people 90, 98-9, 164-5
'one-size-fits-all' approach 169
Operational Efficiency Programme (HM Treasury) 83, 140-1
Osborne, G. 43
Ostrom, E. 211
O'Toole, F. 41, 200
Out of the Crisis (Deming) 141-2

P

Pantazis, C. 96
Parkinson, M. 90
Parry, G. 96
Parston, G. 159, 175
'partnership working' 180
path dependence 121-2, 128, 130
People's Lottery 129
personalisation 158, 159, 160, 161, 162,
 163, 164-5, 167-8, 169, 173-4, 207
Peters, B.G. 119
Phillips, A. 188-9
Pickett, K. xii, 90, 204, 210, 211
place shielding 91-3, 170, 205-6
Places for People 205
Ponzi scandal 8
Portsmouth City Councils 163-4
Portugal 6, 9, 14, 41, 58, 100
postwar economy xi-xii, 26-30, 136,
 182-3
Pre-Budget Report (2009) (HM
 Treasury) 6, 8, 13, 77, 80
PricewaterhouseCooper (PWC) 213
Private Finance Initiative (PFI) 41, 43,
 86, 87, 206
private sector xi, 41, 77, 81, 86
privatisation xi-xii, 41, 46, 76, 79, 81,
 137
'public choice theory' 136-8
Public Partnership Agreements (PPAs)
 86, 87
Public Sector Net Borrowing (PSNB) 6
Public Sector Net Debt (PSND) 4-5,
 9, 14, 17
Public Service Agreements (PSAs) 86,
 138
public service delivery models 205-6
Public Services 2020, Commission on
 212
'punctuated equilibrium' (PE) models
 120
Purchasing Power Parities (PPP) 41-2
*Putting the Frontline First: Smarter
 Government* (HM Government) 92,
 213

Q

Quantitative Easing (QE) programme 8,
 12, 43, 44, 74, 77, 78
Quantum Fund 39
Quantum Game Theory 208
Quirk, B. 91

R

RCT Homes (housing association) 93
recession 5, 6-10, 11, 12, 14-17, 111-33,
 162

Reed, H. 90
Reeves, R. 207
Reinhart, C. 5
Retail Prices Index (RPI) 77
retrenchment 168-9, 175
Revenue and Customs, Her Majesty's
 (HMRC) 147
Ridley, N. 184, 186, 187
Right to Buy (RTB) 6, 137
risk 200-1
Robert Barton Trust (RBT) 97-8
Robinson, W. 40
Rogers, J. 131
Rogers, W. 36-7
Rogoff, K. 5
Roland, T. 33
Roosevelt, F.D.R. 26, 27, 28, 55, 65, 214
Rowan, W. 211-12
Roxburgh, C. 200
Royal Bank of Scotland (RBS) 44, 81
Rural Communities, Commission for
 90, 165

S

Sandel, M. 206, 210
Sarkozy, N. 63, 66
Schmidt, H. 63
Schweickart, D. 206
Seddon, J. 149
Sen, A. 204
Servan-Schreiber, J.J. 32
Seven Locks Housing Association 93
Shaheen, F. 100
Sharpe, J. 183
Silguy, Yves-Thibault de 56
Simmons, R. 157, 159
Simms, A. 204
Single European Act (1986) 53, 54-5, 56
Sklair, L. 39
Slater, J. 33
small and medium-sized enterprises
 (SMEs) 4, 8, 59, 60-1
social behaviour 90, 102-4
Social Care Green Paper (2009) (DoH)
 168
social housing 93-4, 143-7, 157, 158,
 161, 163-4, 172, 205, 209
 see also housing markets
social justice 208-11
social services 83, 86, 89, 157, 158, 159,
 164, 166
The Socialist Challenge (Holland) 34
sovereign debt 4, 9, 14, 74, 76, 200, 202,
 214
Spaak Report 54
Spain 6, 9, 14, 41, 64, 100
The Spirit Level (Wilkinson and Pickett)
 xii

Stability and Growth Pact (EU) 64, 65, 67, 75, 81
'state overload' thesis 136
Stewart, J. 185, 186
Stiglitz, J. 199, 201, 203, 208, 210
Stoker, G. 185, 186
Streek, W. 120
'strong politics' 189, 190, 192, 194
Strong and Prosperous Communities (White Paper 2006) 185
Structural Adjustment Programmes (SAPs) (IMF) 46, 81
Stuckler, B. 95
sub-prime lending 7, 8, 51, 66
Sullivan, H. 116
Summers, L. 51
Sunstein, C. 170
Surviving the Crunch (Audit Commission) 16
sustainability 77-8
Sweden 103
'systems thinking' 19, 136, 141-7, 149, 150, 151-2

T

'targets and terror' approach 136-41
Tax Increment Funding (TIF) 205-6
taxation xii, 8, 9, 12, 13, 25, 45, 80, 201
Thaler, R. 170
Thatcher, M. xi, 6, 7, 26, 37-8
Thelen, K. 120
'thin politics' 189, 190, 192
Thompson, R. 39
Total Place/Total capital approaches 91-3, 170, 205-6
Toynbee, P. 204
Toyota Production System (TPS) 142, 151
trade unions xi, 29, 36, 37, 101
Trans-European Transport Networks (TENs) 56, 65
'Transition' movement 126
'transnational capitalist class (TCC)' 39-40
'transnationalisation' 32, 39, 40, 45, 46
Treasury (UK) 7, 33, 36, 77, 83, 140
Treasury (US) 51, 55, 58, 65
TREES Group (Leicester) 173
trust 199-200
Tunstall, R. 91
two-tier approach 171-2, 175

U

'Undisclosed and unsustainable: Problems of the UK business model' (CRESC) 40-1, 44
unemployment 6, 9, 15, 25, 53, 95, 99-100, 104, 105, 129, 165, 201

Union Bonds 55-6, 57, 58, 59, 60, 66
United Nations Development Programme (UNDP) 41
United States xii, 7, 8, 36-7, 38, 55, 60, 65, 80, 103, 202
banking sector 51-2, 77, 78
Bretton Woods conference (1944) 25, 26-30, 31-2

V

Vaitilingham, R. 99
Vale, D. 105
Van Cleemput, P. 96
velocity of circulation 74, 75
vulnerable groups 19, 79, 80, 86, 90, 94-102, 105, 166, 169, 171, 194

W

Wainwright, H. 192
Walker, D. 204
welfare model 169, 175
White, Harry Dexter 26, 27
White, W. 7, 13
Whitehead, M. 96
Whyte, B. 95
Wilkinson, R. xii, 42, 90, 204, 210, 211
Wolf, M. 43-4
Woolworths 8
Work Foundation 165
Work and Pensions, Department for (DWP) 104, 143-7
World Bank 28, 41-2, 57, 73
World Trade Organisation (WTO) 40

Y

Young Foundation 95
Youth Access 100